Catholicism Against Itself

VOLUME TWO:
*Including: their suppression of the Bible,
elevation of "Tradition" over the Bible,
creation of the priesthood,
worship of Mary and the "Saints,"
blasphemous scandals of the popes,
and anti-biblical "sacraments"*

By O.C. Lambert

2024 REVISED EDITION

"If it be not identical in belief, government, etc., with the primitive Church, then it is not the Church of Christ" (*Catholic Facts,* 27).

Charleston, AR
COBB PUBLISHING
2024

Published in the United States by:
Cobb Publishing
CobbPublishing.com
Editor@CobbPublishing.com
479.747.8372
ISBN: 978-1-960858-16-0

PREFACE TO REVISED EDITION

In an effort to get as much information available to interested readers, O.C. Lambert produced this second volume of *Catholicism Against Itself*, this one focusing on many of the Catholic practices and heretical teachings, as exposed in official Catholic books.

Believing this to be more of a reference volume than a book one would read cover to cover, Lambert occasionally repeated quotations, because they would apply under multiple headings. He wanted you, the reader, to look through the chapter headings and find what you wanted to read about.

This revised edition, published in 2024, has made no changes whatsoever to any of the quotations he provides from Catholic sources, because (as he says later in this very book) it is important that you see the actual quotes, even if it has words spelled wrong or poor grammar.

However, we have taken the liberty of revising some of Lambert's words, correcting some of his grammar and punctuation, and on a few occasions removing some unnecessary wordiness.

We hope you find this volume to be as valuable as we do.

O.C. LAMBERT

PROLOGUE AND DEDICATION

Here, after long years of labor, I present to the world *Catholicism Against Itself, Volume II,* dedicated from a deep sense of gratitude, to a host of loyal friends over the world who believed in the validity and importance of my efforts, and without whose assistance I might have been borne down by the magnitude of the undertaking, in which case this volume would have been an impossibility. This is completely original research, struggling against the popular current. I have been buoyed up also by the appreciation of those whom I have rescued from this benighting system, and the hope that in the future multitudes may be brought from darkness to light. My greatest incentive, however, has been the hope of pleasing Him whose we are, and to be able to answer when my name is called in that Great Day.

The magnitude of this undertaking and the multiplicity of subjects covered has made it necessary to confine this vast amount of material into the smallest possible circle. This fact has compelled me to adopt a simple unadorned style, which I hope the reader will understand.

Just as miners pile up mountains of ore so that refiners may have it available, it is my hope that other hands may fashion this material into invincible armament for the global conflict toward which humanity is hastening. Not only may the enemies of righteousness be routed, but may their fortifications be demolished and the millions who are captives be liberated and join in the song of deliverance as we follow the Prince of Peace, the Captain of our salvation!

PREFACE

VOLUME I is a general treatment of Catholicism while Volume II deals particularly with the absurd, contradictory, fictitious, paganistic, unscriptural priesthood and sacramental system.

Catholic authorities rarely attempt to prove anything, but content themselves with bold assertions and seldom seem concerned or embarrassed with the inconsistencies and contradictions of their tangled history and doctrines. This is probably due to the fact that they know that Protestants spend very little time or money in finding out just what the facts really are. Protestants, in their effort to be fair, dismiss the whole thing with the statement, "They have a right to their religion." Catholics are trained not to trust their own minds and are lulled into submissive complacency by the opiate, "Whatever the Church teaches is right."

Catholics have borrowed profusely from pagans, the world over, and for centuries.

When we have made an exhaustive examination of their literature we are astonished by the persistent effort to discredit the Bible, and to carefully outlaw every freedom loved by mankind: freedom of thought, freedom of speech, freedom of the press, and freedom of worship.

They labor unceasingly to condition the minds of men to the point of accepting their presumptuous and blasphemous pretention to authority. They make every effort to frighten and intimidate the "laity" into accepting the preposterous and shadowy aura of pretended holiness of the priesthood and sacraments. Catholicism is a religion of fear. This frightening atmosphere is augmented by the wholesale blackmail called confession and its twin-forgery absolution.

Catholicism dethrones and demotes both God and Christ, but exalts the fictitious "Mother of God."

Catholic authorities further awe the laity into submission and intimidate non-Catholics into silence with their baseless claim to superior scholarship. It is our purpose to explode this myth.

Probably nothing has done more to induce the laity to accept their dictum than the belated claim to infallibility of the pope. I say, "belated," for this claim is less than one hundred years old. But if this is accepted no proof is necessary.

The exposé of this volume is merciless toward these vicious arrangements and their perpetrators, but prayerfully gentle toward the millions who have been imprisoned by this satanic system. This is an untiring effort to turn the light of reason, history, and scripture into the dark, foul, and moldy recesses of this diabolical abode of demons.

Much time and space will be given to holding up the light of God's word, which is so beautifully and completely displayed in the Bible. Let us never, for a moment, forget the statement found in the Catholic *New Testament* (2 Tim. 3:16-17). The following are renderings of this same statement, as they are found in six different Catholic translations.

"Every scripture is inspired of God and profitable for teaching, for correction, and for training in justice, in order that the man of God may be perfect, fully equipped for every good work" (*Westminster Version*).

"All Scripture, inspired of God, is profitable to teach, to reprove, to correct, to instruct in justice, that the man of God may be perfect, instructed for every good work" (*Douay Version*).

"Everything in the scripture has been divinely inspired, and has its uses; to instruct us, to expose our errors, to correct our faults, to educate us in holy living; so God's servant will become a master of his craft" (*Knox's Translation*).

"All Scripture is inspired by God and useful for teaching, for reproving, for correcting, for instructing in holiness, that the man of God may be perfect, fully equipped for every good deed" (*Kleist and Lilly Version*).

"Every scripture is divinely inspired and is profitable for instruction, for reproof, for correction, for training in rectitude; that the man of God may be perfect, completely equipped for every good work" (*Spencer's Translation*).

"All Scripture is inspired by God and useful for teaching, for reproving, for correcting, for instructing in justice; that the man of God may be perfect, equipped for every good work" (*Confraternity Version*).

Those six translations were made by Catholic scholars and this is believed and accepted by all other scholars. Note that all six translations say that everything in the Scriptures is inspired of God. Yet, we will present many statements from Catholic authorities denying the inspiration of the Scriptures. These translations also say that the man of God, armed with the Scriptures, is "fully" and "completely" equipped for every good work. This one statement demolishes, forever, the claim for Tradition. None of which is even hinted at in the Bible! If it is not in the Bible it is not a good work!

The reader cannot fail to see that this chimerical thing called Tradition is as much without foundation as a mirage on the ocean. The scripture predicts that men will, "turn away their hearing from the truth and turn aside rather to fables" (2 Tim. 4:4, *Confraternity, Catholic version*). It is because of this truth, that abundant evidence will be given showing that Catholic authorities not only blaspheme the Bible, in many statements, but seem unafraid to deliberately delete and mistranslate it.

Tradition" is one incredible succession of fables!

These are severe charges, and the Catholic hierarchy has done such a magnificent job of camouflage that at this point many, who call themselves Protestants, will be tempted to close this book and read no more.

You owe it to yourself to withhold judgment until the end. I pray that you will, and that your conclusion will be honestly and sincerely made.

Has it not occurred to you that if this were slander the Catholic hierarchy would have appealed to the courts, long ago?

CONTENTS

INTRODUCTION

There has been far too much irresponsible writing and ranting against the corruptions of Roman Catholicism which have consisted of erratic charges and unsupported assertions without the proof of documentary evidence. These voluminous vituperations have been more detrimental than beneficial and have closed the avenues of approach to hearts of many who otherwise may have become "doers of the word, and not hearers only."

The author of this volume, and the subject of this sketch, has long been a collector of evidential sources in the field of this treatise, and he speaks and writes "as one having authority," not as a mere scribe, or a novice. His library contains rows of shelves of authoritative works, books, encyclopedias, out-of-print volumes and scores of fragments and treatises, recovering from many centuries the lethal testimony of the ages against the papal hierarchy of Rome. Armed with this documentary historical evidence, along with his chief offensive and defensive armament, the Bible, he has been in the field of battle against Roman Catholicism for more than forty years. He has lived and preached in the strongholds of Catholicism, and on constantly re-occurring occasions in private and public clashes with the priests of Rome, amid the clamor of the hostilities of their devotees and votaries, almost as Paul in Ephesus, the "beasts" of Romanism railed against him, reviled and threatened him. In every situation and upon every occasion, Brother Lambert maintained a calm composure and certitude, knowing that he had the armor of truth and the authenticated evidence of history for every indictment against the Roman priesthood and hierarchy.

Along with the ability that attends age and experience in his own right, O.C. Lambert had in earlier years the enviable opportunity of association with the pioneers of the restoration cause. He was among the legion of the early preachers who attended the Nashville Bible School, before its name was changed to David Lipscomb College, having entered that school prior to the death of its founder, David Lipscomb. In correction of an error made by this writer some years ago, that Brother Lambert had "sat at the feet" of David Lipscomb, he stated that he had not shared this honor with some who claim it, but did live nearby the Lipscomb home after entering that school, was in the Lipscomb home many times and drank milk from his cow! Of a truth, the towering influence of Lipscomb and Sewell—and of other patriarchs of Tennessee, in this cradle of the church in the great Southland of the U.S.A.—touched the life of O.C. Lambert and contributed to the making of the man that he has been in the world and in the church.

Born in Marion County, Alabama, September 16, 1890, Brother Lambert is seventy-four years of age. The Lord has blessed him bountifully and abundantly, as he enjoys better health now than at any previous time since his youth, and is active and busy writing his books and preaching the Word. He was baptized in 1902 and began preaching in 1910; and his labors have carried him into forty-five states and half the provinces of Canada. He has visited no less than one thousand churches of Christ in the United States and Canada. He has had many public discussions with Catholics and Protestants, and has authored numerous books. Among these valuable printed contributions are the books: *Rumblings from Rome, Russellism Unveiled, Catholicism Un-American, Catholicism against Itself,* volume I, and now volume II of that title.

These books have had not only a wide circulation among members of the church of Christ, but have been sold all over the world to various Protestant groups. These publications are inestimable in worth to readers and students inside and outside the church in combatting the evils and the errors, the doctrines and the dogmas, both religiously and politically of the Roman Hierarchy.

Essentially *Roman Catholicism* is not a church—it is a political state, a government, for which its devious religious organization is

12

but a springboard. Its disguised political system operates under the religious mask. Its most effective propaganda among the misguided peoples of all nations, including this United States of America, is the claim to be the custodians of true religion against the encroachments of atheistic Communism. But *Roman Catholicism* is itself not more or less than a rival system of *Communism,* having as its immediate aim and ultimate goal the complete political and religious regimentation of every man in every land. The officials of its multiple-organization are *termites* in our society and all of our people need to be equipped with an effective *insecticide* of information.

The author of this work, O.C. Lambert, has provided this necessary product. He is not an amateur, he is a veteran in the field, and has committed to the printed page the result of maturity in research, a veritable library of resources made available to readers within libraries, in two masterful volumes against the most monstrous system of error and evil man has ever conceived or the world has ever known in the form of a *religio-political* organization—namely, *Roman Catholicism.*

The *first section* of this volume presents a great mass of shocking blasphemy against the Bible, which a Romanist hates with a venom more deadly than do infidels themselves. The *second section* contains sources of vital information concerning Catholic tradition versus the Bible, and reveals the groundless and contradictory character of its claims. The *third section* paints the abysmally dark picture of priesthood depravity, a black history of popery. The *fourth section* is an exposure of the unscriptural Sacraments of the Catholic chinch, showing them to be of human origin and not by divine institution and authority.

In a final word, with respect to *Roman Catholicism* we are facing a battle with two fronts—the political and the religious. The tentacles of this religio-politico monster are fastened to our government and the infiltration of its propaganda in our society exceeds that of Communism, and is no less dangerous to the nation

13

and to the church. The books of O.C. Lambert are a clarion call to arms—let us awake, arise, and gird ourselves for battle. "Stand therefore, having your loins girt about with truth, and having on the breastplate of righteousness."

FOY E. WALLACE, JR.

CHAPTER I

Jews in Old Testament Changed the Law

WHEN the Law of Moses was given, the Jews were cautioned against adding to or taking from the law.

Jews Must Not Change Law

"And now, O Israel, hear the commandments and judgments which I teach thee: that doing them, thou mayst live, and entering in mayst possess the land which the Lord the God of your fathers will give you. You shall not add to the word that I speak to you, neither shall you take away from it: keep the commandments of the Lord your God which I command you" (Deut. 4:1-2 *Catholic Douay Version*).

In spite of this warning the Jews set aside God's law and put their "traditions," the commandments of men, in its place.

"Brethren, the will of my heart, indeed, and my prayer to God, is for them unto salvation. For I bear them witness, that they have a zeal of God, but not according to knowledge. For they, not knowing the justice of God, and seeking to establish their own, have not submitted themselves to the justice of God" (Rom. 10:1-3, *Douay*).

"Then came to him from Jerusalem scribes and Pharisees, saying: Why do thy disciples transgress the traditions of the ancients? For they wash not their hands when they eat bread. But he answering, said to them: Why do you transgress the commandments of God for your tradition?. . . You have made void the commandments of God for your tradition. Hypocrites, well hath Isaias prophesied of you, saying: This people honoreth me with their lips: but their heart is far from me. And in vain do they worship me, teaching doctrines and commandments of men" (Matt. 15:1-9, *Douay*).

15

This is exactly what Catholicism has done in our day.

"But there were also false prophets among the people, even as among yourselves there will be false teachers, who will bring in destructive divisions, and deny the Lord who bought them, bringing upon themselves speedy destruction. And many will follow after their wantonness, by reason of whom the way of truth will be maligned, and in their covetousness they will make their profit of you with feigned words; from of old their judgment lieth not idle, and their destruction slumbereth not" (2 Pet. 2:1-4, *Westminster, Catholic Version*).

"For my people have done two evils. They have forsaken me, the fountain of living water, and have digged themselves cisterns, broken cisterns, that can hold no water" (Jer. 2:13, *Douay*).

"Because they have acted folly in Israel, and have committed adultery with the wives of their friends, and have spoken lying words in my name, which I commanded them not: I am the judge and the witness, saith the Lord" (Jer. 29:23, *Douay*).

"The prophets prophesied falsehood, and the priests clapped their hands: and my people loved such things: What then shall be done in the end thereof?" (Jer. 5:31, *Douay*).

"Thus saith the Lord: "Stand in the court of the house of the Lord, and speak to all the cities of Juda, out of which they come, to adore in the house of the Lord, all the words which I have commanded thee to speak unto them: leave not out one word" (Jer. 26:2, *Douay*).

"To the law rather, and to the testimony. And if they speak not according to this word, they shall not have the morning light" (Isa. 8:20, *Douay*).

"And the earth is infected by the inhabitants thereof: because they have transgressed the laws, they have changed the ordinances, they have broken the everlasting covenant" (Isa. 24:5, *Douay*).

Must Not Add to Law

"Every word of God is fire tried: he is a buckler to them that hope in him. Add not anything to his words, lest thou be reproved and found a liar" (Prov. 30:5-6, *Douay*).

Present Day Prophesied of

"I will raise them up a prophet out of the midst of their brethren like to thee: and I will put my words in his mouth, and he shall speak to them all that I shall command him. And he that will not hear his words, which he shall speak in my name, I will be the revenger. But the prophet, who being corrupted with pride shall speak in my name things that I did not command him to say, or in the name of strange gods, shall be slain" (Deut. 18:18-20, *Douay*).

Must Not Break One Commandment

"He therefore that shall break one of the least commandments, and shall teach men so, shall be called the least in the kingdom of heaven. But he that shall do and teach, he shall be called great in the kingdom of heaven" (Matt. 5:19, *Douay*).

To *break*, means to "annul, subvert, to do away with; to deprive of authority whether by precept or by act" (*Thayers Greek Lexicon*). This the Catholics have done with the entire New Testament pattern. They made immersion "obsolete" and substituted pouring. They have set aside a married eldership for an unmarried priesthood. They have annulled the Lord's Supper and substituted for it the Eucharist and the Mass, as different from the Lord's Supper as night is from day. They have "deprived of authority" the command, "Call no man father" (Matt. 23:9). And so it is with the entire New Testament law!

There Can Be No Argument

There can be no argument: the Scriptures "fully" and "completely equip" "for every good work." All translations of the Bible,

Catholic or Protestant, agree on this point.

This, in reality, cuts the advocates of Catholicism off from any other source of authority. Logically they are forbidden to use, or try to justify, anything not found in the Scriptures. The doctrines, the worship, and government of the Catholic Church are made up of thousands of things not once hinted at in the Scriptures. They talk much of a "Rule of Faith," which when boiled down means, "Forget the Bible and listen to the priests!"

The Bible a Perfect Law of Liberty

Since all are compelled to agree that a law that "equips for every good work" is perfect, we are prepared for another Scriptural passage in the translation of which Catholic and Protestant Bibles are in perfect agreement:

"But he who has looked carefully into the perfect law of liberty and has remained in it, not being a forgetful hearer but a doer of the work, shall be blessed in his deed" (James 1:25).

So we have a law today and it is perfect. For an analogy let us think of a circle. If we change the circle in any respect it ceases to be a circle. Also if we change the perfect law of liberty in any respect it ceases to be the perfect law of liberty. We ought to be able to see clearly why a man is warned, in so many passages, not to add to, or to diminish from the scripture.

The most transcendent quest that can claim the attention of mortal man is to find the way to eternal happiness when this fleeting earthly existence comes to an end. If there is any undertaking that should be characterized by earnestness, charity, and mutual helpfulness it is this. No thoughtful individual should close his mind to truth, for he who does makes himself his own enemy. If there is no future life, then man is the most unfortunate of living things, for no other being is capable of anxiety with reference to it. We would be "of all men most miserable." When we follow the Bible we cannot be wrong! Then, and only then, can our minds be

18

free of anxiety and our hearts filled with hope.

Innumerable evidences are all about us of an infinite intelligence, who, instead of confusion that would characterize blind chance, has provided almost unbelievable harmony everywhere. "The fool hath said in his heart there is no God" (Psalms 14:1). "The heavens declare the glory of God; and the firmament showeth his handiwork" (Psalms 19:1).

The pitifully benighted pagans were, for centuries, cheated and deluded by oracles, fakers, and witch doctors. In our own day men and women sometime claim a great following by pretending to deliver revelations. Unfortunately there are abroad many religious racketeers. A great intelligence capable of creating such a universe is certainly capable of revealing his will to man. One who has made man "a little lower than the angels," and given him dominion over this creation, is giving evidence every moment of His love. Surely this one who loves us so, has not failed to reveal dependable answers to life's great questions.

Those who believe the Bible, believe it gives that light, for it says:

"But is now made manifest by the appearing of our saviour Jesus Christ, who hath abolished death, and hath brought life and immortality to light through the gospel" (2 Tim. 1:10). "Again a new commandment I write unto you, which thing is true in him and in you: because the darkness is past, and the true light now shineth" (1 John 2:3). This revelation was given complete nineteen hundred years ago, according to Jude:

"Beloved, while I was making every endeavor to write to you about our common salvation, I found it necessary to write to you, exhorting you to contend earnestly for the faith *once for all* delivered to the saints" (Jude 3, *Confraternity Version*). Note carefully the wording of the Catholic New Testament: "*Once for all* delivered."

Paul, speaking as one of the inspired Apostles, tells us that

19

they, at that time, had all wisdom, so there was none to be given centuries later, as Catholics claim:

"Wherein he hath abounded toward us in all wisdom and prudence" (Eph. 1:8).

The following Scripture states clearly that the Apostles, in the early church, had all the revelation:

"Go, stand and speak in the temple to the people all the words of this life" (Acts 5:20, *Confraternity Version*).

"I have kept back nothing that was for your good" (Acts 20:20, *Confraternity Version*).

"I have not shrunk from declaring to you the whole council of God" (Acts 20:27, *Confraternity Version*).

"For this cause I, Paul, the prisoner of Christ Jesus, on behalf of you the Gentiles (bend my knees to the Father)—for you have surely heard of the gracious commission of God given me in your regard, how by revelation *the mystery* was made known to me, as I have written in brief above. By reading that you can perceive my insight into the mystery of Christ, which was not made known to other generations of the sons of men, as now it hath been made known to his holy Apostles and prophets in the Spirit—that in Christ Jesus through the gospel the Gentiles are coheirs and concorporate and comparticipant in the promise" (Eph. 3:1-6, *Westminster-Catholic Version*).

"For in him dwelleth the fulness of the Godhead corporeally: and ye are filled in him, who is the head of all principality and power" (Col. 2:9-10, *Douay*).

"As all things of his divine power which appertain to life and godliness, are given us, through the knowledge of him who hath called us by his own proper glory and virtue" (2 Pet. 1:3, *Douay*).

"But when he, the Spirit of truth, has come, he will teach you *all* the truth" (John 16:13, *Confraternity Version*). The spirit came to the Apostles in Acts 2, so, after this they had all the truth!

CHAPTER II

Discount the Bible

The Dilemma of Catholicism

THE CATHOLIC CHURCH occupies a very difficult position, which makes it necessary for her to contradict herself continually. For the benefit of American Protestantism, she has labored to present herself as an ardent lover and defender of the Bible, for she knows that Protestants, whom she hopes to inveigle into her fold, are not yet ready to take seriously a religious body which scorns and ignores that sacred Book. To her devotees, whom she wishes to have accept her teaching without regard for, and most of the time in exact contradiction of the Bible, she presents an image of skepticism, antagonism, indifference and contempt.

There has been presented, in Volume I, more than a hundred quotations from authentic, official Catholic books which unmistakably commit her to this unenviable position. Millions, they claim, got along wonderfully for hundreds of years without the Bible, implying that if they could, so can we. Therefore, they reason, we do not really need the Bible. Catholic authorities assert that the Catholic Church has always been independent of the Bible. This means you do not need a Bible, by which to run the Church. Popes and councils have decreed "reading of the Bible is not for all." The clear conclusion from this is a Catholic may live his entire life acceptably and never read one word of the Bible. They do this in face of "Holy Writ."

"Even in this present age of paper and of printing numberless Catholics live admirable and even sublime lives of faith, hope and charity without any direct reading of Holy Writ" (A *Catholic Commentary on the Holy Scriptures*, 11).

"Now these were more noble than those in Thessalonica who

received the word with all eagerness, daily searching the scriptures, whether these things were so" (Acts 17:11, *Douay*).

Thus, daily scripture reading is a noble thing. They assert further that parts of the Bible are not fit for children or the ignorant to read. This clearly implies that Bible reading is dangerous. There were also presented in Volume I countless statements to the effect that we should keep this dangerous book from our children as we would a sharp knife. We are assured by Catholic authorities that reading the Bible has led millions to the utter rejection of Christ. We are told of one of their very important saints, who herself, could not read or write, who with commendable discernment refused admittance, as an inmate of her monastery, a young lady who wished to bring this dangerous book with her. Volume I produced ample evidence that for about five hundred years it was considered a "crime" for a bookseller to sell a Catholic Bible to a Catholic in his own language. The bookseller was fined, and the "dangerous" book taken forcibly by the priest.

In spite of all these damaging facts the hierarchy boasts that they wrote the Bible, and have kept it through the centuries.

Boasting for the Benefit of Protestants

"Who preserved this book during the previous fifteen hundred years? From whom did the Reformers receive it? Who kept it safe through all dangers; in the midst of conflagration, wars, and the destructive torrents of barbarian incursion? Who copied it over and again, before the art of printing? The Roman Catholic Church did all this; and yet flippant and dishonest writers still accuse her of having concealed this book of life from the people" (*History of the Protestant Reformation.* Archbishop Spalding, 293).

They must have been very inefficient writers to have left out of the Bible the Pope, cardinal, archbishop, subdeacon, abbot, abbess, priests, monks, nuns, monasteries, sacraments, the worship of Mary, and the thousands of other things which go to make up

22

Catholicism. They must have been very careless custodians judging from the following:

The Bible a Mere Wreck!

"If we act honestly, we must confess that we have no certainty if we proceed on these lines, that we have the whole of the Christian faith or can ever obtain it; it is something which the Apostles had, but which has, perhaps, now to great extent been lost; we have some pieces of it, but not with any certainty the whole. It is, as has been said, a mere wreck which has come down to us" (*Plain Facts for Fair Minds,* George M. Searle, 24-25). Searle was a professor in the Catholic University of America. My copy of this book is dated 1915. Eight hundred and ninety thousand copies had been printed up to that date. This shows conclusively that this is a representative Catholic appraisal of the Bible. Besides this, the book bears the *Imprimatur* of an archbishop.

Catholic Authorities Contradictory

"The text of the Hebrew Bible is one of the best attested and most reliable of all those bequeathed to us by antiquity" (*20th Century Encyclopedia of Catholicism,* Vol. 63, *Biblical Criticism,* Jean Steinmann, 74).

"The Greek New Testament was the most frequently copied of all ancient texts and boasts the largest number of manuscripts. The variation of detail in these manuscripts are numerous, but they do not affect in the slightest the substance of the text, which is better guaranteed than that of any other ancient work" (*20th Century Encyclopedia of Catholicism,* Vol. 63, Jean Steinmann, 76).

No Error in the Bible!

"All error is excluded from the Bible since God is its principal Author; if it contains error, God himself would be responsible for that error, but this is impossible because of His infinite knowledge and truthfulness. Hence everything in the original books is infallibly true in the sense intended by the author" (*Catholic Dictionary, Vatican Editon,* 483).

This is a true statement, but diametrically opposed to the many quotations following, to the effect, that the writers of the Bible were ignorant, unlearned men and that their statements are not to be accepted as true. Infidels have for centuries blasphemed against the Bible and the reader will see that all this blasphemy is accepted and triumphantly displayed by Catholic authorities. Catholicism is simply a form of unbelief!

The Bible a Dangerous Book!

The Council of Trent went on record, four hundred years ago, that the Bible was dangerous for our children and that to have it in the language of the people so they might read it for themselves did "more harm than good." She has not changed because the highest authorities make the same statements in almost identical words today (See Vol. I, 32-34).

Dangerous Like Sharp Knives and Fire for Babies!

"For example, if it be a question of our using the Bible in the vernacular (the language of the people—O.C.L.), explain the belief and teaching of the Church in this matter.

"It is said that we deprive the Faithful of the word of God, which is the soul's daily bread. We may answer this falsehood by stating that while indeed the Scripture is our soul's daily bread, Mother Church proportions it to our needs. Just as parents do not give the whole loaf to their children, or a knife with which to cut it lest they injure themselves, so it is the duty of the Church, of the priest or the preacher, to distribute the spiritual bread of the word of God to the people in portions suited to their requirements.

"It is said that the Word of God is the light of the world. Well indeed do we admit this truth. But we do not place a lighted candle

24

in a child's hands, lest he burn himself' (*The Priest, His Dignity and Obligations,* by "St. John Eudes," 99).

This man wrote about three hundred years ago. Cardinal Spellman had this book reprinted under his Imprimatur in 1947. This means that these sentiments are still indorsed by the highest Catholic authorities. The Bible is still believed, by the Catholic hierarchy, to be a dangerous book!

Bible Not a Safe Book!

"From all of which it must be abundantly clear that the Bible alone is not a safe and competent guide because it is not now and has never been accessible to all, because it is not clear and intelligible to all, and because it does not contain all the truth of the Christian religion" (*Finding Christ's Church,* John A. O'Brien, 20). The following would be amusing, if it were not tragic!

Forbids Bible Because She Loves It So!

"If occasionally she has seemed to restrict its use or its diffusion this, too, was through an easily comprehensible love and a particular esteem for the Bible, that the sacred book might not like a profane book be made a ground for curiosity, and endless discussion, and abuses of every kind" (*Catholic Encyclopedia,* XV, 9).

Catholicism Enemy of Bible Reading!

"The Catholic Church is opposed chiefly by three enemies; the civil power, which seeks to rule the Church and become omnipotent in all departments of society; Bible reading Protestantism; and infidelity" (*History of the Catholic Church,* Richard Brennan, 242).

We shall see as we proceed with this work that infidelity is not an enemy of Catholicism if we are thinking of unbelief in the inspiration and authority of the Bible. Infidelity is her principle ally! Catholicism itself is a system of unbelief.

"But first it must be clearly understood whom we have to oppose and contend against, and what are their tactics and their arms. In earlier times the contest was chiefly with those who, relying on private judgment and repudiating the divine traditions and teaching office of the Church, held the Scriptures to be the one source of revelation and final appeal in matters of faith" (*Great Encyclical Letters,* Leo XIII, 281).

It will be remembered by those who have read Volume I that members of the laity have either one or the other of two attitudes (Vol. I, 40) "blank indifference or puzzled hostility"! That should be expected from the hierarchies persistent efforts to picture the Bible as a dangerous book.

Bible "Unsuited" to the Young!

"More than this, parts of the Bible are evidently unsuited to the very young or to the ignorant, and hence Clement XI condemned the proposition that the reading of the Scripture is for all. These principles are fixed and invariable but the discipline of the Church with regard to the reading of the Bible in the vulgar tongue (language of the people—O.C.L.) has varied with varying circumstances" (*Catholic Dictionary,* Addis and Arnold, 82).

The Catholic Church cannot, at this time, bum one at the stake for possessing and reading the Bible, but it has been done thousands of times through hundreds of years. The "principle" of wishing to keep the Bible away from people "is fixed and invariable." She reduces Bible reading to a minimum by a changed "discipline!" It is quite effective judging by the following:

Sell 2000 Bibles Per Year!

"One of the chief reasons for the neglect of the Liturgy has been the Catholic neglect of the Bible. . . Hitherto the annual sales of the Douay Bible in the United States have been about two thousand copies" (*The Story of American Catholicism,* Maynard, 608). This book was issued in 1942.

26

One Bible to 11,000 Catholics

We are informed that there are three hundred forty-nine bishops in the United States. This figures about six Bibles per year for each bishop. Some dioceses comprise a whole state. Catholic authorities claim forty-four million Catholics. While I do not have the number that was claimed twenty-three years ago, we will be conservative and suppose that they claimed only one half as many members, at that time. This would figure one Bible for each eleven thousand Catholics! Their present "discipline" for keeping the Bible away from the "laity" is proving impressively effective. In my long experience with middle aged Catholics, I have found that they almost invariably say that they have never had a Catholic Bible in their hands. All this tells a story!

For 300 Years Catholic Attitude One of Anxious Mistrust, Blank Indifference, Puzzled Hostility

"Yet it must be admitted that for a long time Catholics lagged behind in this field. For nearly three hundred years their attitude toward the Book of Books was one of anxious mistrust" (*20th Century Encyclopedia,* Vol. 60, Henri Daniel-Rops, 10).

"In my experience, the laity's attitude toward the Bible is one of blank indifference, varied now and again by one of puzzled hostility. The clergy, no doubt, search the Scriptures more eagerly. And yet, when I used to go around preaching a good deal and would ask the parish priest for a Bible to verify my text from there was generally an ominous pause of twenty minutes or so before he returned, banging the leaves of the sacred volume and visibly blowing on the top" (*Trials of a Translator,* Ronald Knox, 21-22).

Catholics Afraid of Bible!

"I have said that I am not writing primarily for Catholics; nevertheless I should certainly wish to include them among my readers. Sometimes they seem to feel an almost instinctive dread of

Holy Scripture. The result no doubt of centuries of controversy; they have been happy and content within the Church, and have no desire to begin wrangling about texts and such things, especially now, when they are so liable to be confronted with blank contradictions of Scripture rather than with rival interpretations. They may even have a feeling that devotion to the Scriptures is something rather Protestant" (*Back to the Bible,* by Cuthbert Lattey, 15).

Is the Bible a Catholic Book?

One of the advertisements, so widely publicized, by the Knights of Columbus is entitled, *"The Bible Is a Catholic Book."* Another one bears the caption, "Yes, the Bible Is a Confusing Book!" It is easy to see that these two statements, as so many Catholic statements, are conflicting and confusing. I am sure that to one who is attempting to make the Bible fit Catholicism it is disconcerting.

The truth is, as will be amply shown in subsequent chapters, Catholic "tradition" is the world's most confusing system.

If the Bible is a Catholic book, written by Catholics, how can Catholic authorities account for everything distinctively Catholic being left out?

How can they account for the passage: "A bishop then, must be one with whom no fault can be found: faithful to one wife. . . He must be one who is a good head of his own family, and keeps his children in order by winning their full respect; if a man has not learned how to manage his own household, will he know how to govern God's Church?" (1 Tim. 3:1-4, *Knox's Translation*)

The Catholic Church does not allow a bishop to marry at all, while their Bible says "he must!"

Why did they write in the Bible (Gen. 2:18) "And the Lord God said: It is not good for man to be alone: let us make him a help like unto himself?"

Why did they write with reference to the Lord's Supper, "But

28

let a man prove himself, and so let him eat of that bread *and* drink of the cup" (1 Cor. 11:28, *Confraternity Version*)? For centuries the Catholic Church has denied the "cup" to its members.

Why did they write the Bible as it is, and now feel the necessity of putting footnotes at the bottom of the page, in an effort, to keep their subjects from believing what is in the text?

Is it not strange that they would write, "Nor are you to call any man on earth your father" (Matt. 23:9, *Confraternity Version*) and at the same time call every priest "father"?

If they wrote the Bible why do they claim that it is a dangerous book which has led millions to the rejection of Christ? Why, then, is it dangerous for children to read it?

Bible Dumb and Difficult

If they wrote the Bible why is it such a "dumb and difficult book"?

"Through Luther, although Calvin seems to have been the first to announce Monobiblicism clearly, the Bible became the arm of the Protestant revolt. A dumb and difficult book was substituted for the living voice of the Church, in order that each one should be able to make for himself the religion which suited his feelings. And the Bible open before every literate man and woman to interpret for themselves was the attractive bait used to win adherents" (A *Catholic Commentary*, 11).

Catholic authorities tell us, over and over again, that the Bible is a difficult and confusing book. In one of the Knights of Columbus advertisements we find the following statement:

Bible Not Clear

"Scholars who devote their lifetime to the study of the Scriptures are the first to admit the difficulties that beset them. They know the inspired writings are not the clear and easy guide to Christian understanding that so many seem to think."

All the many statements that we present are clearly intended to inspire the laity with a disrespect for the Bible. The result will be to limit Bible reading to a minimum. In this way they "steal the word of God" from the people as was done of old (Jer. 23:30). This is their new "discipline"!

The Bible an Accident—Not a God-given Book

"But nothing was further from the minds of the writers, and of the Apostles generally, than that these writings be gathered together and made into a book, which would be accepted as a complete statement of the doctrine of Christianity. Any one of them would have been shocked had he known that his letters would in time be made use of by heretics in an attempt of usurping the place of the authoritative teacher, the Church of Jesus Christ. That compositions intended to meet certain local circumstances should be accepted everywhere as an infallible guide in faith and morals independent of any authority to interpret them, is distinctly wrong" (*Our Faith and the Facts,* Donovan, 348).

Catholic authorities insist that with only God's word, the Bible, man would be continually plagued with doubt and uncertainty.

Another Knight of Columbus advertisement entitled, "Why the Bible Alone Is Not Enough" is a fanciful promise of freedom from this God-made uncertainty, and is held out to those who leave the Bible alone and turn their souls over to the priests!

What a pity it is, what a tragedy to the human race, that millions have been hindered, discouraged, and even forbidden in the reading of God's word, the Bible. Should only one, of those millions, be brought to the realization that the Bible is God's book and that it is just as divine as the one who gave it, that it can answer all of man's questions, solve all his problems and finally bring him home to God, I shall feel that I have not wasted my time. If they will read it, respect it, and obey it, the author of this book will have been amply repaid for his long hours of research and work.

30

WHY READ THE BIBLE?

To those who have wondered why they should read the Bible, the following reasons are given:

Bible Reading Christ's Custom

"And he came to Nazareth where he was brought up: and he went into the synagogue according to his custom on the sabbath-day; and he rose up to read.

"And the book of Isaias the prophet was delivered to him. And as he read he unfolded the book, he found the place where it was written:" (Luke 4:16-17, *Douay*).

Daily Bible Reading Is Noble

"Now these were more noble than those in Thessalonica, who received the word with all eagerness, daily searching the scripture, whether these things were so" (Acts 17:11, *Douay*).

Bible Reading Profitable

"All scripture, inspired of God, is profitable to teach, to reprove, to correct, to instruct in justice. That the man of God may be perfect, instructed for every good work" (2 Tim. 3:16-17, *Douay*).

Bible Reading a Command

"Search the scriptures, for you think in them to have life everlasting; and the same are they that give testimony of me" (John 5:39, *Douay*).

The Bible Our Judge

"He that despiseth me, and receiveth not my words, hath one that judgeth him; the word that I have spoken, the same shall judge him in the last day" (John 12:48, *Douay*).

The Bible Is Everlasting

"Heaven and earth shall pass away, but my words shall not pass away" (Matt. 24:35, *Douay*).

"The grass is withered, and the flower is fallen: but the word of our Lord endureth for ever" (Isaias 40:8, *Douay*).

"For ever, O Lord, thy word standeth firm in heaven" (Psa. 119:89, *Douay*).

The Bible Is Pure

"The words of the Lord are pure words: as silver tried by the fire, purged from the earth, refined seven times" (Psa. 11:7, *Douay*).

Greatest Miracle of the Ages!

We see that Catholic clergymen, like others who reject the Bible, have many contradictory guesses as to how and when this earth, and especially man, came into being. These guesses by unbelievers are exploded by time and a new set of guesses are advanced. The Bible story of creation is the only explanation that never has to be revised.

Accidents are never harmonious or perfect. Type spilled and picked up in the dark never printed a poem. A cyclone which gathers a great variety of things; when it is over, this array of material is never a beautiful residence with the windows in place and locks on the doors. "The fool hath said in his heart: There is no God" (Psa. 13:1, *Douay*)

God Is

To recognize God, an infinite intelligence, behind it all, prepares us to accept, at face value, the saying of our Lord, "with God all things are possible" (Mt. 19:26, *Douay*). To accept the Bible account is entirely reasonable. The unbeliever's guesses are not only shifting and contradictory but unreasonable and impossible of belief.

Man Did Not Write the Bible

If any man, or set of men had written the Bible, it would be like other man-made books, out of date and useless. Instead, after nineteen hundred years, it is continually the world's "best seller." The reason is evident: it supplies man's every need, it tells him where he came from, and where he is going. It is equally interesting and profitable to youth and age. Its philosophy fortifies man for every misfortune and enables him to look with happy anticipation beyond death. It provides us with hope, "the anchor of the soul," enabling man to ride out all the storms of life. It is the mirror in which we behold all our blemishes. It is the chart and compass, when without it all would be lost.

It has been the counsellor of the greatest of earth who feel insignificant and humble in its presence. The nations most affected by it have been the most progressive.

Bible World's Greatest Miracle

The fact that the Bible has always been a "best seller" is not our only reason for knowing that it is not a human product, but its brevity, the circumstances of its writing, its unity, the exactness of its predictions and their fulfillment, the majesty and perfection of its morality, and its many marvelous wonders stamp it as divine.

Having diligently read and studied this book, since I first learned to read, I can join the psalmist of old and say:

"Oh, how I love thy law! It is my meditation all the day."

CHAPTER III

Catholics Do Not Believe the Bible!

I WILL now present a number of shocking, official statements expressing contempt for the Bible and for anyone who respects and believes it!

"It matters very little, of course, whether Lot's wife was actually turned into a pillar of salt. No one who believes in the infinite power of God would question the possibility of such a thing.

"If we conclude that it is, however, a legendary element in a story that the author had used and passed on without comment, it is a principle, as a piece of sound interpretation that also follows the papal injunction *Divine Affiante Spiritu.* That we must determine at all cost the Biblical author's literary forms if we are to know his meaning."

"In other words it is not very likely that such accounts are to be taken as factual histories of what actually happened, but rather as stories, probably with some basis in fact, which teaches some lesson" (*Question Box Column in The Witness,* July 24, 1958).

Ridicule the Story of Creation Bible Cannot Be True!

"Can the age of the human race be figured out from the information we have in the Bible?"

"No, several attempts have been made to determine the age of the world and the age of the human race from the testimony of the Bible, but they have failed. It was thought that the computation of the age of the human race was simply a matter of adding up the ages of the Patriarchs descending from Adam. However, the Biblical lists of the Patriarchs is not guaranteed to be complete nor is the precise significance of the ages assigned to be certain. So the problem is a scientific one, the solution to which rests with sources outside the Bible. Recent scientific discoveries are responsible for pushing the age of man farther and farther back but early man is still shrouded in mystery. Some anthropologists think that man is about 20,000 years old; others 100,000 or more. At least we are sure that the once-believed 4,000 years from Adam to Christ could not be so. Man is much older than that" (Question Box Column in diocesan newspapers). The only thing that author is sure of is that the Bible cannot be true!

Man 600,000 Years Old—Prehistory!

"A tentative 600,000 years can be given for the earliest appearance in these regions, and although these figures have been disputed, there are today few prehistorians prepared to allow less than 400,000 years since the origin of mankind" (*20th Century Encyclopedia of Catholicism,* Vol. 29, Nicolas Corte 77).

Blaspheme Bible!—Man 500,000 Years Old

"When theologians get into the field of science they try to tell us the time, place and manner of man's creation. Scientists have many sound studied reasons for believing that man's history on earth must date back at least thirty thousand years, and possibly a good half million. So they have little patience with the theologians who demand that it be encompassed into the traditional six thousand. Their daily work in the biological science is based on the sound theory that living things have reached their present perfection by a long process of evolution. So we naturally meet only amusement or irritation when we come before them with our imaginative notion of a divine sculptor, who came down to earth on the sixth day, dressed in a workman's smock, blended dust into moulder's clay, and proceeded to fashion man into his own image" (*Question Box Column, Our Sunday Visitor* (Lone Star), Nov. 2, 1958).

Man Millions of Years Old!
Bible Writers Ignorant, Childish!

"What is the effect of the impact of this new knowledge upon religious faith? Does the Christian religion, born two thousands years ago in Palestine in a prescientific age when people entertained childish notions of the universe which have long since been outmoded, possess validity in the age of science in which we now live? To the student whose knowledge of religion does not extend much beyond the catechism or lessons of the Sunday School, the new knowledge is apt to be somewhat disturbing. Coming with the idea of the world created in six days of twenty-four hours each, and the concept of Adam suddenly springing full blossomed from the slime of the earth about six thousand years ago, science's new picture of the world existing for thousands of trillions of years, of the slow evolution of life from lower to higher forms over many millions of years, or man having his physical antecedents in lower organisms, of humanity's long climb from his lowly habitation among the caves of the earth to the mountain peak of present civilization, and his probable duration upon this planet for millions of years—these are likely, at first sight, to be somewhat unsettling" (New *Knowledge and Old Faith,* John A. O'Brien. Ph. D., Imprimatur Cardinal Hayes. Apr. 13, 1935, Page 5).

Thus, we are told that man was not created, as the Bible says, but "evolved" as infidels say!

Don't Believe Story of Flood

"Is the story of the Deluge in the Bible a historical fact or are we to look upon this as a parable?

"We need have no doubt about the actual occurrence of the Deluge. It has been explained in a true historical sense by the Fathers of the Church, theologians, Catholic and non-Catholic writers. The existence of this story among many people, as has been handed down by independent traditions, is the best possible argument for the historical character of the facts which it relates.

"Modern Scripture scholars say that the flood did not cover the entire world, that we need not think that it destroyed all the human race then existing, though the author of Genesis probably believed that it did—and we may believe it too if we want to. Best thing is to see the Flood a symbolic story based on historical fact, the purpose of the story being to teach God's punishment of mankind's sin and his mercy for the sake of the just" (*Lone Star Catholic,* 6/14/59).

This denies the account, given by Moses, in the Catholic Bible:

"He (God) said: I will destroy man, whom I have created, from the face of the earth, for it repenteth me that I have made them. . . He said to Noe: The *end of all flesh* is come before me. . . for they overflowed exceedingly: and *filled all on the face of the earth. . .* and *all the mountains under the whole heaven were covered, the water was fifteen cubits higher than the mountains which it covered.* And *all flesh was destroyed* that moved upon the earth, both of fowl, and of cattle, and of beast, and of all creeping things that creep upon the earth: and *all men. . .* and *Noe only remained, and they that were with him in the ark"* (Gen. 6:13; 7:18-23, Italics for emphasis).

They Do Not Believe Jesus!

Jesus says all were taken away;

"And as in the days of Noe, so shall also the coming of the son of man be. For in the days before the flood they were eating and drinking, marrying and giving in marriage, even till that day in which Noe entered into the Ark, and they knew not till *the flood came, and took them all away"* (Matt. 24:37-39, *Douay Version.* Also Luke 17:26-27).

They Do Not Believe Peter!

"Which had been sometime incredulous, when they waited for the patience of God in the days of Noe, when the ark was a-building: *Wherein a few, that is eight souls, were saved by water*" (1 Pet. 3:20).

Catholics do not believe Moses; they do not believe Peter and they do not believe Jesus. All of them attest the Bible story of the flood!

Africa the Birthplace of Man!

The Bible is very plain that the Garden of Eden, the place of the creation of man was in Asia (Gen. 2:8-17) but Catholic authorities do not believe this as evidenced by the following:

". . .Africa may well have been the birthplace of the primitive members of the species *Homo Sapiens*" (*20th Century Encyclopedia of Catholicism*, Volume 30, Remy Collin, 64).

The Bible Classed as Ignorance!

"And this is one of the most important advances made by exegesis, under the pressure of scientific research itself, during the last half century. Today it is readily accepted that the Bible is not to be consulted as if it were a scientific treatise, and that such seemingly scientific facts as are to be found in it *have no other value than to inform us of the ideas current at the different times at which the books composing it were written*" (*20th Century Encyclopedia of Catholicism*. Volume 29, Nicolas Corte, 94).

How do they have the temerity to speak of the Bible as the "Holy Scriptures"?

Bible Not History—Confused

"His (Ezekiel's) book is amazingly confused. It claims to have been written in exile at Babylon. But the many obvious and curious editorial tricks have given rise to the hypothesis that the oracles were uttered in Palestine, then touched up and published at Babylon. . . Numerous obscurities in the text . . . it is admitted today that Jonas is a long parable. Habacuc and Zacharias show strong apocalypic influence. . . it has not reduced the value of these texts or cast doubt on their inspiration" (*20th Century Encyclopedia of Catholicism,* Volume 63, Jean Steinmann, 99).

In the same way they dispose of Job, Psalms, and Ecclesiastes.

Bible Not History

"Similarly, when we come to the stories of the Patriarchs, Moses and the conquest of Canaan, we are confronted not so much with history in the technical sense of the word as with a heroic epic. In the old traditions the details of the Patriarchs' lives smack of an intentional poetry which, in the eyes of the inspired writers, cast no more discredit on the reality of these people than the poetry of the *Song of Roland* on the reality of Charlemagne. . . The Principles of ancient law and various topographical details all support the historicity of the Patriarchs, even *if the stories of their lives do not belong to a literary form that can technically be described as history"* (*20th Century Encyclopedia of Catholicism,* Volume 63, Jean Steinmann, 88).

"Hai (Ai) was already in ruins in the time of Josue (Joshua), but he is made to capture the town" (Ibid, 92).

"Criticism enables us to read *the so-called historical books of the Bible* without making too many blunders" (Ibid, 95).

Story of Creation Myth!

"It is for the exegetes and the theologians and, in the last resort, for the teaching authority of the Church, to discriminate between what is mythical in the Biblical texts and what in the myth deserves to be retained as true. That a serpent spoke is a myth" (*20th Century Encyclopedia of Catholicism,* Volume 29, Nicolas Corte, 120-121).

Catholics Are Evolutionists—Have Changed!

"Father Ewing stated that the question of evolution affords us an excellent example of how Catholic theologians can change their opinion, without challenging the *immutability of Catholic doctrine*.

"He recalled that 100 years ago Darwin's theory seemed to many Catholic thinkers to call into question some sections of Scripture, especially the book of Genesis.

"To those who believe that theologians were too slow to accept the evolution of man's body, the Jesuit scientist replied that at the time of the publication of *Origin of the Species,* scientific evidence for evolution was 'scant indeed'" (J. Franklin Ewing, S.J., *Brooklyn Tablet,* 12/5/59).

This is great Jesuit logic. Catholic changes in doctrine show the impossibility for Catholics to change!

Claim Paul Was Mistaken, Charge He Misled!

"It may be granted that certain counsels (i.e. to the father of a family) are influenced by the Apostle's personal belief in the proximate return of Christ" (*Pastoral Medicine,* Ruland and Rattler, 327).

This evidently alludes to I Cor. 7 where Paul advises against marriage because of "the present distress" (verse 26) and this writer infers that Paul therefore expected the immediate end of the world! The context shows clearly that this is not what is meant. I am sure that this is true for another reason. Paul in 2 Thes. 2:1-3 warns against ignorant men like "Pope Gregory, the Great," who had that false notion!

"And we beseech you, brethren, by the coming of our Lord Jesus Christ, and of our gathering together unto him: that you be not easily moved from your sense, nor be terrified, neither by spirit, nor by word, nor by epistle, as sent from us, as if the day of the

Lord were at hand. Let no man deceive you by any means, for unless there come a revolt first, and the man of sin be revealed, the son of perdition, who opposeth and is lifted up above all that is called God, or that is worshipped, so that he sitteth in the temple of God, showing himself as if he were God" (2 Thes. 2:1-3, *Catholic Translation*). Paul warned against belief in the immediate return of Christ. But listen to Gregory:

Pope Gregory "The Great" Badly Mistaken!

Catholic Encyclopedia, in commenting on Gregory, who is claimed as bishop of Rome (590-604) speaks of "his clear expectation of a speedy end of the world" (VI, 780). This authority also says:

"He was not a man of profound learning, not a philosopher, not a controversialist, hardly even a theologian in the constructive sense of the term" (*Catholic Encyclopedia,* VI, 786).

This pope expected a speedy end of the world nine hundred and sixty-four years ago and it has not ended yet! It was the pope who was mistaken and not the inspired apostle!

Catholics Charge Bible Is Fables!

"The events related in Holy Scripture are only occasionally correlated with events of secular history and are seldom dated according to **an** era or epoch. . . Those that precede the time of Abraham, cannot be determined even approximately. *In Genesis 5 and 10, we have fables* of chronological units, but for various reasons the numbers given in our present text are considered corrupted and *the fables themselves incomplete. . .* During the period of the two kingdoms we come to the first dates on which all authorities agree, because they are found recorded on Assyrian monuments" (*Catholic Dictionary, Vatican Edition,* 212).

41

Writer of Genesis Ignorant!

"The Biblical narrative was written by an eye witness (flood, O.C.L.), or by someone writing not long after the event, and must be understood, not according to our ideas, but according to his, *who wrote the things in as far as known to him* . . . It is impossible to fix the time of the deluge, since the dates mentioned in the three available texts of Scripture disagree both as to the year from Adam and as to the year before Christ mentioned in the text and ancient tradition is 3100, but scientists demand that the deluge be placed at a much earlier time" (*Catholic Dictionary, Vatican Edition,* 287).

Bible Ridiculous Folklore

"The chapters with which the Bible begins, the book of Genesis, obviously belong to a complex species of literature in which history, popular tradition and folklore, moral teaching and cosmogonical revelation are all mixed together and borne aloft on the wings of admirable poetry. As for the actual history to be found in the Bible, it is perfectly obvious that it does not obey the often ridiculously artificial criteria of the 'historical science' of today" (*20th Century Encyclopedia of Catholicism,* Volume 60, Henri Daniel-Rops, 52).

Claim Bible Only Ignorance!

"Here is a chapter that presents formidable difficulties. Ever since Galileo it has been the object of learned discussion. Moses described God's creating the universe in six days. But science has proved that our earth broke off from the sun millions of years ago. The gradual cooling and hardening of this earth, the formation of continents and seas, the invasion of glaciers, form an epic narrative of staggering time proportions. Only in quite recent times did this earth bring forth the animals and vegetation of today, these having evolved gradually from different forms. Can the six days of which Moses speaks be these long periods described by geologists?

"Answering the oft-repeated query, the association replies: 'Certainly they are not'. *Moses knew nothing of modern science: his picture of the universe is quite naive, no further advanced, in fact, than that of the people among whom he lived three thousand years ago.* But no human mind has ever surpassed him in the ultimate explanation which he gives of the universe in his first words: 'In the beginning God created the heavens and the earth'" (*Getting the Most Out of the Bible,* O'Brien, 16).

Stopping the Sun Only Hyperbole!

"The stopping of the sun by Josue is told in a miniature epic poem and looks very much as though it is only an Eastern hyperbole" (Henri Daniel-Rops, *20th Century Encyclopedia of Catholicism,* Vol. 60, 52).

Sun Only Appeared To Stand!

"Thus (to apply the doctrine of the *Encyclical-Providentissimus Deus* to a well-known passage) in Joshua 10:13, it is said that the sun stood still: details are not supplied such as to enable us to determine with precision, what exactly happened, but it would be a sufficient explanation to say that the sun only appeared to stand still" (Cuthbert Lattey, *Back to the Bible,* 41).

Bible Writer Totally Devoid of Talent!
Bible Most Boring!

"Inspiration does not prevent the author of *Leviticus* from being the *most boring of lawyers,* the compiler of the chronicles from being *totally devoid of talent* or the author of the Apocalypse from making *many syntactical mistakes* in his Greek" (Henri Daniel-Rops. *20th Century Encyclopedia of Catholicism,* Volume 60, 47).

Bible a Poor Book—Loyola Better!

"Yet it does happen that some devout Christians experience a certain disappointment when they open the Bible. They expect to find uplifting and heartwarming phrases and are *faced instead with dry lists of ritual observances, fierce imprecations of some of the prophets* and the enigmatic sentences of the Apocalypse—if not the matrimonial adventures of the Kings. It must be admitted that the Bible in no way resembles a manual of devotion; apart from the Gospels and sapiential books, *it has little to offer the believer nourished on the Imitation or even the Spiritual Exercises of St. Ignatious of Loyola"* (Henri Daniel-Rops, *20th Century Catholic Encyclopedia,* Volume 60, 112-113).

Bible Platitudinous and Dull!

"Some parts of the book flash with the sparkle of genius, others are *undeniably platitudinous and dull"* (Henri Daniel-Rops, *20th Century Catholic Encyclopedia,* Volume 60, 27).

Must Accept Catholicism without Change

The Catholic Church has not hesitated to change everything from the pattern given in the New Testament: she has a different name, different beliefs, different practices and a different government.

Claim Bible Crude

"Scripture offers in the *crude state,* as it were, what theologians have subsequently classified, thought out and elaborated" (*20th Century Encyclopedia of Catholicism, What is the Bible,* Henri Daniel-Rops, Volume 60, 108).

Catholic Books Better Than Bible!

"In *other spiritual books* the truths of the Bible are presented more fully, and in a more modern and familiar style, so that we can hardly wonder that they are, as a rule *preferred"* (*Plain Facts for Fair Minds,* Searle, 154).

". . . if the sacred books are permitted everywhere . . . in the vernacular, there will by reason of the boldness of men arise therefrom *more harm than good"* (Council of Trent, recorded in *Decrees of the Council of Trent,* Schroeder, 273-278). This was four hundred years ago, but Pope Leo XIII made the same statement about seventy-five years ago (*Great Encyclical Letters of Leo XIII*).

Bible Without Plan

"From a literary point of view it is *absurd* to talk of the *'plan of the Bible"'* (Henri Daniel-Rops, *20th Century Encyclopedia of Catholicism,* Volume 60, 28).

Catholicism Not Like the Bible
Bible Not Clear!

"The Bible is silent or at least is *not* clear on a number of matters such as the baptism of infants and exact number of the sacraments, concerning which the church follows tradition" (*National Catholic Almanac,* 1943,128).

This is an admission that Catholicism is not like the Bible.

As we will see when we come to the chapter dealing with "The Virgin Mary," that Mary, in the Catholic system, is above Christ and God! All of which is foreign to the New Testament.

No Scripture To Support Mary Doctrine

"Can it be said that the Blessed Virgin, like Christ also distributes all grace? There is no text in Scripture to support it" (*The Virgin Mary,* Guitton, 138).

CHAPTER IV

Catholics Contradict the Bible

"PROBABLY because Mary Magdalene—*after the Mother of God*—first beheld the risen savior" (The Holy Sacrifice of the Mass, Gihr, 490, emphasis added).

The Catholic Bible Says...

"Now when he had risen from the dead early on the first day of the week, *he appeared first to Mary Magdalene*" (Mark 16:9, Confraternity Catholic Version).

The Bible being true, this Catholic book is wrong!

Bible One Mediator—Catholics Have Thousands!

"For there is one God, and one Mediator between God and men, himself man, Jesus Christ" (1 Tim. 2:5 *Confraternity Catholic Translation*). Catholic teachers contradict this. The *National Catholic Almanac,* (1961, Page 358), says there were 413,034 priests in the world at that time. "St. John Eudes, says priests are "Gods" (*The Priest, His Duties and Obligations,* 13). You will note that Catholics, in referring to priests as "Gods," by capitalizing the word deify the priests. They also insist that there are nearly one half million "Gods." All these priests are "mediators" besides more than nine thousand "saints," including Mary, who are between Catholics and God. Mary is the *Mediatrix (Glories of Mary,* Liguori, 169).

A Priest a Mediator

"It is really God who calls you to the priesthood, to help him in the work of the salvation of souls. He wants you to be a mediator between heaven and earth, to speak to men of God, to speak to God of men and their needs" (*Our Priesthood,* Bruneau, 22).

Bible Teaching Impossible—Changed to Pouring!

"The church at one time practiced immersion. This was up to the thirteenth century. The Council of Ravenna, in 1311, changed the form from immersion to pouring. It is well known, however, that the church had good reasons for doing this, that she had the power to legislate on the matter, and that immersion was not the only accepted form of Baptism up to the time of its change.

". . . The sick, however, could not be baptized by immersion. St. Paul must have used either the sprinkling or pouring, when he baptized the jailer, and his whole household, as recorded in the Acts of the Apostles. Many other cases could be cited where immersion was impossible" (*Our Faith and the Facts,* Donovan, 399).

Immersion Practically Obsolete

"Immersion was the method generally employed in the early Church. The Greeks still retain it; but though valid, for obvious reasons immersion has practically become obsolete in the Latin Church (Roman Catholic—O.C.L.)" (*Catholic Dictionary, Vatican Edition,* 471).

This also shows that the Roman Catholic church split off from the Greeks.

Titus 1:5-7 uses *presbyter* and *bishop* interchangeably in the Catholic translations, but Catholics have tried to confuse this matter because in Catholic doctrine, *a presbyter* is one office and *bishop* is another. In Acts 14:22 we read: "And when they had appointed *presbyters* for them in every Church" (*Confraternity Version*). In the *New Testament* church each congregation had a plurality of bishops, but Cannon 8 of the Council of Nicea forbad two bishops in one city (*Disciplinary Decrees of the General Councils,* 34).

47

Again Catholics contradict the Bible!

Wresting the Scriptures

"In his (Paul's) opinion the words (presbuteros and episcopos) were at one time used one for the other, but there has been a gradual adaptation of names corresponding with the progressive evolution of the hierarchy. . .

"Thus the way was prepared for the still later use of the word *episkopos* to denote the rulers of the church, the successors of the Apostles, i.e., bishops in the modern sense of the word" (*A Catholic Commentary,* 1144).

Law Changed at Last Supper!

"The *Old Testament* went out of force at the Last Supper, the First Mass. The *New Testament* came into force" (*New Interpretation of the Mass,* Borgmann, 81).

The Bible tells us very plainly that the handwriting of ordinances was done away when Jesus was nailed to the cross (Col. 2:14), and that the New Covenant began to be operative after the death of Christ (Heb. 9:11-17).

Catholics Think Saul and Absalom Lived at Same Time!

". . . it (42nd Psalm) was originally written by King David when exiled from his house and home by the treachery of his son Absolom and his kinsman Saul" (*History of the Mass,* O'Brian, 184).

The facts are that Saul was not related to David or Absalom, and had been dead for years when Absalom rebelled.

Contradict the Bible!

Catholic writers say of Christ:

". . . the son is equal in everything to His Father and the same God with Him" (*History of the Church,* Noethen, 176).

48

The Catholic Bible says: "The Father is greater than I" (John 14:28, *Confraternity Version*).

Again Catholics Contradict the Bible

"If we know not the place of his (Joseph's) birth, we know at least that he resided ordinarily at Nazareth, where according to common opinion he pursued the trade of a smith" (*Life of the Blessed Virgin,* Kelley, 164).

The Catholic Bible says: "Is not this the carpenter's son?" (Matt. 13:55, *Confraternity Version*).

In the Bible people were baptized "the same hour of the night" (Acts 16:32-34). In the Catholic Church they do not do this but put them through a long period of training.

"Let a catechumen be instructed for three years" (*Sources of Theology,* I, Palmer, 51).

Long Hair on Christ

A Catholic book says: "Images of Christ retain the long hair parted in the middle and flowing to the shoulders" (*Catholic Dictionary, Vatican Edition,* 429).

In the Catholic Bible we read: "Does not nature itself teach you that for a man to wear his hair long is degrading?" (1 Cor. 11:14, *Confraternity Version*).

Put Pants on Christ, says Priest

"Milwaukee (AP)—A leading Roman Catholic educator suggested Friday that young artists be encouraged to portray Christ as a smooth shaven, short haired, trousered man of today.

"The Rev. E.M. Catish, professor of art at St. Ambrose College, Davenport, Iowa, told delegates to the National Catholic Educational Press Congress that 'we must fashion a Christ who will be no stranger to our time.'

"'Pictorial representations of Christ which we see in our

49

churches, schools and homes usually show Christ gowned, bearded and wearing long marcelled tresses,' said Father Catish.

"'These bearded-lady Christs are strangers to our age—if not to all ages.'

"'Youthful artists,' he said, should be urged to 'defeminize Christ, to return his trousers, to restore his masculinity.'

"'At the same time,' Father Catich added, 'I do not think it vulgar to suggest that we give Christ a shave and a haircut'."

How Catholics Baptize

A Catholic book says:

"The oil of Catechumens is exorcised in this minor unit. The oil of the catechumens is so called because it is for the use of the sacrament of baptism, whereby the catechumens are received into the membership of the Holy Church. Before the pouring of the water in the rite of baptism, the catechumen is anointed with the oil of the catechumens on the breast and on a spot between the shoulders, which corresponds to the spot on the breast just anointed. When anointing the catechumen, the priest says: 'I anoint thee with the oil of salvation in Christ Jesus, Our Lord, that thou mayest have life everlasting'" (*New Interpretation of the Mass*, Borgmann, 140).

This is not like the Catholic Bible, which reads:

"And as they went along the road, they came to some water; and the eunuch said, 'See, here is water; what is there to prevent my being baptized?' (And Philip said, 'If thou dost believe with all thy heart, thou mayest.' And he answered and said, 'I believe Jesus Christ to be the Son of God.') And he ordered the chariot to stop; and both Philip and the eunuch went down into the water, and he Baptized him. But when they came up out of the water, the Spirit of the Lord took Philip away, and the eunuch saw him no more, but he went on his way rejoicing" (Acts 8:35-40, *Confraternity Version*).

50

Reject Statement of Jesus in Matthew 19:9 as Misleading!

Catholic writers insist that there is no just cause for divorce but they admit they have difficulty with their Bible:

"The Protestants who base their doctrine of divorce on our Lord's reply, as related by Matthew, consider divorce permissible in the church. The text of Matthew is difficult, because of the clause, 'except it be for fornication.' But considering it in its context together with the parallel texts, it is hard to imagine how Protestant moralists could have based their doctrine of divorce upon it. A principle of such important matters must be sought where it is expressed without danger of it misleading the reader. We find it in Mark 10, Luke, 16, and I Corinthians, 7. Here the clause, 'except for fornication' is entirely omitted and no one can explain away the truth of the indissolubility of marriage from these texts" (*Catholic Dictionary, Vatican Edition*, 302).

Here the writer blasphemously says that what Jesus says in Matthew 19:9 would mislead the reader. He says, virtually, that Jesus contradicted Himself and that what he said in Matthew 19:9 is not true!

Disregard I Timothy 3:6
"St." Ambrose a Bishop before Baptism!

Catholic writers teach that a man may be made a bishop before baptism, as the following shows:

"When striving to hold an orderly election of a bishop to that see in 374, the people acclaimed him, although out of reverence for baptism he was still only a catechumen preparing for it" (*Catholic Dictionary, Vatican Edition*, 35).

In contrast to this Paul said:

"He must not be a new convert" (1 Tim. 3:6, *Confraternity Catholic Version*)

51

Public Confession Unreasonable—Pope Leo I

"Confess, therefore, your sins to one another" (James 5:16, *Confraternity Version*).

Pope Suppressed Bible Teaching!

"I determine to have all means suppressed, so that the confession of the kind of sins committed by individuals should not be published written in a little book, since it suffices that the guilt of their consciences be made known to the priest only, in secret confession. . . Let so unreasonable a custom be done away: lest many should be repelled from the remedies of penitence, either because they are ashamed, or because they fear that their deeds may be disclosed to their enemies' " (quoted in *History of the Confessional,* Hopkins, 143).

Brands Bible Teaching Presumption!

"In 459 he (Leo I, 'The Great') forbad public confession, as never having been commanded by the Church." He says that it was a "presumption against the Apostolic rule, secret confession being sufficient" (*Lives and Times of the Roman Pontiffs,* Chevalier Artaud de Montor, I, 303-304).

Formally Abolish Bible Teaching!

"Communion 'under both kinds' entirely and formally abolished in 1416 by the Council of Constance" (*Lives and Times of the Roman Pontiffs,* Chevalier Artaud de Montier, I, 111).

"Communion under both kinds was the prevailing usage in Apostolic Times" (*Catholic Encyclopedia,* IV, 176).

"'This cup is the new covenant in my blood; do this as often as you drink it, in remembrance of me. For as often as you shall eat this bread AND DRINK the cup, you proclaim the death of the Lord, until he comes.' Therefore whoever eats this bread or drinks the cup of the Lord unworthily, will be guilty of the body and the

52

blood of the Lord. But let a man prove himself and so let him eat of that bread AND DRINK OF THE CUP; for he who eats AND DRINKS unworthily, without distinguishing the body, eats AND DRINKS judgment to himself" (1 Corinthians 11:25-29, *Confraternity Version*).

I capitalize the words in the forgoing passage to emphasize the fact that the Lord intended for all to drink of the cup.

Two Popes Condemn Present Practice!

"In the fifth century Pope Gelasius commanded the laity to receive under both kinds" (*Question Box*, 446, 1913 Edition).

Glasius is said to have become bishop of Rome in the year 492.

"True, Leo and Gelasius emphatically condemn persons who abstained from the Chalice" (*Catholic Dictionary*, Addis and Arnold, 202).

Catholic authorities thus admit that they countermanded the will of the Lord and in this way popes "exalt themselves above God" (2 Thessalonians 2:4)!

It was in the eleventh century that an effort to do away with the Lord's will, in this matter, was started and after three hundred years this apostasy was finally completed. This "bringing in" of "damnable heresies" was predicted by Peter (2 Peter 2:1-3).

After 1414 What Bible Teaches Is Heresy!

"In the thirteenth session (1414, June 15) the lawfulness and expediency of giving communion to the laity under one species were affirmed, and those who obstinately maintained the contrary were to be treated as heretics" (*Catholic Dictionary*, Addis and Arnold, 219).

The Catholic boast of never changing is clearly refuted, and two popes thus declared to be heretics! This is another instance convicting Catholics of reversing the Lord's arrangements.

Reversing Bible Teaching!

"Woe unto them that call evil good, and good evil; that put darkness for fight, and light for darkness; that put bitter for sweet, and sweet for bitter" (Isaiah 5:20, *Douay, Catholic Version*).

Catholic writers claim that a person receives both the body and blood in the bread only. Why didn't the Lord think of that? Why then, do the priests have to have the wine any more than anyone else?

They claim there are two great reasons why Catholic authorities took the fruit of the vine from the members. First: fear that someone would spill a drop of the precious blood of Christ. Why did Christ not foresee this dreadful possibility? Second: is the "repugnance of some." Is it a valid reason for discarding the Lord's arrangement, just because some do not like it?

I strongly suspect that the third and real reason was, that the priests like wine better than they do unleavened bread!

What an Empty Boast!

"If only one instance could be given in which the church ceased to teach a doctrine of faith which had been previously held, that single instance would be a death blow to her claim of infallibility" (*Faith of Our Fathers,* Gibbons, 61).

Provided English Bible in Self Defense!
One Hundred-Sixty Years Late!

Volume I presents abundant evidence that the Catholic authorities, in England, waited one hundred and sixty years before providing an English Version of the Bible. The reason that they waited so long is because for five hundred years before and during the Reformation it was pronounced a "crime" for a Catholic to have a Bible that he could read. (Volume I, 49-53). During this period Wycliffe and others were supplying English Bibles in defiance of the Catholic hierarchy. These Bibles "were a misery to nearly everybody" (A *Catholic Commentary,* 35).

The Bible is still dealing Catholics misery and always will, for we have learned how different Catholicism is from the Bible—by Catholic scholars' own admission! The rebelling laity were asking thousands of unanswerable questions about such unscriptural things as the priesthood, the sacraments, including penance; the exaltation of Mary, purgatory, and nearly everything else about this satanic system.

They Read Catholicism into the Bible!

Wrest the Scriptures

"The same council (Trent, 1545-1563 A.D.-O.C.L.) speaks of Scripture as insinuating (innuit) this truth, and more can scarcely be said. One text indeed, so translated in our *Douay* Bible, would certainly seem to settle the question—viz. Ephesians 5:31-32, 'For this cause shall a man leave his father and his mother, and shall adhere to his wife; and they shall be two in one flesh. This is a great sacrament, but I speak in Christ and in the Church.' But we venture to think that this is not the true sense of the Vulgate. . . Indeed, though the word *sacramentum* occurs in fifteen other places of the *Vulgate,* it cannot possibly mean a sacrament in any one of them. We translate accordingly, 'This mystery is great, but I speak with reference to Christ and the Church' . . . We have the authority of Estius for this interpretation, which is that adopted by modern scholars, and he denied that the ancients appealed to this text to prove marriage a sacrament" (*Catholic Dictionary,* Addis and Arnold, 545-546).

It was in 1884 that Catholic scholars admitted the Catholic English Bible falsely translated the words of Paul. But it was not until nearly sixty years later (1941 A.D.) that the Catholic English Bible was corrected on this point. The present English Catholic translation says "mystery" just as Protestant versions have always read! This is only one of the many like instances.

"There is sometimes in such passages a fulness and a hidden depth of meaning which the letter hardly expresses and which the laws of interpretation hardly warrant. Moreover the literal sense itself frequently admits other senses, adopted to illustrate dogma or to confirm morality. Wherefore it must be recognized that the Sacred Writings are wrapped in a certain religious obscurity, and that no one can enter into their interior without a guide" (*Great Encyclical Letters of Leo XIII*, 285).

To a Catholic the Lord's word is not trustworthy!

CHAPTER V

Delete and Mistranslate the Bible

Deliberately Mistranslate to Promote Worship of Mary!

"THIRDLY, the *Vulgate* even in its purest form is not declared to be perfect. Such perfection was, indeed, attributed to it by Post-Tridentine theologians, but was utterly denied by many Catholic Scholars at the time (Hody, p. 509, seq.), and now probably would be affirmed by nobody. Franzelin sets this exaggerated view aside as little better than fanatical.

"Fourthly, Franzelin admits the lawfulness of holding that texts directly intended to teach dogmatic truth may have been omitted in the *Vulgate;* and again, that when such texts are given, considerable alterations may have been made in their form. For example, he grants that we are at liberty in Genesis III, 15 to reject the *Vulgate* (or supposed *Vulgate*) reading, 'She shall crush thy head'; as an error, for 'He shall crush thy head'; and similarly we may deny the correctness of the rendering *'ante Luciferum'* (Psalms CIX, 3), *'fundetur'* (Luc. XXII, 20), *'in quo omnes peccaverunt'* (Romans V. 12), *'omnes quiden resurgemus'* (1 Cor. XV, 21)" (*Catholic Dictionary,* Addis and Arnold, 856, 857).

Thus Catholics claim the right to change and delete the word of the Lord. No one who fears God would do this!

Refuse To Correct This Now!

"Charles Hodge, the author of highly esteemed commentaries, when informed that his quotation from Genesis iii, 15. . . was a serious inaccuracy, refused to change it on the ground that this translation had passed into use" (*Catholic Encyclopedia,* IV, 500).

Errors Left in on Purpose!

"It (the *Clementina Vulgate*) was not a perfect text of the *Vulgate*. The preface disclaims any such exaggerated praise—nay admits that imperfections have been left 'of set purpose,' lest offence should be given to the people, as well as for other reasons" (*Catholic Dictionary*, Addis and Arnold, 583).

Vulgate Mistranslated Genesis 3:15, Corrected Lord's Mistake!?!

"The second point of difference between the Hebrew text and our version concerns the agent who is to inflict the mortal wound on the serpent: our version (English) agrees with the present *Vulgate* text in reading 'she' (*ipsa*) which refers to the woman, while the Hebrew text reads "his' (*autos, ipse*) which refers to the seed of the woman. According to our version (*Douay*) and the *Vulgate* reading, the woman herself will win the victory; according to the Hebrew text, she will be victorious through her seed. In this sense does the Bull *'Ineffabilis'* (Pius IX, Dec. 8, 1854, Defining the Immaculate Conception) ascribe the victory to Our Blessed Lady. The reading 'she' (*ipsa*) is neither an intentional corruption of the original text, nor is it an accidental error; it is rather an explanatory version expressing explicitly the fact of Our Lady's part in the victory over the serpent, which is contained implicitly in the Hebrew original" (*Catholic Encyclopedia*, XV, 464 B).

Thus Pope Pius IX endorsed a mistranslation.

"The translation 'she' of the *Vulgate* is interpretative; it originated after the fourth century and cannot be defended critically" (*Catholic Encyclopedia*, VII, 675).

Penance Is Not Repentance

"Sins committed after baptism are forgiven on repentance and on doing penance" (*Pope Innocent III and His Times,* Clayton, 176).

The Douay version reads 'do penance' (Acts 2:38) and the Confraternity version, 'repent.' The *Douay* was put out in self-defense, and this is one of many deliberate mistranslations to answer her critics. This does not square with her thousands of books based on the *Douay*. Here is a sample:

"The spirit of sacrifice, springing thus from the great sacrifice of the cross, is the source of these austerities, voluntary macerations, penances, fastings, bodily inflictions, and other satisfactions, which have ever been dear to the fervent members of the Catholic Church" (*Miscellanae*, Archbishop Spalding, 424).

All this admits that the *Douay* of Acts 2:38 was a mistranslation. The new *Confraternity* reads exactly like the Protestant Version. Does this not prove the Catholic wrong and the Protestant right?

They Mistranslate Proverbs 18:22

"He that hath found a *good* wife, hath found a good thing." Footnote to *Douay* states that "good" is not found in the Hebrew.

Mistranslates Priest for "Elder"

"This word (etymologically 'elder' is from *presbuteros, presbyter*) has taken the meaning of *"sacerdos'* " (*Catholic Encyclopedia, XII,* 406).

"The elders (in early church,—O.C.L.) (*presbuteroi*) formed a kind of council" (Ibid).

"The word *presbyter* soon lost its meaning of 'ancient' and was applied only to the minister of worship and of the sacrifice (hence our priests)" (*Catholic Encyclopedia, XII,* 406).

Jerome "appears to assert the full equality of priests and bishops" (*Catholic Encyclopedia, XII,* 416).

Catholics Admit Apostasy

"Thus the way was prepared for the still later use of the word *episkopos* to denote the rulers of the church, the successors of the Apostles, i.e. bishops in the modern sense of the word" (A *Catholic Commentary*, 1144).

Catholic Translation by Inquisitors

John X:6: "If any one abide not in me, he shall be cast forth as a branch, and shall wither, and they shall gather *him up and cast him into the fire and he burneth*" (*Catholic Encyclopedia*, VIII, 35).

In the Catholic *Breviary* where Galatians 2:7-9 is cited in order to support the idea of the supremacy of Peter, the statement that Peter was the Apostle to the Circumcision (Jews) is left out in three citations. The divine writer states that Paul was the Apostle to the Gentiles (all nations)! (*Catholic Breviary,* Volume 2:602, 605, 608).

Elder and Priest

The Greek word *Presbuteros,* old man, is translated in the *Douay* (the self-defense translation) as *priest.* A priest is almost invariably made of a very young man. It would be a contradiction of terms, or an impossibility, to have a young old man. It is clearly evident that this was a deliberate mistranslation to silence the criticism that there were no officers in the early church called priests. This false translation was retained for about three hundred and fifty years, but the new *Confraternity* version translates it *presbyter.* This is simply bringing the Greek word over and avoiding a translation. It is interesting to note that in a glossary, in the back of the *Confraternity, presbyter* is defined as an elder in the *New Testament* Church. Thus admitting that the Catholic Bible was in error for centuries, and Protestant versions correct!

Another Scripture that was evidently used against the Catholic Church, with telling effect, concerned the sacraments. The idea of sacraments did not occur to Catholic leaders for about fifteen centuries and was only completed and fixed by the Council of Trent

60

about 1550. This was evidently one point that produced the "misery," complained of by Cardinal Allen, when appealing to the pope for permission to get out the *Douay* Bible. The critics were calling attention to the fact that the Bibles, gotten out by Wycliffe and others were silent on the sacraments, which was by that time one of the most profitable of Catholic inventions. All Protestant Bibles have always read, "This is a great mystery" (Ephesians 5:32). *The Douay* was made to read, "This is a great sacrament." For centuries this was triumphantly pointed to as proof that "sacraments" are in the Bible! But *Catholic Dictionary,* more than eighty years ago pointed out very clearly that this was a mistranslation. It was not until 1941, when the *Confraternity,* now their standard, appeared, reading exactly as all Protestant versions have always read, "This is a great mystery." This, again, is an admission that the Catholic Bible has been in error for three hundred and fifty years, and the Protestant Bible correct!

Mistranslation Provides Women for the Priest!

Catholic writers very candidly admit that until one thousand years after the birth of Christ, priests of the Catholic Church were married men. The *King James* translation of I Corinthians 9:5 reads: "Have we not power to lead about a sister, a wife, as well as the other Apostles, and as the brethren of the Lord, and Cephas?"

Paul and Barnabas were bachelors. The brethren of the Lord and the other Apostles, including Cephas, or Peter, were married men. They were carrying their wives with them.

The Catholic Bible says that the bishop *"must* be the husband of one wife" with the right kind of children. It is now an inflexible law of the Catholic Church that the bishop must not, under any circumstances, be married! (Note: the Catholic Church has since permitted married denominational preachers who convert to Catholicism to become priests and remain married. But this is not an option for anyone else—*Editor.*)

A Catholic priest may not marry, but he may have a woman,

and most of them do. This has been true for centuries. When men began to have Bibles, in spite of the prohibitions of the Catholic Church, the "laity" evidently challenged this unscriptural arrangement. To counter this the *Douay* was made to read:

"Have we not power to carry about a woman, a sister, as well as the rest of the Apostles, and the brethren of the Lord, and Cephas"?

Think of this: the Lord had brothers, despite the fact that Catholics deny it. This translation says that all of them were carrying about women, but could not have a wife. Cephas, or Peter, was carrying about a woman, but could not carry about his wife (Matthew 8:14)!

A footnote at the bottom of the page reads:

"Some erronerous translators have corrupted this text by rendering it, *a sister, a wife.* " According to this gem of Catholic scholarship and "infallible" exegesis: it is a corruption to render *gune* as a *wife* in chapter 9, but not a corruption *when they rendered it that way* ("wife") fifteen times in Chapter 7!

This is a glaring, deliberate mistranslation to allow all priests to have their women!

CHAPTER VI

The Canon

THE CATHOLIC claim of superiority, advanced for uncritical and uninformed people, concerns what is called the Canon of the Bible. It is a fact that the Catholic Bible contains seven books, and other parts of books, not included in the Protestant Bibles. It is the boast of Catholic writers that the "Canon" of the Bible was infallibly settled nearly sixteen hundred years ago, and that Protestants have taken several books from the Bible. Let us examine the facts. If this were true, then all Catholic writers through the Middle Ages would have known it!

Catholic Uncertainty on Gelasius I (492-496)

"For a long time the fixing of the canon of the Scriptures was attributed to Gelasius, but it seems now more probably the work of Damasus (367-385)" (*Catholic Encyclopedia,* VI, 406).

Protestantism and the Bible

"The divine inspiration of the Bible and the official list or Canon of inspired books are known to us only through Tradition and are taught by the living and infallible authority of the Catholic Church. When the Protestant Reformers rejected Tradition and the teaching authority of the Church, they repudiated the only solid proof for the existence of inspiration and of the Canon of the Bible" (*National Catholic Almanac,* 1955, 248).

Why is this "living and infallible authority" so uncertain about the Canon of Scriptures?

"This was the celebrated *Vulgate,* the official text of the Catholic Church, recognized by the Council of Trent as the only authoritative version of the Scriptures. Pope Sixtus, in 1590, and Pope Clement in 1593, revised minor parts, but from the date 404 A.D. it stands untouched, except for minor revisions just mentioned. From it comes the authoritative translation into English known as the *Douai* Bible" (*Our Faith and the Facts,* Donovan, 350). So the original Greek and Hebrew versions are not authoritative!

Trent Fixed Catholic Canon in 1546

"The canon of scripture was fixed as it now stands: the council (Trent —O.C.L.) approved, as authentic, the old edition known as the *Vulgate,* and 'consecrated', said the Fathers, by the usage of so many centuries.' 'In order,' continues the decree, 'to restrain petulant spirits, the holy ecumenical council decrees that, in matters of faith and morals, no one, relying upon his own private judgment, shall rashly presume to interpret the sacred scriptures in a sense either contrary to that of the Church, to which alone it belongs to judge of the true sense of scripture, or contrary to the unanimous consent of the Fathers and of Catholic Tradition' " (*Pastor's History of the Popes,* IV, 138-139).

"The Tridentine list or decree was the *first* infallible and effectually promulgated declaration on the Canon of the Holy Scriptures" (*Canons and Decrees of the Council of Trent,* Schroeder, 17).

"The Fathers of the Third and Fourth centuries who wrote about the Scriptures indicate no firm and general agreement about the Canon of either the *Old* or *New Testament,* but there seems to have been growing uniformity except that Jerome raised some doubt about those seven books of the Second Canon which were not included in the Hebrew Bible.

"At the third council of Carthage in 397 the books of the Canon were listed as we know them today; and eight years later Pope St. Innocent I wrote a letter in which he gave the same listing of canonical books. From that time (405) there was *rather general agreement* about the Canon, especially after the Eastern churches gave formal approval of the same list at their council in Trullo, in Constantinople in 692. *However there was no definition of the matter until the Council of Trent, in 1546"* (*Operation Understanding,* July 5, 1964).

Uncertainty about the Apocrypha was admitted long after Damasus (367-385) or Gelasius I, (492-496).

Doubt Concerning Second and Third John

"The canonicity of these two letters was long disputed. Eusebius puts them among the Antilegomena. They are not found in the Peshito. The Canon of the Western Church includes them after the fourth century; although *only Trent's decree set the question of their canonicity beyond the dispute* of such men as Cajetan" (*Catholic Encyclopedia,* VIII, 437).

Of the Fourth Book of Esdras

"There was a very spirited discussion in the council of Trent about the propriety of putting this book on the list of canonical Scriptures. Some of the Fathers, considering its rare worth in general and the lofty tone of its sentiments, argued strongly in favor of it, while others opposed it. The latter, however, ruled; and so it yet remains" (*History of the Mass,* O'Brien, 198).

"(d) Fourth Book of *Esdras.*—The personage serving as the screen of the real author of this book is *Esdras (Ezra),* the priest-scribe and leader among the Israelites who returned from Babylonia to Jerusalem. In fact the two canonical books associated with his name, together with a genuine literary power, a profoundly religious spirit pervading *Fourth Esdras,* and some Messianic points of contact with the Gospels combined to win for it an acceptance among Christians unequalled by any other apocryphon. Both Greek and Latin Fathers cite it as prophetical, while some, as Ambrose, were ardent admirers of it. Jerome alone is positively unfavorable. Notwithstanding this wide-spread reverence for it in early times, it is a remarkable fact that the book never got a foothold in the Canon or liturgy of the church. Nevertheless, all through the middle ages it maintained an intermediate position between canonical and merely human compositions, and even after the council of Trent, together with *Third Esdras,* (it was included in) the official edition of the *Vulgate"* (*Catholic Encyclopedia,* I, 603).

Once in Catholic Bible—Now Left out!

The following item, included in the Catholic Bible before 1550 is now left out:

"*Prayer of Manasses (Manasseh).*—A beautiful penitential prayer put in the mouth of Manasses, King of Judah, who carried idolatrous abominations so far. The composition is based on *II Paralipomenon, XXXIII,* 11-13, which states that Manasses was carried captive to Babylon and there repented; while the source refers to his prayer as recorded in certain chronicles which are lost. Learned opinion differs as to whether the prayer which has come down to us was written in Hebrew or Greek. Several ancient manuscripts of the *Septuagint* contain it as an appendix to the *Psalter.* It is also incorporated in the ancient so-called *Apostolic Constitutions.* In editions of the *Vulgate* antedating the Council of Trent, it was placed after the books of *Paralipomenon.* The *Clementine Vulgate* relegated it to the appendix, where it is still to be found in reprints of the standard text. The prayer breathes a Christian spirit, and it is not entirely certain that it is really of Jewish origin" (*Catholic Encyclopedia,* I, 605).

Trent Fixed Catholic Canon Feb. 8, 1546

"The council in the meanwhile had applied itself to a subject which the Legates had brought forward in the general congregation of February the 8th: the establishment of the canon of Holy Scripture as the foundation and bulwark of the defense of Church doctrine. Here clear definition was all the more necessary as the Reformers appealed in the first instance to the *Bible,* certain portions however, of which they rejected. The question therefore has to be examined, whether all the books of the *Old* and *New Testaments* in common use were to be regarded as parts of Holy Scripture; and also a point of no less importance, what respect was due together with the written word to that ecclesiastical tradition which the Protestants had entirely discarded" (*Pastors History,* XII, 259).

Trent "Canonized" Judith But Cannot Be True!

"*Judith,* The Book of, is an *Old Testament* chronicle which takes its name from the valiant woman who by her courage, resourcefulness, and confidence in God saved the city of Bethulia from destruction at the hand of Holofemes general of Nabuchodonoser, King of Ninive. The present state of the text is very confused. It is highly probable that the Greek version is derived from a Hebrew or Chaldaic original. The two Hebrew versions now extant are different, one of them agreeing with the Greek. St. Jerome wrote his *Vulgate* translation with the help of a Chaldaic version, but the admitted carelessness of this work makes it difficult to determine which of the two texts, the Greek or the Chaldaic, is closer to the original. The geographical and historical references in the book are also a source of much confusion and debate. For instance, Scripture scholars find it difficult to identify the city of Bethulia with any ancient town in the Plain of Esdraelon where the writer of the Book located it. And again, how could Nabuchodonoser, who became a king 605 B.C., have ruled in Ninive, which was destroyed the year before? The blame for many of these inaccuracies has been laid at the feet of careless translators and inaccurate copyists. The confusion has been such as to lead most non-Catholic commentators to reject the Book of Judith as a narrative of facts; for them it is an allegory. On the other hand, Catholic tradition from the earliest times has always considered the Book as historical, and the council of Trent has defined its character as an inspired writing by placing it among the canonical books of the *Old Testament.* The chronicle ends with a beautiful hymn of thanksgiving which has found its place in the Wednesday Lauds of the *Roman Breviary"* (*New Catholic Dictionary, Vatican Edition,* 523).

Catholic Scholars Doubt Tobias

"*Tobias,* Book of, a canonical book of the O.T. The Book of *Tobias* is a most interesting story about Tobias, an Israelite who was taken from Nephtali to Ninive by the Assyrians in the *8th* century B.C., his son Tobias, and Sara, whom the younger Tobias married at Ecbatana. The book is not recognized as a part of the Sacred Scriptures by the Jews and Protestants; but the church has defined its inspiration. A few Catholic authors have treated the story as wholly or partly fictitious. Like the parable of Lazarus in the Gospel, they claim it was meant by its author only to convey religious and moral instruction. They find difficulty in reconciling certain data of the book with Assyrian history; and the discovery that Achior or Ahikar (Tobias, 11) was a personage in a fictitious story of the Orient seems to them to indicate that the author gives warning that he is not dealing with real facts. However the common view of Catholics has not varied; nearly all Catholic scholars maintain that the book is strictly historical" (*New Catholic Dictionary, Vatican Edition,* 966).

"Most Catholic scholars, however, consider the book historical, at least to some extent. . . The fact that the councils of Trent and the Vatican list *Tobias* among historical books scarcely proves that our book must be viewed in the strictest historical sense" (*A Catholic Commentary,* 394).

The Third Book of Esdras

"Third Book of *Esdras*— This is also styled by non-Catholics the *First Book of Esdras,* since they give to the first canonical Esdrine writing the Hebrew form Ezra. *Third Esdras* is one of the three uncanonical books appended to the official edition of the Vulgate. It exists in two of the oldest codices of the *Septuagint,* viz., Vaticanus and Alexandrinus, where it precedes the Canonical *Esdras*. The same is true of MSS. of the Old Latin and other versions. *Third Esdras* enjoyed exceptional favour in the early ages of the church, being quoted as Scripture with implicit faith by the leading Greek and Latin Fathers (See Comely, *Introductio Generalis*, I, 201). St. Jerome, however, the great minimizer of sacred literature, rejected it as apocryphal, and thenceforward its standing was impaired" (*Catholic Encyclopedia*, I, 605).

Jerome Called Extra Books Apocrypha

"St. Jerome evidently applied the term to all quasi-scriptural books which in his estimation lay outside the canon of Holy Writ, and the Protestant Reformers, following Jerome's catalog of *Old Testament* Scriptures—one which was at once erroneous and singular among the Fathers of the Church—applied the title Apocrypha to the excess of the Catholic canon of the *Old Testament* over that of the Jews. Naturally, Catholics refuse to admit such a denomination, and we employ 'deuterocanonical' to designate this literature, which non-Catholics conventionally and improperly know as the *'Apocrypha'*" (*Catholic Encyclopedia*, I, 601).

Trying To Get Back to Jerome's Vulgate:

"Pius X continued the work of his distinguished predecessor through the issuance of several letters, chief of which are the Apostolic letter of 18 Nov., 1907, in which he gives instructions regarding the methods to be employed in the teaching of Sacred Scriptures in the Seminaries; a letter written 3 Dec., 1907, addressed to Abbot Gasquet, authorizing him to begin the revision of the Vulgate with a view to reproducing as far as was possible the original text of St. Jerome; and the Apostolic letter, *'Vinea Electra,'* 7 May, 1909, through which medium he officially established the Pontifical Biblical Institute at Rome" (*New Catholic Dictionary, Vatican Edition*, 117).

Jerome, Greatest Catholic Scholar, Claimed His Vulgate Was "Exact"

"To preserve for future times, and irrevocably to fix the text of the Sacred Scriptures, the pope had just caused St. Jerome to furnish, under his personal supervision, an exact translation from the original Hebrew. This is the version which the council of Trent afterwards declared *Authentic*. In the course of this immense labor, besides the encouragement of the pope, St. Jerome received also that of the most illustrious Roman ladies, who made the sacred text their only study. Sts. Melania, Marcella, and her sister Asella, Paula and her daughter Paulina, Lea and Fabiola, and the virgin Eustochium, members of the most illustrious houses of the time, became the disciples of the austere anchoret of Palestine, who has made their names and their virtues immortal in his eloquent works. The pope lavished upon St. Jerome the honors due to his talents, but painful to his modesty" (*General History of the Church*, Darras, I, 522).

"There remained, however, attention to accuracy of translation from original manuscripts. This work was intrusted by the church of St. Jerome, the greatest Bible scholar the world has known. With a staff of helpers the work was done by him from the years 383 to 404 A.D. His research included both testaments" (*Our Faith and the Facts*, Donavan, 349).

St. Jerome, the "greatest Bible scholar the world has ever known" (their words, not mine), rejected the extra books!

Jerome Most Eminent Biblical Scholar

"If we do not become the masters of Biblical lore, our adversaries will supplant us and this will not be for the better. Few subjects are more vital at this moment to the cause of Faith, few more dextrously used by those who are against the church. Remember rather the advice of St. Jerome, the most eminent Biblical scholar:

Cadentem faciem pagina sancta suscipiat" (*Our Priesthood,* Bruneau, 60).

We have presented official Catholic statements to the effect that Damasus I fixed the Canon (*Catholic Encyclopedia,* VI, 406). This was supposed to have been A.D. 382 (*New Catholic Dictionary, Vatican Edition,* 117). If this were true why did Pope Gregory the Great reject the Apocrypha? This is a complete refutation of the usual claim!

This next quotation is one of the most devastating facts:

Pope Gregory the Great Rejected Apocrypha (540-604)

"Even Pope St. Gregory the Great inclined to the view (of Jerome) and speaks of the disputed books as 'books which though not canonical, are received for the edification of the Church' *Lib. Mor.* 19, 21, PL 76, 119" (*A Catholic Commentary,* 18).

"St." Hilary refused to call "extra books" canonical (Henri Daniel-Rops, *Twentieth Century Encyclopedia of Catholicism,* Vol. 60, Page 33).

Faulty Bible Means Fallibility

On pages 54-58 of Volume I (revised edition, 2022), I presented much evidence that the Catholic church admits unhesitatingly she has never had a correct Bible either in Latin or English for fifteen hundred and fifty years! If she were infallible, this would not, and could not be true.

Confusing Catholic Laws Refutes Claim of Infallibility
Canon Law Confusing Even to Clergy!

Think how many human laws 262 popes could make through all the centuries! The following quotation states that two of them issued nearly nine thousand!

"Alexander III is said to have issued thirty-nine hundred and thirty-nine decrees and Innocent III over five thousand" (*General Legislation in the New Code of Canon Law,* 42).

"Moreover, not a few ordinances, whether included in the *Corpus Juris* or of more recent date, appear to be contradictory; some have been repealed, others had become obsolete by long disuse; others, again had ceased to be useful or applicable in the present condition of society. Great confusion was thus engendered and correct knowledge of the law was rendered very difficult even for those who had to enforce it" (*General Legislation in the New Code of Canon Law,* 70).

They tell the people that the Lord ordained the heirarchy so as to explain or make plain the will of God for them, but according to this statement, even the priests could not understand their man-made laws! How, then, did they expect the "laity" to understand them?

Bishops Could Not Understand Catholic Law!!!

"'The body of ecclesiastical laws' said the Bishops of the Province of Naples, 'has become in modern times an almost unbearable burden— *Ingens camelorum onus—;* contradictory texts abound in it, giving rise to endless disputes; often it is impossible to ascertain what is really the obligation'" (*General Legislation in the New Code of Canon Law,* 71).

Where is the boasted Catholic certainty? How can they have the temerity to admit this situation and at the same time claim infallibility for those who created such a babel of confusion? As another example of how burdensome and perplexing this maze of human doctrine became, let me say that just the "Bulls" of the popes from 450 to 1857 filled forty-one volumes! And this did not include the countless laws formulated by synods and councils. It is no wonder that a cry of despair went up from the Bishops for relief from this medley of confusion. The French bishops said:

Bishops Buried Beneath the Law!!!

"It is very evident and has long been recognized by all and pro-claimed everywhere that some revision and reformation of Canon Law is necessary and very urgent. For, owing to the changes that have taken place in society, many laws have become useless and others very difficult if not impossible to observe; of others it is doubtful whether they are still in vigor or not. Finally in the course of centuries, their number is so multiplied and they have been heaped up in voluminous collections that, in a sense, we may say, we are buried beneath the laws. Hence it is that the study of Canon Law is beset with almost inextricable difficulties, the door is open to disputes and litigations, consciences are troubled with a thousand anxieties and the people are driven to despise the law" (*General Legislation in the New Code of Canon Law,* Ayrinhac, 71. See also *Catholic Encyclopedia,* I, 645 and IX, 64).

CHAPTER VII

The Divine Pattern

WHEN Moses received the elaborate directions for building the Tabernacle (which is used as a type of the Lord's Church by the writer of the Hebrew letter) he was cautioned, "See that thou make all things according to the pattern that was shown thee on the mount" (Hebrew 8:5, *Confraternity Version*). The divine writer was calling this up as a warning to men in this dispensation to "make all things according to the pattern." The main purpose of this book is to give a clear outline of the divine pattern for the Lord's Church, and to picture it so no one can fail to see that the Catholic Church is the great apostasy from the divine pattern, having discarded every feature of the pattern and substituted for the Lord's directions. "This people honors me with their lips but their heart is far from me; but in vain do they worship me, teaching for doctrines precepts of men" (Matthew 15:8-9, *Confraternity Version*).

The Name of the Church

There was only one Church, in the beginning, and it was called the Church of Christ (Rom. 16:16) because Christ built it (Matt. 16:18), bought it (Acts 20:28), and is the head of it (Eph. 1:22-23). It is His body (Eph. 1:23). It is also called the Church of God (Cor. 1:1 and II Cor. 1:7). We have no need for other names if the original condition still remains. Why not all be one and restore the divinely given name? This is a part of the divine pattern. I am glad that most those who have departed from the Bible have chosen a different name, this keeps them from being quite so deceptive.

Simplicity in Christ and the Church

The law of entrance into the Church is so very simple: faith, repentance. confession and baptism. Immersion alone is baptism. "But I fear, lest by any means, as the serpent beguiled Eve through his subtilty, so your minds should be corrupted from the simplicity that is in Christ (2 Cor. 11:3).

An honest reading of the New Testament would show, crystal clear, its simplicity. Each congregation was separate from every other, and managed its own affairs without outside interference. Elders, sometimes called bishops and pastors, superintended its activities; not as lords but as teachers and examples. These elders were assisted by a plurality of deacons (servants). There were evangelists who spent their time preaching the gospel, but they occupied no official place in the congregation. It is easy to see how practically all religious groups have departed from this simplicity.

New Testament Church Worship Simple

There was no ritual, no breviaries, no eucharist, no mass, no liturgy, no worship of Mary, no prayers for the dead, no candles, no holy water, no incense, no sign of the cross, no robes, no confessional, no penance, no sacraments, no sacramentals, no clergy, no laity, no hierarchy, no religious titles and none of a thousand other things which are characteristic of Catholicism. *New Testament* worship consisted of Bible study, the Lord's Supper, singing (without musical accompaniment), prayers and contribution—The Lord's Supper and the contribution were attended to once a week, on the first day of the week.

Any deviation from this arrangement, so clearly outlined in the *New Testament,* is a repudiation of the divine pattern.

"In vain do they worship me, teaching for doctrines precepts of men" (Matt. 15:9, *Confraternity Version*).

This book is an effort showing how the Roman Catholic

Church has, through its long history, drifted away from every vestige of the divine pattern.

Let us, for example, imagine a situation hundreds of years in the future, long after the popular game of baseball has been discontinued and forgotten. A man finds a rule-book describing the game, giving its name, its organization, and participation rules. He arranges for two teams of nine men each. They play just as the rule-book explains. This man has not invented a game. He has only restored a game that was invented long ago.

If the *New Testament* had been forgotten hundreds of years and we find one, if we adhere to its rules, we would not have a new church, but only a *New Testament* church. This is what we hope to accomplish by this book: help the reader to find and to identify the *New Testament* church. And at the same time impress upon him the seriousness of making and keeping all things according to the pattern. To be fearful of adding to or taking from the words written in the book. To be diligent in study and prayerfully careful not to be blinded by those who claim the right to change, add, to or take from the divine pattern. The Roman Catholic Church has always claimed this right, by her own admission. Ample proof of this has been given in the proceeding chapters of this book.

Be Sure with Your Bible!

"You are always sure of your ground when you stand on a Scriptural Rock" (—Cardinal Gibbons as quoted in *Our Priesthood,* Bruneau, 60).

CHAPTER VIII

Tradition

CATHOLIC authorities sneer at the Bible, insisting that it is not inspired, but is simply the result of men writing the ignorance of the age in which they lived. They ask men to turn away from the Bible and to settle everything by "history," which they would have us believe is a very dependable record of "Tradition." One Catholic writer contrasts the unwritten constitution of the British Empire with our written *Constitution,* clearly expressing a preference for our own. He insists that an unwritten one is capable of being interpreted by a citizen in any way to suit himself. This same reasoning applied to Catholic unwritten "Tradition" would mean that it is also very uncertain. I am sure that Catholic authorities would prefer something written to something unwritten, particularly with reference to all contracts, financial and otherwise.

Unwritten, Elastic, Unreliable

"We may go still further: the American thought of his constitutional rights as something indeed defined by a document but as also inherent in the law of nature. An elastic constitution and a haphazard assortment of laws—many of which were obsolete and uninforced—seemed plainly to contradict the concept of fundamental and immutable law so dear to the American mind. Flux and confusion were intolerable to him, and he saw how in such a state of indefiniteness tyranny could very easily appear under the guise of law—even under guise of a constitution which precisely because it was unwritten, could be made to bear almost any interpretation" (*Story of American Catholicism,* Maynard, 139).

An Interesting Paraphrase

I think of my God-given rights as something defined by the Bible. An elastic law, like "Tradition" and a haphazard assortment of laws, (many of which are obsolete and unenforced), which characterize Catholicism, plainly contradicts my conception of immutable law. This divinely inspired law, the Bible, never becomes obsolete. There is nothing indefinite about it. Such indefiniteness would be intolerable to me. I cannot see how Catholic "shifting indefiniteness" can be tolerated, even by Catholics themselves.

This conglomeration of man-made laws has fortified the most intolerable tyranny, mental, physical and moral that has ever afflicted the earth! The Bible aptly characterizes it as the "working of Satan" (2 Thes. 2:9)!

While admitting the "vagaries" of "tradition," Catholics in the following quotation assert that the Catholic Church is divinely guided. Think how absurd it is for them to claim inspiration for tradition and at the same time, by other official statements, deny the inspiration of the Bible.

Vagaries of Tradition!

"This infallibility is to control the vagaries of Tradition, for Tradition, of its very nature, tends to exaggeration, as we find in legends of ancient people. Exaggerated, they destroy themselves, but in the bosom of God's Church those truths forever retain their character unchanged and unchangeable" (*Explanation of Catholic Morals,* Stapleton, 69).

What is palmed off on the trusting "laity" is really a potpourri of ignorance, fraud, forgeries, legends, and especially paganism. It is admitted to be contradictory, uncritical, unreliable, and worthless as history! Furthermore, it contradicts the Bible at every turn.

In spite of this, Catholic authorities insist that tradition is divinely inspired, and leaves no doubts in the minds of Catholics. It is declared to be enough to guide Catholics without the Bible. We are told, numberless times, that we cannot depend on the Bible, which is "a mere wreck," made up by ignorant and misguided people. We are sagely informed that we must believe *all* tradition!

It is enlightening to have an abundance of quotations, from official Catholic sources, admitting that ignorance, fraud, and general unreliability have always characterized the hierarchy, and tradition. There is no real history of the early church except that which is found in the Bible.

Priesthood and Tradition Eliminate Doubt

The hierarchy says:

"What Catholics *do* believe is that the church, not the individual, must interpret and explain Christ's teachings, including those set forth in the Bible. Christians outside the Catholic fold do not of course accept this authority, but for Catholics it eliminates the doubts, confusion and misunderstanding which inevitably results from individual interpretations. The intolerance of the Church toward error, the natural position of one who is the custodian of truth, her only reasonable attitude makes her forbid her children to read or to listen to heretical controversy, or to endeavor to discover religious truths by examining both sides of the *question" (Explanation of Catholic Morals,* Stapleton, 35).

Not Allowed to Reason or Think

"Once he does so (joins the Catholic Church—O.C.L.), he has no further use for his reason. He enters the Church, an edifice illumined by the superior light of revelation and faith. He can leave reason like a lantern at the door" (*Explanation of Catholic Morals,* Stapleton, 76).

Cannot Choose Religion

"Many non-Catholics today find this viewpoint difficult to understand, for with them religion is a matter of human opinion. They believe that a man is free to choose his religious beliefs as he chooses the style of his coat, or his political opinion" (*Question Box,* 192).

Do as Jews Did—Follow Priests!

"But in those times the faithful did not attempt to interpret scripture for themselves. For the Jewish people in the pre-Christian era, the synagogue was their voice of spiritual authority; and the *Old Testament* was preached to them by the Rabbis and fathers of their faith. In like manner, the Catholic Church was the custodian of the inspired writings of the *New Testament* Gospel nearly four centuries before these writings were collected into a single book and formally declared to be inspired.

"Today Catholics listen to one authoritative voice—the Church—in the interpretation of God's word" (*Knights of Columbus Ad., "The Bible Is a Confusing Book!"*).

That most Jews did this, was to their undoing. They were to listen to God's word, not to man's interpretation.

"And *these words which I command* thee this day, shall be in thine heart; and thou shalt *teach them* diligently unto thy children, and shall *talk of them* when thou sittest in thy house, and when thou walkest by the way, and when thou liest down, and when thou risest up. And thou shalt bind *them* for a sign upon thine hand, and *they* shall be as frontlets between thine eyes. And thou shalt write them upon the post of thy house, and on thy gates" (Deut. 6:6-9) .

They were to do this for God's word, not for some man's interpretations!

The Bible tells us how disastrous it proved to be, to those who listened to the interpretations of their leaders:

"For the leaders of this people cause them to err, and they that are led of them are destroyed" (Isa. 9:16).

In the course of this study we will see how fatal it would be, for anyone, to follow Catholic leaders.

"Why do thy disciples transgress the traditions of the elders? for they wash not their hands when they eat bread. But he answered and said unto them, Why do ye also transgress the commandment of God by your tradition?. . . But in vain they do worship me, teaching for doctrines the commandments of men. . . Let them alone: they be blind leaders of the blind. And if the blind lead the blind, both shall fall into the ditch" (Mt. 15:2-14).

"But they also have erred through wine, and through strong drink are out of the way; the priests and the prophets have erred through strong drink, they err in vision, they stumble in judgment" (Isa. 28:7).

"The priests said not, Where is the Lord? and they that handle the law knew me not: the pastors also transgressed against me, and the prophets prophesied by Baal, and walked after things that do not profit" (Jer. 2:8).

"The prophets prophesy falsely, and the priests bear rule by their means; and my people love to have it so: and what will ye do in the end thereof?" (Jer. 5:31).

". . . from the prophet even unto the priests every one dealeth falsely" (Jer. 8:10).

"For both prophet and priest are profane; yea, in my house have I found their wickedness, saith the Lord" (Jer. 23:11).

"So the priests and, the prophets and all the people heard Jeremiah speaking these words in the house of the Lord. Now it came to pass, when Jeremiah had made an end of speaking *all that the Lord had commanded him* to speak unto all the people, that the priests and the prophets and all the people took him saying, Thou shalt surely die" (Jer. 26:7-8).'

"Her priests have violated my law, and have profaned my holy things: they have put no difference between the holy and profane, neither have they showed difference between the unclean and the clean, and have hid their eyes from my sabbaths, and I am profaned among them" (Ez. 22:26).

"And as a troop of robbers wait for a man, so the company of priests murder in the way by consent: for they commit lewdness" (Hosea 6:9).

"Her prophets are light and treacherous persons: her priests have polluted the sanctuary, they have done violence to the law" (Zephaniah 3:4).

"For the priests' lips should keep knowledge, and they should seek the law at his mouth: for he is the messenger of the Lord of hosts. But ye are departed out of the way; ye have caused many to stumble at the law; ye have corrupted the covenant of Levi, saith the Lord of hosts. Therefore have I also made you contemptible and base before all the people, according as ye have not kept my ways, but have been partial in the law" (Mal. 2:7-9).

It was the priests who led in having the Son of God crucified. Yet in spite of all this abundance of evidence concerning the wickedness of the priests and prophets of the *Old Testament,* this Knights of Columbus Advertisement insists that it was the duty of the people to turn their souls over to these bad men, and that it would have been wrong for the people to read the Bible for themselves! Will we not believe that God *is* God? Will we not listen to *His* warnings and heed them? Hear again the prophet of old: "For the leaders of this people cause them to err; and they that are led of them are destroyed" (Isa. 9:16). Such a serious statement, given by divine authority, should be given careful consideration by all God-fearing people. As we proceed with an unfolding of Catholic history and practice, we see striking similarity between religious leaders then and now. Peter warned of this:

"But there were false prophets also among the people, even as there shall be false teachers among you, who privily shall bring in damnable heresies, even denying the Lord that bought them, and bring upon themselves swift destruction. And many shall follow their pernicious ways; by reason of whom the way of truth shall be evil spoken of" (2 Pet. 2:1-2),

The thesis of this book is to demonstrate that this is exactly what the Catholic Church has done.

DRUNKEN PRIESTS TO BE FOLLOWED?!?

We have already quoted Isaiah 28:7 showing how the terrible apostasy of priests and prophets is associated with strong drink.

The Catholic Church produces a very great portion of liquor in thousands of monasteries using the slave labor of monks and nuns! The Catholic hierarchy is the greatest foe to prohibition. A great many priests are alcoholics! See volume I, pages 156-157 for documented proof of this. The bishops, through their diocesan newspapers, advertise "110 proof" liquor which is produced in monasteries!

"Drunkenness is not a new failing with the hierarchy. The following is an account of conditions among them seven hundred and fifty years ago.

"Then there is heavy drinking in clerical circles and bishops are among those who sit up all night carousing. It is known that organized drinking bouts take place, clergy competing with clergy in the consumption of intoxicants and endeavouring to outdrink one another. What is the result of this drunkenness? The absence from choir of priests who should be at Matins, inability to say Mass. Some bishops indeed rarely say Mass at all and make light of the very idea of assisting at Mass. When these prelates do assist they behave without decorum, hardly attending to the service, choosing rather to talk with laymen and discuss diocesan business" (*Pope Innocent III and His Times,* Clayton, 177).

There are many things in the Catholic system of religion that are hard for Christians to believe. Knowing what the Bible teaches concerning drunkenness they cannot conceive of religious leaders indulging themselves in drinking sprees and carousing. Nevertheless this is true and it might be well, at this time, to cite other things along this line and give their authority for so doing.

There is a formula, in Catholic books of authority, for blessing a distillery and "St." Thomas, Archbishop of Canterbury (1118-

1170), is the "Patron Saint of Brewers," to whom Brewers can appeal for divine help! (Strange But True Column, Operation Understanding, Aug. 18, 1963). So is "St," Amand (*New Catholic Dictionary, Vatican Edition,* 34).

Liquor Influenced Conclave In Selecting a Pope!

"With Hildebrand across the Alps and only eight months after Stephen's installation the Papal throne became empty again. Some said it was poison, and whether the whispers were true or not the dying Pope was sufficiently apprehensive of what might happen after his death to beg, with his last breath, that there should be no election until after the return of Hildebrand. He died and his wishes were ignored. The suspicion that his end bore the stain of murder was strengthened by the unseemly haste with which the old factions now moved to present their candidates. The Counts of Tusculum were by a great show of arms and liberal donations of liquor to the fickle mobs, successful with their protégé John Mincius, Bishop of Villetri, who now took the highly significant name of Benedict X" (*Pageant of the Popes,* Farrow, 113-114).

Liquor Men Prominent Catholic Leaders

"We shall not deny that as a natural result of these facts and conditions, the Church has suffered. Saloon keepers made themselves leaders among their countrymen, guided them in the novel road of American politics, and sought to represent them in religious affairs. They became officials in Church societies, Marshals in Church processions, Chairmen in Church meetings. They contributed liberally—as a matter of business—to Church works, and paid rent for prominent pews. Catholic opinion in regard to intemperance and to the saloon was in some degree perverted, and things were done and allowed which appear at first sight inexplicable to persons more conversant with American ideas and practices. At times, clergymen feared to offend the potent saloon keeper; they softened the tone of their denunciations of intemperance; if total abstinence was mentioned, emphasis was laid on the peril of running into the Manichean heresy—that liquor itself was morally bad. At church fairs and picnics liquor was sold. At their annual outings, religious societies kept their own bar and paid high tribute to it; at certain church fairs, punch bowls were voted to the most popular saloon keepers; Catholic papers admitted into their advertising columns paid notices of saloons and liquor stores, and, in one instance, a brewery invaded the grounds of a monastery" (*The Church in Modern Society,* I, Archbishop John Ireland, 332-333).

In the foregoing statements we get a clear glimpse of the satanic machinations which are employed in selecting "His Holiness," "The Roman Pontiff," who claims to be vicar (substitute for) of God and Christ! There is a call to all good people of the earth to join in eliminating this terrible evil from both the religious and political life of the whole world. Both of these are on the brink of disaster in this, our own country, the greatest country on earth!

The moral conditions of the clergy is an exact parallel to the depravity of Jewish priests and prophets whose condemnations have already been quoted from the *Old Testament.* The priests and prophets of that day broke the law of God themselves and led the people into such abominable disobedience that the whole nation was destroyed. *Yet, in spite of this, Catholic leaders tell us that we should follow the priests as they did!*

Should we follow the Catholic hierarchy when they make the following confessions?

"We all, prelates and clergy, have gone astray from the right way, and for long there is none that has done good; no, not one" (Pope Adrian VI, *Pastor's History of the Popes,* IX, 135).

Concerning this same pope, Adrian VI, *Catholic Encyclopedia,* I, 60, says:

"Appalling tasks lay before him in this darkest hour of the papacy. To extirpate inveterate abuses, to reform a court which thrived on corruption, and detested the very name of reform. . .

Two days later he received the triple crown. History presents no more pathetic figure than that of this noble Pontiff, struggling single-handed against insurmountable difficulties. . . His exaggerated acknowledgement that the Roman Court had been the fountainhead of all the corruption in the Church was eagerly seized upon by the Reformers as a justification of their apostasy."

Catholics Admit Error

"And history shows only too plainly that the Church, in their sense of the term, has varied in its doctrine, taught dogmas at various times and at various places at the same time, inconsistent with each other, and therefore to a considerable extent erroneous" (*Plain Facts,* Searle, 34).

Admit Forgery and Ignorance
Now Needs Revising!

"There was need of revision which is not yet complete, ranging over all that had been handed down from the Middle Ages under the style and title of the Fathers, the Councils, the Roman and other official archives. In all these departments forgery and interpolations, as well as ignorance had wrought mischief on a great scale" (*Catholic Encyclopedia,* XII, 768).

Yet Catholic authorities counsel us to follow them as the Jews followed their leaders!

God speaking through his prophet Jeremiah pronounced a woe upon the leaders of the Jews. Listen: "Woe be unto the pastors that destroy and scatter the sheep of my pasture! saith the Lord. Therefore thus saith the Lord God of Israel against the pastors that feed my people; Ye have scattered my flock, and driven them away, and have not visited them: behold, I will visit upon you the evil of your doings, saith the Lord" (Jeremiah 23:1-2). Why would the Lord do such a terrible thing to the priests? Hear the reason, given by this same prophet of God. "For both prophet and priest are profane; yea, in my house have I found their wickedness, saith the Lord. . .

86

they commit adultery, and walk in lies: they strengthen also the hands of evildoers, that none doth return from his wickedness: they are all of them unto me as Sodom, and the inhabitants thereof as Gomorrha" (Jeremiah 23:11, 14). God was faithful in his promise made to the Jews of that day. Do we count him less faithful under similar conditions today? "The Lord is not slack concerning his promise, as some men count slackness; but is longsuffering to us-ward, not willing that any should perish, but that all should come to repentance" (2 Peter 3:9).

Tradition—Its Source

This anomalous thing called "Tradition" is a conglomeration of paganism, purported "revelations," forgeries, customs, "discipline," dogmas, canons of Councils, bulls and encyclicals of popes, statements of the "saints" and "Fathers," and in fact anything that they wish to draw from, but let us not forget that none of it is even hinted at, much less mentioned, in the Bible.

"Tradition—We speak here of those sources which rest on mere tradition, and which, unlike the remains, are themselves no part of the fact. They are (1) Collections of acts of the martyrs, of legends and lives of the saints. (2) Collections of the lives of the popes (*Liber Pontificalis*) and of bishops of particular churches. (3) Works of ecclesiastical writers which contain information about historical events; to some extent all ecclesiastical literature belongs to this category. (4) Ecclesiastico-historical works, which takes on more or less the character of sources, especially for the time in which their authors lived. (5) Pictorial representations (paintings, sculptures, etc.). The foregoing are accessible in various collections, partly in editions of the works of particular authors (Fathers of the Church, theologians, historians), partly in historical collections which contain writings of different authors correlated in content, or all the traditional sources for a given land" (*Catholic Encyclopedia*, VII, 371).

Church Alters Ancient Writings

"When the Church studies the ancient monuments of her faith she casts over the past the reflection of her living and present thought and by some sympathy of the truth today with that of yesterday, she succeeds in recognizing through the obscurities and inaccuracies of ancient formulas and portions of traditional truth, even though they are mixed with error" (*Catholic Encyclopedia,* XV, 10).

"Moreover, not a few ordinances, whether included in the *Corpus Juris* or of more recent date, appear to be contradictory; some have been repealed, others had become obsolete by long disuse, others again had ceased to be useful or applicable in the present condition of society. Great confusion was thus engendered and correct knowledge of the law was rendered very difficult even for those who had to enforce it" (*General Legislation in the New Code of Canon Law,* Ayrinhac, 70).

Forged Tradition

"Substituting of false documents and tampering with genuine ones was quite a trade in the Middle Ages" (*Catholic Encyclopedia,* VI, 136).

"Writers of the fourth century were prone to describe many practices as of Apostolic institution which certainly had no claim to be so regarded" (*Catholic Encyclopedia,* III, 484).

We, all people, should have convictions. Convictions should be based on facts—facts of history and divine law. Read any history of the Catholic Church and note its many changes and additions. Search the scriptures and be impressed with God's law and its changeless character. "My covenant will I not break, nor alter the thing that is gone out of my lips" (Psa. 89:34). We are under God's covenant, the *New Testament,* but we have the same covenant-keeping God. He will not, and human beings *must* not, change his covenant!

Catholic authorities have changed and do change God's arrangements whenever they choose, and for whatever reason they feel would suit their purpose best. By their own admission they bear testimony to this fact. So many church leaders have forgotten, or perhaps never knew, that to "Fear God, and keep *His* commandments: . . . is the whole duty of man" (Ecclesiastes 12:13). Does our trouble stem from the fact that we have no fear of God? The Jews wanted peace, just as we do, but they could not have it. God speaking through the Apostle Paul told them why: "There is no fear of God before their eyes" (Rom. 3:18).

They had a warning, which they could have heeded, but they did not. "Ye *shall not* add unto the word which I command you, neither shall ye diminish aught from it, that ye may keep the commandments of the Lord your God which I command you" (Deut. 4:2). Are we, like the Jews, going to continue to ignore this same warning? We find it repeated in God's last and final message to man. "For I testify unto every man that heareth these words of the prophecy of this book. If any man shall add unto these things, God shall add unto him the plagues That are written in this book: And if any man shall take away from the words of the book of this prophecy, God shall take away his part out of the book of life, and out of the holy city, and from the things that are written in this book" (Revelation 22:18-19). What a terrible thought! I can only repeat with Simon, the sorcerer, "Pray ye to the Lord for me, that none of these things which ye have spoken come upon me."

CHAPTER IX

Catholics Do Not Claim to Follow the Bible

Tradition, being the only adequate exponent of the doctrine of Christ, is therefore, the only competent and legitimate interpreter of the scriptures. The dead letter has need of the living voice of tradition for its explanation. Moreover, the church alone preserves the scriptures and defines their integrity, because she believes them to be the orally revealed doctrine of Christ, the utterances of the same Holy Ghost who inspired them, and because she puts upon them their true meaning and interpretation, while heretics garble many passages, entirely rejecting others, and explain all to suit their own whim and fancy" (A *Manual of Church History,* John Alzog, 302).

It was hundreds of years after the *New Testament* time before anyone began to think up this "Catholic interpretation" theory. In *Catholicism Against Itself,* Vol. 1, appear a number of official Catholic admissions, very vital to the present point. The only book used by the Church for hundreds of years was the Bible. No one believed the pope to be infallible. One of the principal reasons was they had not dreamed up the idea of a pope at that time. It would hardly be possible for one to believe in the infallibility of the pope who had never heard of a pope! These official statements assure us that they had the Bible and all people read it freely. I will repeat one of these statements which flatly contradicts one of the most common Catholic assertions, to the effect that people did not read the Bible for several hundred years because there was no Bible to read!

"There was far more extensive and continuous use of Scriptures in the public service of the early Church than there is among us" (*Catholic Dictionary,* Addis and Arnold, 509).

90

Augustine who is claimed as one of the greatest "saints" and authorities in the Catholic Church (354-430), and his contemporary, "St." Cyril of Alexandria, rejected the present day Catholic doctrine concerning tradition and contended for only what the Bible teaches.

Augustine and Cyril of Alexandria Rejected Tradition

"St. Augustine allows that the things openly stated in the Scripture contains the whole sum of faith and morals. . . A Christian may find in the Bible all he needs to know explicitly in order to be saved, a fact that is undeniable . . . St. Cyril of Alexandria tells his catechumens that he will have them believe nothing he tells them except he can prove it out of the Scripture" (*Catholic Dictionary,* Addis and Arnold, 801).

Present Claims Contradict Augustine and Cyril

"That there are such truths is evident, for on many vital points of the Christian faith the Bible is either silent or does not speak with sufficient clearness, e.g., the baptism of infants, exact number of the sacraments, etc. Moreover, before our four Gospels and the other books of the *New Testament* were written a whole generation of Christians knew the teaching of Christ and the duties of a Christian life through the preaching of the Apostles and their co-workers. . . It is worthy of note that in all the controversies with the heretics the first defenders of the faith took their stand on Tradition even more than on the Bible" (*New Catholic Dictionary, Vatican Edition,* 969).

This admits that the Bible does not teach infant baptism or sacraments, very prominent Catholic practices. When we reach the "sacraments," in our study, we will have official Catholic admissions to the fact that no one in the Catholic Church, including popes, knew anything about the seven sacraments for thirteen hundred years after Christ! Catholics make a big point of the Apostle Paul recommending "traditions." The word translated *traditions* simply meant "something received." There is a vast difference between that which has been received from God through the Apostles in the Bible and that which has been ordained of men. The Church in Jerusalem "continued steadfastly in the apostles' doctrine" (Acts 2:42). This is what we are contending for today.

"The most of the fourth century, the controversy with the Arians had turned upon Scripture, and appeals to past authority were few" (*Catholic Encyclopedia,* VI, 2).

Claim Tradition Divinely Revealed

"Isn't there danger of error creeping into circulation when teaching is passed from one generation to another by word of mouth?

"There would be, 1, if the Church did not have the guidance of the Holy Spirit, and 2, if tradition were principally oral, as you understand it. But the Church's Tradition is chiefly 'written.' She has preserved the writings of learned saints of all centuries from the time of the Apostles. Then, as we have already seen, she possesses the decrees of General Councils beginning immediately after the age of the martyrs. Remember that the Tradition which we believe contains the word of God is *Divine* Tradition, not human. Divine Tradition is the divinely revealed truth taught orally by Christ and His Apostles which is not found in the Bible, though recorded for all time by churchmen in the early age of the Church" (*Father Smith Instructs Jackson,* Noll and Fallon, 58).

Catholic Teachings Based on Presumptuous Error!
Catholics in Conflict with Bible!

"Innocent III formally admits the possibility of this conflict. Some persons, he says, may be free in the eyes of God but bound in the eyes of the Church; *vice versa,* some may be free in the eyes of the Church but bound in the eyes of God: for God's judgment is based on the very truth itself, whereas that of the Church is based on arguments and presumptions which are sometimes erroneous"

(*Catholic Encyclopedia,* V, 684).

Bible Crude Beside Tradition!

"Scripture offers in the crude state, as it were, what theologians have subsequently classified, thought out and elaborated" (Henri Daniel-Rops, *Twentieth Century Catholic Encyclopedia,* Vol. 60, 108).

Holy Ghost Guides Catholics to Make Mistakes!

"It is true that the Church's leaders may make a mistake in placing a book on the Index, but the one mistake in the condemnation of Copernicus and Galileo is a clear testimony of the guidance of the Holy Ghost, even when the Church is giving a non-infallible decision" (*Question Box,* Conway, 207).

The writer of this must have gotten a hearty laugh at the expense of those naive enough to believe it!

Human Books Preferred by Catholics!

"In other spiritual books the truths of the Bible are presented more fully, and in a more modern and familiar style, so that we can hardly wonder that they are, as a rule, preferred; and that though Catholic families generally have a Bible, it is more venerated than read" (*Plain Facts for Fair Minds,* Searle, 54).

Catholics Do Not Need Bible!

"It is that of having for an authority in all ages, for a means of deciding all doubtful points, not a book alone, or a book with authorized interpreters, *but simply authorized interpreters of the faith* such as the Apostles were, with a book perhaps to help them, but still not absolutely needing that book for the discharge of their office any more than the Apostles did for theirs" (*Plain Facts for Fair Minds,* Searle, 33).

"They (apostles) consigned to unwritten tradition many revealed truths and thus made the Church from the beginning independent of their writings" (*History of the Church of God,* B.J. Spalding, 253).

The following quotation admits that it was the Council of the Vatican, less than a hundred years ago, which declared that Catholics must believe in "Tradition," that it is infallible, inspired, that it is better than the Scriptures, and, therefore, we do not need a Bible!

Tradition Inspired, Infallible
Tradition Better Than the Bible!

"The Vatican Council has decreed as an article of Faith that Tradition is a source of theological teaching distinct from Scripture and that it is infallible. . . As Revelation, it must have come from the Apostles as received from the lips of Christ Himself or been handed down by the Apostles at the dictation of the Holy Ghost. . . Whereas much of the teaching contained in the books of the Bible could not be determined without Tradition, Tradition as a source of Faith would suffice without Scripture" (*The Question Box Column, Brooklyn Tablet,* Nov. 8, 1958).

Bible Impossible—Catholics Must Legislate!

"The Church at one time practiced Baptism by immersion. This was done up to the thirteenth century. *The Council of Ravenna, in 1311, changed the form from immersion to pouring.* It is well known, however, that the Church had good reasons for doing this, that she had the power to legislate on the matter, and that immersion was not the only accepted form of Baptism up to the time of its change. . . The sick, however, could not be baptized by immersion. St. Paul must have used either sprinkling or pouring, when he baptized his jailer, and his whole household, as recorded in the Act of the Apostles. Many other cases could be cited where immersion was impossible" (*Our Faith and the Facts,* Donovan,

94

399).

This says that what the Lord required was "impossible" of observance, and that Catholics had to step in and rectify the Lord's mistake! God says that: "his commandments are not grievous" (hard). Catholics say that they are hard and some of them *impossible* to keep. Jesus says: "My yoke is easy and my burden is light" (Matt. 11:30). "Let God be true, but every man a liar" (Romans 3:4).

Space will not allow us to explode all the ignorant assumptions of these Catholic authors, but I will notice one. This "authority" asserts that the jailor could not have been immersed and assumed he was baptized in the jail. The Bible plainly states that the jailor "brought them out" of the jail before he was baptized. This shows how little regard they have for the Bible and how carelessly they read it. For the reader's benefit it might be well, at this point, to call attention to another apparent discrepancy made by many Catholic writers. You will notice in Donovan's explanation of why the jailor could not have been immersed he spelled the word "jailer." The *Douay* version gives it "gaoler." Some, in reading these hundreds of quotations, may attribute these discrepancies to my carelessness, not realizing that quotations *must* be exact.

Bible Absolutely Untenable
Catholics "Unerring"

"There is still an easier means of setting forth most clearly the falseness of Protestantism, namely by showing that its *rule of faith* is absolutely untenable and contrary to the will of Christ. When this basis is overthrown the whole edifice of the Reformation crumbles of itself. . .

"We Catholics profess also the greatest respect for the *Holy Scripture* (What a falsehood!—O.C.L.), but we receive it from the hands of the Church, which (by) virtue of her infallibility, guarantees its inspiration. Moreover, with the Scriptures we receive from the same hand with equal veneration, Tradition, that is, the word of God not contained in the Sacred Scriptures. Finally, far from claiming, like Protestants, that everyone has the right to determine the meaning of Scripture, far from declaring every man the judge and arbiter of his belief, we say that it belongs to the Church, assisted by the Holy Spirit, to fix the Catalogue or canon of the Holy Scriptures, to determine the meaning of the sacred text and unerringly interpret tradition. In a word, *the Catholic Rule of Faith is the* teaching authority of the Church; her living and infallible voice and doctrine" (*Christian Apologetics,* Deviviers-Messmer, 354-355).

After reading the many quotations, that have already been presented, is it not plain to the reader that Catholic authorities show the greatest disrespect for the Scriptures? They deny their Divinity; they ridicule the Bible writers as woefully ignorant men and they say that men, not God, have the right to determine the meaning of the Bible. They also say that they are guided by the Holy Spirit in reversing what the Holy Spirit said in the Bible!

Catholics Deny Even One Change!

"If only one instance could be given in which the Church ceased to teach a doctrine which had been previously held, that single instance would be the death blow of her claim of infallibility" (*Faith of Our Fathers,* Gibbons, 61).

"The Catholic church cannot be reformed. The doctrine is perfect and hence, can never be reformed" (*Faith of Our Fathers,* Gibbons, 61).

Catholicism Has Constantly Changed!

"While the church remains essentially the same despite the changes which she undergoes in time, the changes help to exhibit more fully her internal and external life. . . If we turn to the life of the Church, ecclesiastical history treats of the development of ecclesiastical teaching, based on the original supernatural deposit of faith, of the development of ecclesiastical worship in its various forms, of the utilization of the arts in the service of the Church, especially in connection with worship, of the forms of ecclesiastical functions, of the different ways of cultivating the perfect religious life, of the manifestations of religious life and sentiment among the people, and of the disciplinary rules whereby Christian morality is cultivated and preserved and the faithful are sanctified" (*Catholic Encyclopedia,* VII, 366).

Let us repeat here a very important quotation:

"And history shows only too plainly that the Church, in their sense of the term, has varied in its doctrine, taught dogmas at various times, and at various places at the same time, inconsistent with each other, and therefore to a considerable extent erroneous" (*Plain Facts for Fair Minds,* Searle, 34).

Admit Absurd Traditions
Christ's Clothes Grew!

"The cathedral of Trier (Fr. Treves), Germany, and the parish Church of Argenteuil, France, both claim to possess the seamless garment of Christ, *tunica inconsutilis* (John 19) for which the soldiers cast lots at the crucifixion. The Trier tradition which affirms that the relic was sent there by St. Helena, is substantiated by a tablet of the 6th century and several documents of the 12th century. The coat of Argenteuil is mentioned in a document dating from 1156 as the *cappa pueri Jesu* (garment of the child Jesus). The intermingling of these two traditions gave rise to the legend that the garment woven by the Blessed Virgin for the child Jesus grew with him during his whole life on earth. Modern advocates of the Argenteuil tradition now claim the Trier relic is not the *tunica inconsutilis* but the outer garment of Christ. The veneration of both these relics has been the occasion of many pilgrimages" (*New Catholic Dictionary, Vatican Edition,* 450).

Mary's Baby Clothes Grew too!

This is affirmed in Apocryphal and Legendary Life of Christ,

Donehoo, 21:

"Her raiment, which was always of the natural colours, never became foul nor wore out nor tore, but that which her mother put upon her on the day she gave her to the temple, remained upon her until the day of her death; As regards that which Mary increased daily, the raiment became greater with her." Catholics affirmed the same of John the Baptist (*Ibid.,* 111).

No Early Traditions

Catholic authorities carefully explain that "tradition" is just as old as the information we have in our Bible. Let us now notice a number of quotations admitting that there are no "traditions" that go back within hundreds of years of the *New Testament* period. In fact the only reliable records are those in the New *Testament.* There are no Roman records for hundreds of years after the *New Testament.* These admissions could hardly be more damaging to Catholic claims.

"And all this, we have reason to think, may well happen again, to an ever increasing extent . . . In the fifth century, the German and Arab invasions made an end of all culture of the West, and it was not till the eleventh century that the thread of tradition was again recovered" (*The Virgin Mary,* Guitton, 88).

Catholic writers rely heavily on *Eusebius' History,* especially when they attempt to establish a line of popes all the way back to Peter. The following statement from Eusebius shows how groundless this sort of pretended evidence really is. Eusebius wrote three hundred years after the Church was established.

"We are attempting a kind of tractless and unbeaten path. . . we are totally unable to find even the bare vestiges of those who may have traveled the way before us; unless, perhaps, what is only presented in the slight intimations, which some in different ways have transmitted to us in certain partial narratives of the times in which they lived" (*Eusebius History,* 2).

"The records of the second century are so scanty as to throw but little light on the subject (Appeal to Rome)" (*Catholic Encyclopedia,* XII, 267).

Tradition Worthless

"Even respecting the fields of Apostolic missions, they are self-contradictory or confused. In general their details are scientifically worthless unless confirmed by independent authorities, which rarely happens. Much of their apocryphal matter was taken up by the offices of the Apostles in the Latin *Breviaries* and *lectionaries* composed in the seventh and eight centuries at an extremely uncritical period" (*Catholic Encyclopedia,* I, 610).

Tradition of Peter Fades Out 400 Years Too Soon!

"*Peter and Paul,* Saints, Feast of, one festival used for these two great Apostles because, according to tradition, they were martyred on the same day, in Rome. It goes back to the fifth century" (*Catholic Dictionary, Vatican Edition,* 750).

No Roman Tradition!

"Tertullian, one of the most famous Latin Apologists, open(s) the long series of the Christian writers born in Northern Africa. Up to the time of Augustine, practically all the great names in the history of Christian literature will be African. During the same period, Rome herself will produce little or nothing" (*History of Christian Philosophy,* Gilson, 44).

What were the thirty popes of Rome doing throughout this period? The fact is, that the Roman "history" of those years is a forgery!

Obscurity of Early Rome, Tradition without Foundation!

"The precise date at which the Roman Church was founded we

do not know, nor the date at which St. Peter first went to Rome. But it is universally the tradition of this primitive Christianity that St. Peter ruled the Roman Church and that at Rome he gave his life for Christ in the persecution of Nero.

"We do not know very much about the first development of the Roman Church. The obscurity which, in these centuries, veils so much, veils this, too, very largely" (*A Popular History of the Church,* Philip Hughes, 15,16).

Know Nothing of Early Rome

"About the origins of Christianity in Rome itself we know nothing. It is already a flourishing church when, in 56, St. Paul refers to it. Three years later he himself arrived in Rome, a prisoner, for the hearing of his appeal to Caesar. St. Peter first appeared there, *apparently,* some three years later, about the time St. Paul, acquitted, had left the city" (*A Popular History of the Church,* Philip Hughes, 19).

One of the biggest claims of the Catholic Church is that the Roman Church was always supreme. In the light of the foregoing and the following quotations, if for no other reason, we are forced to conclude that such a claim is preposterous.

Rome Not Supreme in 325

"For this dogmatist (Novatus, O.C.L.), this (pretended) champion of ecclesiastical discipline, when he attempted to seize and usurp the episcopate not given him from above, selected two desperate characters as his associates, to send them to some small, and that the smallest, part of Italy, and from thence, by some fictitious plea, to impose upon three bishops there, men altogether ignorant and simple, affirming and declaring, that it was necessary for them to come to Rome in all haste, that all the dissension which had there arisen might be removed through their mediation, in conjunction with the other bishops" (*Eusebius' History,* 249).

100

Rome Lost Its Traditions

"This seems to be especially true of Rome, which possessed so few authentic Acta (*Acts of the Martyrs*) in spite of the number and fame of the martyrs; for the Romans had apparently lost the thread of their traditions as early as the second half of the fourth century" (*Catholic Encyclopedia,* IX, 744).

Errors and Inaccuracies in Catholic Tradition Must Be Doctored!

"When the Church studies the ancient monuments of her faith she casts over the past the reflection of her living and present thought and by some sympathy of the truth today with that of yesterday she succeeds in recognizing through the obscurities and inaccuracies of ancient formulas the portions of traditional truth, even when they are mixed with error" (*Catholic Encyclopedia,* XV, 10).

No Record of Early Church Except in Bible

"The sources from which the historian must reconstruct the story of primitive church are, from the point of view of his task, far from ideal. There are no diaries, memoirs, or correspondence of the chief actors, no dossiers of official papers, no systematically filed records, certificates, and statistics. There are only the summary lives of Our Lord we call the Gospels. There are letters from various Apostles to different communities of believers, and, in the next two centuries, a none too voluminous collection of polemical, apologetical, and expository writings. But nowhere save in the Acts of the Apostles, is there, for nearly three hundred years, anything that can be called a contemporary historical record. The precious facts, very often, are no more than the carefully gleaned *obiter dicta* of the theologians and the controversialists, of the unbelievers and the heretics too, no less than of the Catholic writers" (*Popular History of the Church,* Hughes, 2, 3).

101

No Evidence of Peter at Rome!

A "dogma" is a statement by the pope about something for which there is not a shred of evidence!

"It was not divinely revealed that St. Peter was Bishop of Rome, but it is a dogmatic fact, i.e., an historical truth so certain and so intimately connected with the dogma of the primacy that it comes under the divine, infallible teaching authority of the Church" (*Question Box,* 1929 Edition, 145).

So, you can see that Catholics, themselves, say that the tale about Peter being Bishop of Rome is a "made up" story. And did you notice that they also say that this dogma *must* be believed in order to substantiate another dogma concerning the primacy?

Tradition Untrustworthy

"In the sixth and seventh centuries pilgrims to Jerusalem were led to believe that the actual chalice was still venerated in the Church of the Holy Sepulchre, having within it the sponge which was presented to Our Saviour on Calvary . . . At a much later period two other vessels have been venerated as the chalice of the Last Supper. . . The fact is that the whole tradition is untrustworthy and of late date" (*Catholic Encyclopedia,* III, 561).

Tradition Shifting and Uncertain

"And while ordinary tradition is by its very nature shifting and uncertain, the Holy Ghost preserved the tradition of truth in the Church" (*Our Faith and the Facts,* Donovan, 353).

Tradition Capricious Admixture of True and False

"Why should we not deal similarly with popular tradition? It appeals in just this way to our attention and we have the same motives for mistrusting it. More than once it has been helpful to judicious critics and pointed the way to important discoveries which they would have never made with the sole aid of written documents or monuments. Let us look at the matter another way. Have not all students of historical documents come frequently across the same peculiar, one might say capricious admixture of true and false which meets us at every step in the case of popular traditions? It would be equally rash on the one hand to reject all traditions and place faith only in written testimony or contemporary monuments, and on the other to accord to tradition an implicit confidence merely because it was not formally contradicted by other historical data, though it received from them no confirmation" (*Catholic Encyclopedia*, IV, 507).

Catholic Tradition Developed!

"The whole tradition of venerating holy images gradually and naturally developed" (*Catholic Encyclopedia*, VII, 667).

The truth is that when Constantine dispossessed the pagans from their beautiful temples, filled with exquisite sculpture, the pagans immediately "joined the Church" and demanded that their beloved images be retained.

Catholics Retain Paganism!

"It has been and always will be the intent of tradition of the Apostolic See, to make large allowances in all that is right and good, for the primitive tradition and the special customs of every nation" (*Great Encyclical Letters of Leo XIII*, 308).

Present Argument for Retaining

"If, notwithstanding the precepts of the sound doctrine explained by the Church, ignorance and fraud have introduced some superstitious ideas to alter its purity, was that a reason for abolishing a received, popular, reasonable and consoling institution?" (*Lives and Times of the Roman Pontiffs*, Chevalier Artaud de Montor, I, 197).

Pagan Statue Transformed at Rome!

"On the high altar is a tabernacle of 1123; there is an antique statue transformed into a St. Sebastian by Paolo Campi and a monument of Innocent X" (*Catholic Encyclopedia*, XIII, 174).

Pagan Temples Converted!

"Many pagan temples were converted into Christian Churches" (*History of the Church*, Birkhaeuser, 125).

Catholics Borrowed Buddhism!

"The monasticism and the religious services of Lamaism also present so striking a similarity with Catholic institutions that non-Catholic investigators have unhesitatingly spoken of a 'Buddhist Catholicism' in Tibet. Pope and Dalilama, Rome and the city of Lhasa are counterparts; Lamaism has its monasteries, bells, processions, litanies, relics, images of saints, holy water, rosary-beads, bishops mitre, crosier, vestments, capes, baptism, confession, mass, sacrifice for the dead" (*Catholic Encyclopedia*, XII, 409).

Saints in Place of Pagan Gods!

"Further research has shown the origins of these fanciful details to be pagan rather than Christian, being drawn from the tales of the pagan deities and heroes. After the age of the martyrs, the original truthful Acta were gradually encrusted with these details, so that, with the popular credulity, the romantic elements have quite buried the truthful facts. The fact that the honoring of the Christian saints took the place of the honoring and adoring of the local pagan gods and demigods, offering an opportunity for the abuse of attributing to the saints the deeds of the pagan demigods" (*Catholic Encyclopedia, Vatican Edition*, 552).

Tradition Based on a Misunderstanding!

One of the childishly absurd fables told the trusting laity concerns a white marble house "richly adorned with statues and sculpture. . . which tradition asserts to be the very same building in which the Blessed Virgin dwelt in Nazareth, where she heard the message of the archangel, and where the holy family resided during the childhood and hidden life of the Lord" (*Catholic Dictionary,* Addis and Arnold, 530).

Catholic Encyclopedia states that this "has been numbered among the most famous shrines in Italy." The "tradition" is that Angels transported this building to Italy and placed it at two different locations before finally settling on the little town of Loreto. Why the angels were so uncertain as to finally locating it, "tradition" fails to inform us. The house was supposed to have been carried more than one thousand miles!

SANCTIONED BY 48 POPES

"That the tradition thus boldly proclaimed to the world have been fully sanctioned by the Holy See cannot for a moment remain in doubt. More than forty-seven popes have in various ways rendered honour to the shrine, and an immense number of Bulls and Briefs proclaim without qualification the identity of the *Santa Casa di Loreto* with the Holy House in Nazareth. As lately as 1894 Leo XIII, in a Brief conceding various spiritual favors for the sixth centinary of the translation of the *Santa Casa* to Loreto, summed up its history in these words: 'The Holy House of Nazareth is justly regarded and honoured as one of the most sacred monuments of the Christian Faith: and this is made clear by the many diplomas and acts, gifts and privileges accorded by Our predecessors . . .

"It must be acknowledged, however, that recent historical criticism has shown that in other directions the Loretan tradition is beset with difficulties of the gravest kind. . . When we eliminate certain documents commonly appealed to as early testimonies to the tradition, but demonstrably spurious, we find that no writer can be shown to have heard of the miraculous translation of the Holy House before 1472, i.e., 180 years after the event is supposed to have taken place" (*Catholic Encyclopedia,* XIII, 455).

POPES AND SAINTS APPROVED FALSEHOOD!

"The tradition was approved by *many* popes and *many* saints and many miracles are recorded as having taken place there. Most recent research shows that the tradition is mistaken and rests upon some unexplained misunderstanding. The marvel is mentioned in the Roman Martyrology on December 10, on which day a feast of Our Lady of Loreto is celebrated in some places. There is a nice appropriateness in the fact that under this title, Our Lady is venerated as the Patron of Airmen" (*Question Box Column in Brooklyn Tablet*).

Read the above again and observe how many important features of Catholicism are based on this falsehood: Tradition, Roman Martyrology, Feast Days, "Patron Saint of Airmen," to say nothing of the infallibility of popes, the veracity of Saints, Catholic miracles, etc!

Tradition Divinely Revealed!
Must Believe All Tradition!

"We are bound by divine and Catholic faith to believe all those things which are contained in the Word of God, whether it is Scripture or Tradition, and are proposed by the Church to be believed as divinely revealed, not only through solemn judgment but also through the ordinary universal teaching office" (*National Catholic Almanac,* 1955, 74).

The "ordinary and universal teaching office" means the little priests. Few Catholic laymen ever have any contact with any other. The assertion made here is that Catholics must believe all a priest teaches is being divinely revealed!

106

Dionysius the Areapogite Is Forgery

"Although he openly wove into the genuine Catholic system neoPlatonic (pagan—O.C.L.) thoughts and phrases nevertheless he enjoyed an unparalleled reputation among the greatest scholastics of the Middle Ages because he was supposed to have been a disciple of the Apostles" (*Catholic Encyclopedia,* XIV, 589).

ALL CATHOLICS USED THIS FORGERY UNQUESTIONED FOR 1000 YEARS!

"Neither in the West (Roman Catholic—O.C.L.) was voice raised in challenge down to the first half of the fifteenth century; on the contrary his works were regarded as exceedingly valuable and even sacred" (*Catholic Encyclopedia,* V, 17).

Imagine, if you can, an "infallible" church regarding a huge forgery as sacred!

WRITTEN AND USED TO DECEIVE!

"It is plainly for the purpose of deceiving" (*Catholic Encyclopedia,* V, 13), and intended to "accentuate" clerical "immunity" (*Augustine's Commentary on Canon Law,* I, 26), also, "to create the impression that the author (The forger—O.C.L.) belonged to the time of the Apostles" (*Catholic Encyclopedia,* V, 14). It was further admitted that this forgery was perpetrated "to secure the authority of the Roman Pontiff" (*Augustine,* I, 25). This is the sort of "tradition" of which Catholic authorities boast!

Another Great Catholic Forgery: The Rosary Tradition!

The story that is still told to trusting laymen is that "St. Dominic" who had been appointed the Grand Inquisitor for the purpose of carrying fire and sword to the destruction of those who refused to follow Catholicism, the Albigenses, that at the earnest prayer of Dominic to Mary, she appeared to him, giving specifications for the Rosary. Later, we will see that this story is branded as a false-

107

hood by the *Catholic Encyclopedia!* We are informed that Dominic never heard of a rosary in his life and that it was about two hundred and fifty years after he was dead when Alan de Rupe wrote the forgery including this story. What do you think of the "sanctity" and "infallibility" of those popes, who, for nearly five hundred years have continued to tell this falsehood?

STORY OF ROSARY REVEALED TO DOMINIC!

"At Toulouse, according to tradition, the devotion of the Rosary was revealed to him" (*Catholic Dictionary, Vatican Edition,* 305).

TRUE ROSARY, SOMETIMES CALLED THE DOMINICAN

"*Rosary of the Blessed Virgin,* a form of prayer (vocal or mental), consisting of fifteen decades of Hail Mary's, said on beads, each decade preceded by an Our Father and followed by a Gloria, during the recitation of which the mind meditates or dwells on the principle mysteries of the life, death and resurrection of Our Lord. This is the true Rosary, sometimes called the Dominican, or Rosary of St. Dominic, because its origin has been traditionally attributed to that saint" (*New Catholic Dictionary, Vatican Edition,* 836).

STORY OF THIS TRADITION A "FORGERY"

"The Rosary, says the Roman Breviary, is a certain form of prayer wherein we say fifteen decades or tens of Hail Mary's with Our Father in between each ten, while at each of the fifteen decades we recall successively in pious meditation one of the mysteries of our redemption. The same lesson of the Feast of the Holy Rosary informs us that when the Albigensian heresy was devastating the country of Toulouse, St. Dominic earnestly besought the help of Our Lady (1200 A.D.) and was instructed by her, 'so tradition asserts' to preach the Rosary among the people as an antidote to heresy and sin. From that time forward this manner of prayer was 'most wonderfully published abroad and developed by St. Dominic whom different Supreme Pontiffs have in various passages of their apostolic letters declared to be the institutor and author of the same devotion.' That many popes have so spoken is undoubtedly true, and amongst the rest we have a series of encyclicals, beginning in 1883, issued by Pope Leo XIII, which, while commending this devotion to the faithful in the most earnest terms, assumes the institution of the Rosary by St. Dominic to be a fact historically established. . .

"Impressed by the conspiracy of silence, the Bolandists on trying to trace to its source the origin of the current tradition, found that all the clues converged upon one point, the preaching of the Dominican Alan de Rupe about the year 1470-1475. He undoubtedly was who first suggested the idea that the devotion of 'Our Lady Psalter' (a hundred and fifty Hail Marys) was instituted or revived by St. Dominic. Alan was a very earnest and devout man, but as the highest authorities admit, *he was full of delusions, and based his revelations on imaginary testimony of writers that never existed.* His preaching, however, was attended with much success. The Rosary Confraternities, organized by him and his colleagues at Douai, Cologne, and elsewhere had great vogue, and led to the printing of many books, all more or less impregnated with the ideas of Alan. Indulgences were granted for the good work that was thus being done and the documents conceding these indulgences accepted and repeated, as was natural in that uncritical age, the historical data which had been inspired by Alan's writings and which were submitted according to the usual practice by the promoters of the confraternities themselves. It was in this way that the tradition of the Dominican authorship grew up. . ."

"It is now admitted by Dominican authorities to be a forgery" (*Catholic Encyclopedia,* XIII, 184-186).

SOME INEVITABLE CONCLUSIONS
There are a number of interesting and characteristic things

about this story. It was in that same way that nearly every feature of "Tradition" grew up! The reader should note the number of times that the word "tradition" occurs in this short quotation. This ought to shake the confidence of any good, honest Catholic in Catholic leadership. This important matter originated in the deluded brain of an ignorant man, but he was not so ignorant that he did not know he was writing a forgery and deluding dying men. When Catholics want "traditions" they invent them.

Deny A Single Change!

The following quotation cannot be repeated too many times:

"If only one instance could be given in which the Church ceased to teach a doctrine of faith which she had previously held, that single instance would be a death-blow to her claim of infallibility" (*Faith of Our Fathers,* Gibbons, 61).

Have we not shown hundreds of such changes? I cannot understand how any person having this information before him, could believe that anyone in the Catholic Church is, or ever has been, infallible. Many of the Popes have been astrologers, and yet she now condemns astrology!

CHANGED ON ASTROLOGY

"Catholics are bound in conscience to have nothing to do with astrology" (*Radio Replies,* Rumble and Carty, II, 229).

DENY MISTRANSLATING SINGLE WORD!

"If one small blunder concerning the doctrine of original sin, were made in her twenty centuries of charting the course of men to God, huge blunders would have been made in human happiness. A mistranslation of a single word one thousand years ago might have smashed all the statues of Europe" (*Moods and Truths,* Sheen, 94).

Let us not forget this extravagant boast, by this present-day idol

110

of the Catholic Church, when we later produce a great many ignorant, and quite a few deliberate mistranslations of the Bible!

SHE NEVER CONTRADICTS HERSELF!

"But in dealing with everything that can be urged against her
the Church never finds herself compelled to unsay anything. In answering difficulties from the most diverse points of view, even the
most contradictory, she never contradicts herself, having to unsay
to one opponent what she has maintained in her replies to another"
(*Radio Replies,* Rumble and Carty, III, XII).

Catholic Tradition Additions To Bible Teaching

This fact, I am sure, is evident to the reader, already, and let us
remember that a number of quotations already given admit this
readily. However, I hope you will bear with me, as I give again a
very important quotation: "And history shows only too plainly that
the Church, in their sense of the term, has varied in its doctrine,
taught dogmas at various times, and at various places at the same
time, inconsistent with each other, and therefore to a considerable
extent erroneous" (*Plain Facts for Fair Minds,* Searle, 34).

This surrenders the whole contention.

CHAPTER X

Catholic Law

ALL the unbearable burdens which the hierarchy has bound upon the Catholic Church, in the aggregate, is called *Canon Law*. I have in my library three editions: One was printed in 1503, which was before the beginning of the Protestant Reformation, and during the ugliest, most tyrannical period of Catholic history. The next one I have, was printed in 1696. This was the period when the Catholic Church was burning "witches" and "heretics" by the millions. It was also during this period, Catholic writers admit, that the Bible was forbidden and the most inhuman devices were being invented in an effort to crush the revolt which had been generated by the widespread reading of the Bible. My third edition is the present one which went into force in 1918.

Those who are ignorant of the importance of *Canon Law* vainly imagine that the Catholic Church, that frightful monster of the Dark Ages, has now been transformed into a gentle lamb. The fact is, that all the ugliness of the Dark Ages is still retained in the present law. The only difference is that these offensive laws cannot be enforced as long as the present situation continues.

"The Church is not in a position to enforce these laws, but the right to do so is still radically inherent in the society established by Christ" (*A Commentary on Canon Law,* Augustine, I, 88).

Church Cannot Now Enforce Her Law!

"Although in the extraordinary condition of these times the Church usually acquiesces in certain modern liberties, not because she prefers them in themselves but because she judges it expedient to permit them, she would in happier times exercise her own liberty" (Leo XIII, in *Great Encyclical Letters,* 158).

Freedom Declared Unlawful!

"From what has been said, it follows that it is quite unlawful to demand, to defend, or to grant unconditional freedom of thought, of speech, of writing or worship, as if these were so many rights given by nature to man" (Leo XIII, in *Great Encyclical Letters,* 161).

Canon Law for All Roman Catholics

"There is now no Canon Law, affecting the Universal Church, outside this *Codex* (1918) except (1) the laws of the Oriental Church in union with Rome" (*The Catholic Doctor,* Bonner, 9).

"The Church has the power to do this, and when she acts, 'Whatever is, is light'" (*New Matrimonial Legislation,* C.J. Cronin, 146).

How Catholic Laws Come About!

"Jurisprudence is as a rule the result of a slow and gradual process of development. It originates in the views and conclusions of individual jurists, which gather strength in proportion as the number and authority of the doctors who share them increase, until they become common and solidly probable opinions, which, when they have reached this stage, may in many cases be safely acted upon in practice. . . It began in private opinions, which gradually gained ground till they became the current jurisprudence, and were ultimately consecrated by the authentic declarations of the Holy See" (*New Matrimonial Legislation,* CJ. Cronin, 144).

This is how the Pope arrives at his "infallible" decisions!

When the Pope cannot find what he wants from all these dubious sources, he appeals to "natural law," and he claims that he is the sole interpreter. This gives him unlimited latitude to say whatever he wants!

Catholic Definition of Natural Law

"Natural law, the sum total of the ethical precepts implanted by God in the rational nature of man, through the observance of which he, as a free intelligent being, might attain his natural destiny. It is that universal, unchangeable, eternal law, which St. Paul says is indelibly written by the creator in our hearts or in our very nature, urging us to observe the moral order, to do good, and avoid evil. The ultimate basis and source of the natural law is the eternal law or Divine reason ordering and directing all things in accordance with their natural inclinations to their proper acts and ends" (*New Catholic Dictionary, Vatican Edition,* 665).

According to this definition, if we follow our inclinations and do whatever we feel that we want to do, this is right! This, it seems to me, would authorize every evil thing.

Another Definition of Natural Law

"The natural law which governs human conduct is that which is known to man's reason as manifested by his very nature. It is studied in his appetites and faculties, giving man a knowledge of what he, as a human being ought to do (*The Question Box column in the Brooklyn Tablet,* Oct. 13, 1962).

This could only mean that a person may do what he has a desire to do, or is capable of doing"

"You shall not do there the things we do here this day, every man that which seemeth good to himself" (Deut. 12:8, *Douay*).

"The way of a fool is right in his own eyes" (Prov. 12:15, *Douay*).

"Every way of a man seemeth right unto himself" (Prov. 21:2, *Douay*).

"There is a way that seemeth to a man right, and the ends

114

thereof lead to death" (Prov. 16:25, *Douay*).

The Catholic Bible "clearly refutes the Catholic doctrine concerning "natural law."

"I know, O Lord, that the way of a man is not his: neither is it in a man to walk, and to direct his steps" (Jer. *10:23,.Douay*).

If there were such a thing as "natural law," in the Catholic sense, we would not need a Bible!

Beasts Under Natural Law
Just Instinct!

"Natural law was thus a sort of *Vis a tergo* or instinct common to man and beasts, and the similarity in the laws of various peoples was explained as no more than a manifestation of the same instinct" (*The State and the Church,* Ryan and Millar).

Rousseau Apostle of Natural Religion

Rousseau was a libertine who seemed to recognize nothing as sacred or divine except sex. He did what came naturally!

"He went again to Lyons as private tutor, then to Paris where he met Diderot and the Encyclopedists. Having spent a year in Venice as secretary to the French Ambassador, he came back to Paris, wrote music, and began his liaison with Theresa le Vasseur, a barmaid, by whom he had five children, consigning all of them to a foundling asylum. Later he retired to a cottage in the forest of Montmorency, as the guest of Mme. d'Epinay. . . He was also the creator of a new false philosophy which he calls 'Instinctivism,' and proclaimed the sacredness of sensual passion; he is the Apostle of natural religion, was the enemy of all positive religion, and is responsible for some of the most dangerous social and political errors of the present time" (*New Catholic Dictionary, Vatican Edition,* 838).

The Catholic system appeals to the same "Natural Law" to bolster its dangerous system. She has changed everything the Lord

115

arranged, and thus perverted the plan (Gal. 1:7) and preached another gospel, based partly on "natural law"! Rousseau had as much right to do this as the popes. Since, we are told by Catholic authorities that "natural law," or instinct, is about the same for men as animals, why should men not live like animals? Thousands of the priesthood, including many popes, have done this and fathered illegitimate children just as Rousseau did. Their system is just as dangerous as his!

Natural Law Above Bible Law

"The supreme law is the eternal law, which is the fount of all other laws and precepts. The eternal law is manifested to us through the evolution of reason (natural or moral law), or through a certain sensible sign or positive act of the legislator (positive law). Positive law is either imposed on us immediately by the authority of God (Divine positive law, e.g., revelation), or it is imposed immediately by the authority of man (human positive law). Human law regards either the end of religious society (ecclesiastical law), or the end of civil society (civil law)" (*New Catholic Dictionary, Vatican Edition,* 547).

How different is this burdensome system from that of the Bible, even the *Catholic Bible!*

"For from thy infancy thou hast known the Sacred Writings, which are able to instruct thee unto salvation by the faith which is in Christ Jesus. All Scripture is inspired by God and useful for teaching, for reproving, for correcting, for instructing in justice; that the man of God may be perfect, equipped for every good work" (2 Tim. 3:15-17, *Confraiernity Version*).

According to this there is only one law and it is found in the Bible. If a thing is not found in the Bible, it is not a good work.

"And they bind together heavy and oppressive burdens, and lay them on men's shoulders; but not with one finger of their own do they choose to move them" (Matt. 23:4).

"But he answered and said to them, "Why do you, too, transgress the commandment of God by your traditions?. . . So you have made void the commandment of God by your tradition. Hypocrites, well did Isaias prophesy of you saying, 'This people honors me with their lips, but their heart is far from me'; but in vain do they worship me; teaching for doctrines precepts of men" (Matt. 15:3-9).

Pope Alone Interprets "Natural Law"

"No doubt all theologians recognize the *directive* power of the Pope: that it belongs to him to *interpret* authentically the natural law and the divine law. . . For example, depose monarchs or rulers, release subjects from their oath of allegiance—opinions are divided, and the Church has given no decision. Bellarmine, for example, sustains that he can" (*Christian Apologetics,* Deviviers-Messmer, 511).

The definitions of natural law, already given, simply mean our desires. Why then would it be necessary to have a Pope to tell us what we want? And if that be true why did the Apostle Paul have such a struggle with his desires? (Roman 7:18-25).

We are told that our natural desires are the expression of natural law, yet they tell us fasting is based on natural law. The Catholic law forbidding our eating when we are hungry is simply Catholic law conflicting with natural law! To claim that any Catholic law is based on "Natural law" is tantamount to admitting it is not in the Bible!

"Finally in the strict acceptation of the term, fasting denoted abstinence from food, and as such is an act of temperance finding its *raison d'etre* in the dictates of natural law and its full perfection in the requirements of positive ecclesiastical legislation" (*New Catholic Dictionary, Vatican Edition,* 789).

They Claim Crucifix Talks!

I have, probably, extended this study concerning the sources of Catholic "law" to a point of weariness, but I hope the indulgent reader will bear with me a little further. It is so necessary to demonstrate that Catholic authorities go everywhere except to the Bible for their confusing "law"!

"Had it not been for the voice from the crucifix, which rang in the ears of Francis, he would have been well content to spend his life in the lazar houses of Gubbio" (*Life of St. Francis Assisi,* Magliano, 39).

The following are several similar quotations which not only portray the idolatry of Catholicism but reveals one more way in which they pretend that God reveals Catholic practices. Presently I shall demonstrate, even to a person unfamiliar with the Bible, how false this is.

'St.' Bonaventure Did Not Need Bible!

"Once when a great master of theology came to visit him, he inquired where he had learned so much heavenly science. St. Bonaventure pointed to his crucifix, and exclaimed, 'This is the fountain of all my knowledge; for I desire no other book, save Jesus crucified'" (*Life of St. Francis* Assisi, Magliano, 354).

Do Not Need Bible—Only a Rosary!

". . . St. Margaret of Cortona, who by means of the Rosary, conversed often and long with God."

"It was by constantly saying the Rosary that she was introduced into this happy country of the interior life—a country overflowing with milk and honey. Here she learned more of God in one moment than by reading all the books in the world; she spoke to God, and God spoke to her" (*Devotion of the Holy Rosary,* Muller, 102-103).

Another Ignorant Catholic Saint!

"The great servant of God, Brother Bernard of Corlien, a Cap-uchin, did not know how to read, and his fellow-religious wished to teach him. He went to ask advice from the crucifix, and Jesus answered him from the cross: 'What necessity for books or read-ing! I am your book—a book in which you can always read the love I have borne you'" (*The Devotion of the Holy Rosary,* Muller, 96).

Rosary More Convenient Than Bible!

"What book is so convenient to carry with us as our beads? It can always be about us; in going to our work we can take it in our hands, and say a decade; at night we can put it around our neck or on the arm, and before falling asleep offer to our Mother another decade of prayer" (*Devotion of the Holy Rosary,* Muller, 187).

Bread Talked

In these quotations it is clear that Catholics are taught that Christ is actually on the crucifix, just as they insist that when the priest performs over the bread that it is actually Christ himself. They worship this piece of bread! Thus, we can see how idolatry is carried even further to the point of believing that Christ some-times speaks from this bread and gives instructions. It is easy to see how this would awe ignorant people and influence children who have never known anything else or been allowed to think for themselves, in matters of religion.

"He used to console me out of his great compassion; and if he had trusted to his own convictions, I should not have had so much to suffer; for God revealed the whole truth to him. I believe that he received this light from the Blessed Sacrament" (*St. Teresa's Au-tobiography, 207*).

119

Fabricated Stories

"But the ancient stories were much more probably nothing but the fabrication of some monastic dreamer, who, after pouring over manuscripts that told of Fortunate Isles, retold them with an Irish twist. A romancer, in days where there was hardly any line drawn between sober fact and shining fable, was not necessarily a liar. He did not think of himself as writing history. If, as De Costa points out, the very word 'America' in the Monastikan Britanicum proves the reference fraudulent, we need not charge deliberate fraud. It would merely date the scribe's transcription; he could still have been reworking immemorial traditions" (*The Story of American Catholicism,* Maynard, 3).

Discipline

When Catholic authorities are challenged on their substituting a celibate priesthood for a married eldership, or taking the fruit of the vine from members and giving it all to the priest, or substituting pouring for immersion they say, "That is only discipline." Is it not presumptions blasphemy to talk of applying discipline to the Lord's arrangements? The same stock answer is given for adding to the divine law.

ABOUT COMMUNION UNDER ONE SPECIES

"My non-Catholic neighbors want to know why in the Catholic Church the people do not receive Communion under the species of both bread and wine. What say you?

"It is a matter of the *discipline* of the Church. It was the ordinary practice of the whole Church until the twelfth century for the laity to receive Communion under both kind. But it is now the law for the Latin rite made definitive for this rite at the Council of Constance, in 1415, for the laity to receive under one kind only, namely, under the species of bread" (*Our Sunday Visitor,* Nov. 17, 1963)

120

This is man's arrangement, not our Lord's. The reader should think seriously upon these matters as we go along. Many questions should arise in our minds. One question we might ask ourselves at this point is: Why does the priest drink all the wine, if the wine is not necessary?

Dogma

It seems that when Catholic authorities cannot find the law they want, under any of the fanciful heads already mentioned, that the pope makes it a law anyway. When there is no scripture, no history and no reason for a law of the pope, Catholics must accept it as true and divine anyway. That is the reason why the pope declared himself to be infallible in 1870. You must, then, accept his statements as true whether they are or not!

"The dogmas of the Church on the other hand are true because grounded on the authority of Divine Reason who reveals them. . . Dogmatic facts are certain truths, which though not revealed by God, came nevertheless under the teaching authority of the Church" (*New Catholic Dictionary, Vatican Edition,* 304).

CATHOLICS INTEND TO KEEP ON ADDING!

"Or again, dogma is like a Cathedral still in process of construction; so far we cannot grasp its exact proportions; only the nave is completed; we still have to wait for the placing of the last stone" (*The Virgin Mary,* Guitton, III).

This is so diametrically opposed to the Catholic Bible which states that we have had the complete plan of God for more than nineteen hundred years.

"Beloved, while I was making every endeavor to write to you about our common salvation, I found it necessary to write to you, exhorting you to contend earnestly for the faith *once for all* delivered to the saints" (Jude 3, Confraternity Version).

". . . I have kept back *nothing* that was for your good. . . for I have not shrunk from declaring to you *the whole* council of God"

121

(Acts 20:20, 27, Confraternity Version).

Philosophy

At a recent debate, the priest, who was one of the disputants, gently boasted of how many years he had studied theology and how many years he had studied philosophy, but in the same session tried, in vain, to find 2 Timothy. I think, probably, his people, who were present, may have wished that he had also studied the Bible! I certainly wish all people would.

Here is a sample of Catholic Philosophy (Foolosophy)!

"This remark applies to the so-called creation of Ideas. Their creation is the first of all theophanies. In Ideas God begins to emerge from the most hidden secret of his nature and reveals himself to himself. And indeed, since God is beyond being, he is non-being; as such, God is unknowable not only to us, but to himself, unless he begins to reveal himself to himself under the form of the only objects accessible to intellectual knowledge, namely beings. This is why we had to say that, in producing Ideas, God creates himself, because instead of remaining in his own in accessible transcendency, God then begins to be in something which is his self-manifestation" (*History of Christian Philosophy*, Gilson, 119).

"Let us now consider the divisions of nature insofar as it includes what is not. In a doctrine which, directly or not, derives its inspiration from Plato's *Sophist,* the concept of being and non-being have only a relative value. All being is the non-being of what is not; moreover, there are cases when what is said not to be is more real than what we usually call being. For indeed being can be reasonably defined: that which can be perceived by the senses or understood by the intellect. Consequently, whatever escapes the grasp of these two cognative powers can rightly be called non-being. Applying this definition, Erigena distinguishes five types of non-being. First, that which escapes our senses and our understanding on account of its very perfection; for instance, God, or

122

even the essences of things, which we know only through their accidents. Second, within the hierarchical order of beings, the affirmation of the inferior is the negation of the superior, and conversely, so that what a being is implies the non-being of what it is not. Third, potential being is the non-being of what it will be once it is actualized. Fourth, beings subject to generation and corruption are not, at least in comparison with the immutable Ideas, which are their models. Fifth, in the case of man one can say that he is insofar as he loses this image through his fault" (*History of Christian Philosophy,* Gilson, 116).

It seems impossible to string words together to make less sense. The years a young man spends in the seminary is largely employed in trying to unravel such riddles. This in addition to learning the fables of more than nine thousand manufactured "saints" and the different colors for different occasions, the right robe to wear, the number of candles to burn, and the many Latin "rigmaroles" for different occasions, he has no time left to read or learn anything about the Bible! I have learned, from experience, that priests, as a class, know less than any other religious group. It is evident that they are ignorant of the following scriptures:

". . . stay now at Ephesus, in order that you may enjoin certain persons not to teach a different doctrine, nor to occupy themselves with myth" (1 Tim. 1:3, *Spencer's Catholic Translation*).

"And avoid foolish and unlearned questions, knowing that they beget strifes" (2 Tim. 2:23, *Douay*).

Custom

Catholic Canon Law is contradictory in countless ways. One is with reference to how long it takes customs to change Catholic law. Sometimes their books say ten years, some say twenty, some forty. The following is an example:

"Custom either introduces a new law or abrogates an old one. . . Authors generally hold that for the legalizing of a custom in accordance with or besides the law (*juxta or praeter legem*) a space of ten years is sufficient; while for a custom contrary (*contra*) to law man demand a lapse of forty years. The reason given for the necessity of so long a space as forty years is that the community will only slowly persuade itself of the opportunities of abrogating the old and embracing the new" (*Catholic Encyclopedia,* IV, 576).

They go slowly so the laity will not get alarmed by the change!

Everything About Catholicism Changes

"While the Church remains essentially the same despite the changes which she undergoes in time, these changes help to exhibit more fully her internal and external life . . . If we turn to the internal life of the Church, ecclesiastical history treats of the development of ecclesiastical teaching based on the original supernatural deposit of faith, of the development of ecclesiastical worship in its various forms, of the utilization of the arts in the service of the Church, especially in connection with worship, of the forms of ecclesiastical government and the exercise of ecclesiastical functions, of the different ways of cultivating the perfect religious life, of the manifestations of religious life and sentiment among the people, and of the disciplinary rules whereby Christian morality is cultivated and preserved and the faithful are sanctified" (*Catholic Encyclopedia,* VII, 366).

Forbid Printing Canon Law in English!

Many of the questionable features of Catholic practice are hidden in Latin. In the Foreword to Volume II of *A Commentary on Canon Law,* by Charles Augustine we find the following:

"Semi-official notice received from Rome, in response to our inquiry, caused us to limit our work to a commentary proper, since translations into the vernacular are not only not desired by the authorities, but rather discouraged, nay, at least for the whole Code as such, forbidden. Therefore we had to embody the contents of the Code in the Commentary, and rendered the Latin text into English only when it seemed absolutely necessary, or where no commentary was needed. Some canons have been neither translated nor paraphrased because the persons concerned might have been offended by a translation or paraphrase."

Think on these things!

". . . men loved darkness rather than the light: for their works were evil" (John 3:19, *Douay*).

Babies Must Wear Bonnets!

"The present law of the Church (Canon 1262,2) prescribes that women who assist at sacred functions should cover their heads and be dressed modestly, especially when they approach the Lord's table. So women and girls should wear a hat or a scarf, or a veil or a babushka. Girl babies should wear a bonnet" (*Our Sunday Visitor,* Aug. 25, 1963).

Multiplicity of Catholic Laws

Catholics claim to have had more than two hundred and sixty popes and twenty-one ecumenical Councils. Think what a burden this would become. Jesus said that men would "bind heavy burdens and grievous to be borne, and lay them on men's shoulders" (Matt. 23:4).

Alexander III is said to have issued thirty-nine hundred and thirty-nine decrees and Innocent III over five thousand (*General Legislation in the New Code of Canon Law,* Ayrinhac, 42).

According to the *Hughes-Breckenridge Debate,* page 34, there were one hundred volumes of the Decrees of Councils and Bulls of Popes 140 years ago.

Catholic Laws Unbearable Burden

"'The body of ecclesiastical laws,' said the Bishops of the

Province of Naples, 'has become in modern times an almost unbearable burden—*Ingens camelorum onus*—; contradictory texts abound in it, giving rise to endless disputes; often it is impossible to ascertain what is really the obligation'" (*General Legislation in the New Code of Canon Law,* Ayrinhac, 71).

Where is the boasted certainty of Catholic leadership? How can they have the temerity to admit this situation, and at the same time make a claim of infallibility for those who have created this Babel of confusion? It is no wonder that a cry of despair went up from the bishops!

Bishops Buried Beneath Laws

"It is very evident and has long been recognized by all and proclaimed everywhere that some revision and reformation of Canon Law is necessary and very urgent. For, owing to the changes that have taken place in society, many laws have become useless and others very difficult if not impossible to observe; of others it is doubtful whether they are still in vigor or not. Finally in the course of centuries, their number is so multiplied and they have been heaped up in voluminous collections that, in a sense, we may say, we are buried beneath the laws. Hence it is that the study of Canon Law is beset with almost inextricable difficulties, the door is open to disputes and litigations, consciences are troubled with a thousand anxieties, and the people are driven to despise the law" (*General Legislation in the New Code of Canon Law,* Ayrinhac, 71).

Jesus said: "My yoke is easy, and my burden light" (Matt. 11:30, Confraternity Version). It seems to me that people who have been laboring, all their lives under such intolerable burdens would rejoice to lay them down, believing what Jesus said.

Catholics Say Bible a Tyrant

"From that time (1604) the Bible took the place of the Church in the religion of Protestantism, which far from becoming 'free' substituted the tyranny of a printed page for the voice of universal

Christendom" (*The Catholic History of Great Britain,* Wilmot-Buxton, 217).

All this Catholic fanfare is an effort to dazzle the minds of men, and to induce them to accept the immoral commandments of men rather than the holy precept of the Bible. This should be remembered a little later as we, in this work, present many more unscholarly, and many times, silly interpretations of Scripture, along with many deliberate mistranslations. This is all done in an effort to make it appear that the Bible teaches Catholicism.

Men seem instinctively to want something easy. This system of turning all one's thinking and Bible reading over to another is about the easiest sort of religion in the world. A religion that allows killing, stealing, lying and nearly every other immoral thing is very enticing to the majority of people, and Paul speaks of "the deceivableness of unrighteousness" (2 Thes. 2:10).

Men were commended in Acts 17:10-11 for not being so credulous as to accept anything that was told to them by others, until they had checked the Scriptures themselves.

"And the brethren immediately sent away Paul and Silas by night unto Berea: who coming thither went into the synagogue of the Jews. These were more noble than those in Thessalonica, in that they received the word with all readiness of mind, and searched the scripture daily, whether these things were so."

The True Bible Attitude

It has been pointed out several times what a noble thing it is to shape our lives after the pattern revealed to us in the Holy Scripture. We should study the Bible daily, believe every word of it, obey faithfully all the commandments and trust its wonderful promises. Through all the ages when men have done this, light has spread abroad and progress has been assured. But on the other hand wherever human authority, in any form, has intervened to distort

127

or modify its divine law, progress has been correspondingly impeded.

The Sacred Scriptures show us the way of life. We believe in Christ, repent of our sins, confess that Jesus is the Christ, the Son of God and are buried in baptism for remission of sins. The Lord then adds us to his church and there can be no doubt about it. All congregations are autonomous, without any man, or set of men, to interfere. Christ is our only lawgiver and the *New Testament* contains all his laws, which will never be changed or annulled. Christ is our only High Priest and we all as priests can approach the Father through Him. This is the gospel or good news. Why are men ". . . ever learning and never able to come to the knowledge of the truth" (2 Tim. 3:7, Westminster Catholic Version)?

CHAPTER XI

The Priesthood

IN THIS CHAPTER we will deal largely, by way of official quotations, in giving a complete view of the unscriptural, presumptious Catholic priesthood; their fantastic claims, their immoral arrangements, so as to get a true picture of this papal army, nearly a half million strong, which is endeavoring to bring into captivity the minds of men, and in this way bring about a drastic re-alignment in the entire political and religious structure of the world. It is mainly through her priesthood that the Catholic Church plans to gain the power and money with which to do this terrible thing. Our hope is in understanding the Priesthood and its motives.

The Priesthood, as with every other feature of this hideous system, is entirely without foundation.

A Gigantic Apostasy

"Hold to the form of sound teaching which thou hast heard from me. . . Guard the good trust through the Holy Spirit" (2 Tim. 1:13-14, *Confraternity New Testament*).

"Hold fast the form of sound words, which thou hast heard of me. . . That good thing which was committed unto thee" (2 Tim. 1:13-14, *King James*).

"And the things that thou hast heard of me among many witnesses, the same commit thou to faithful men, who shall be able to teach others also" (2 Tim. 2:2, *King James*).

"As I requested you when I was going into Macedonia, stay now at Ephesus, in order that you may enjoin certain persons not to teach a different doctrine" (1 Tim. 1:3, *Spencer's Catholic Version*).

Catholics, as I will show, admit that there was no Catholic priesthood, no clergy and laity, no hierarchy in the *New Testament* Church, and that it was hundreds of years before Catholicism was noticeably developed and thirteen hundred years after that before it came into full flower. Therefore, Catholicism is a "different doctrine"!

The Catholic Bible clearly shows that there was no clergy in the *New Testament* for every member of the Lord's church preached!

"And at that time there was raised a great persecution against the Church which was at Jerusalem; and *they were all dispersed* through the countries of Judea, and Samaria, except the apostles. And devout men took orders for Stephen's funeral, and made great mourning over him. But Saul made havoc of the Church, entering in from house to house, and dragging away men and women, committing them to prison. They therefore that were dispersed, went about preaching the word of God" (Acts 8:1-4, *Douay Version*). They were *all* dispersed and *all* preached.

Yet in spite of what their own Bible says, the Council of Trent decreed that,

"If anyone saith that all Christians have power to administer the word . . . let him be anathema" (*Canon X Council of Trent* as recorded in *Teachings of the Catholic Church,* De Ligney, S.J., 14).

The Catholic Church has much legislation on this point and it would be considered exceedingly sinful to do as the *New Testament* Church did!

New Testament Church Unlike Catholic Church

"First, there were then hardly any 'clerical' terms as differentiated from 'lay' terms" (*The Mass of the Future,* Ellard, 68).

No Catholic Priesthood!

"The words 'priest', 'priesthood' (heirus, hierateuma) are never applied in the *New Testament* to the office of the Christian ministry. All Christians are said to be priests (1 Pet. 11, 5-9; Apoc. V, 10)" (*Catholic Dictionary,* Addis and Arnold, 692).

Lollards and Wyclif Scriptural
All Christians Are Priests

"The Lollards, less cautious, even than Wyclif, affirmed at the end of the fourteenth century, that every man was equally priest. . . Catholic scholars had somehow to explain the Scripture references to all Christians as priest. To safeguard the unquestioned priestly prerogatives of the higher clergy all sorts of qualifiers were advanced" (*The Mass of the Future,* Ellard, 177).

"The priesthood evolved" (*Catholic Encyclopedia,* XII, 406, 415).

"Priests were not so called in the very earliest Christian times; rather they were the presbyters or elders" (*Mass of the Future,* Ellard, 66).

"The following seems to us on the whole the way the term 'clergy' gradually assumed a technical and restricted sense" (*Catholic Dictionary,* Addis and Arnold, 189).

"The Apostolic Fathers abstain from any mention of a Christian priesthood" (*Catholic Dictionary,* Addis and Arnold, 693).

"*Clergy,* the term *clerus* (Latin, part or portion falling to one by lot) was first applied to the whole Church or people of God as being the Lord's special possession or property (1 Pet. V, 3), but soon it became appropriated to the ministers of religion as belonging to God in a special manner" (*General Legislation in the New Code of Canon Law,* Ayrinhac, 233-234).

Jesus said:

"And call no one on earth your father; for one is your Father, who is in heaven" (Matt. 23:9, *Confraternity Version*).

131

Catholics are required to disobey Christ and call every Catholic priest "father." The priests pretend to be terribly offended if others do not do so. The *Catholic Dictionary* (Addis and Arnold) speaks of the centuries after the Lord commanded this of "a new use of the word Father" (page 342).

"It is a happy development of Catholic custom in these days for all priests to be called 'Father'" (*Pulpit Commentary on Catholic Teaching, The Creed,* Gerrard, 260).

"Originally given to bishops and later to priests" (*Catholic Dictionary, Vatican Edition,* 360).

No Hierarchy in New Testament

"The divine institution of the threefold hierarchy cannot of course be derived from our text; in fact it cannot in anyway be proved directly from the *New Testament,* it is a Catholic dogma by virtue of the dogmatic tradition, i.e. in a later period of ecclesiastical history the general belief in the divine institution of the episcopate, presbyteriate, and diaconate can be verified and thence followed on through the centuries. But the dogmatic truth cannot be traced back to Christ Himself by analysis of strict historical testimony" (*Catholic Encyclopedia,* VII, 334).

"The word (hierarchy) first occurs in the work of *Pseudo-Dionysius* (one of the admitted monstrous forgeries used by the Catholic Church) on Celestial and Ecclesiastical Hierarchies. The signification was gradually modified until it came to be what it is at the present. A hierarchy now signifies a body of officials disposed organically in ranks and orders, each subordinate to the one above it" (*Catholic Dictionary,* Addis and Arnold, 402).

"Some parts of the government system of the Catholic Church are of divine origin; and many of them are human institutions" (*Externals of the Catholic Church,* Sullivan, 19).

"At the end of the fifth century the Roman Church was completely organized" (*Catholic Encyclopedia,* IX, 61).

This is far from the truth for at that time no one had ever heard of a Pope, a Cardinal, a Rosary or a Sacrament!

"One is forced to admit that the gradual corruption of Christianity began very early" (*Catholic Encyclopedia,* XII, 414).

"Writers of the fourth century were prone to describe many practices as Apostolic institutions which certainly had no claim to be so regarded" (*Catholic Encyclopedia,* III, 484).

"If occasionally she seemed to restrict it (The *Bible*) use or its diffusion this too was through an easily comprehensible love and particular esteem for the *Bible,* that the sacred Book might not, like a profane book, be made a ground for curiosity, endless discussions, and abuses of every kind" (*Catholic Encyclopedia,* XV, 9).

Compare the Catholic attitude of restricting the use and discussion of the Bible with that of the Apostle Paul. One citation should be enough. "And he (Paul) entered the synagogue, and for three months spoke boldly, reasoning and persuading about the Kingdom of God. But when some were hardened in disobedience, speaking evil of the Way before the multitude, he left them and withdrew his disciples, discoursing daily in the hall of Tyrannus. This went on for two years, so that all who dwelt in Asia heard the word of the Lord, both Jews and Greeks" (Acts, 19:8-10, *The New Testament in Westminster Version*).

The word of God (Bible) is the only weapon we have in combatting the devil and all should learn to use it skillfully.

"And it is undeniable that the cult of Mary, like everything else of a delicate nature, has been subject to numerous exaggerations and corruptions" (*The Virgin Mary,* Guitton, 178).

"We all, prelates and clergy, have gone astray from the right way, and for long there is none that has done good, no not one" (Pope Adrian, in *Pastors History of the Popes,* IX, 135).

"But when we speak of the legislative power of the Church, we have in mind particularly the power to make new laws in addition to the natural law and divine law" (*The Catholic Doctor,* 8).

We have said quite a bit already about Catholic natural and divine laws but I want to call special attention to the first part of the foregoing quotation. The part that reminds us that the Catholic Church claims the power to make *new* laws. Yet the wise man said: "Add not any thing to his words, lest thou be reproved and found a liar:" (Proverbs, 30:6, *Douay*).

Paul ordained elders (or bishops) in every Church (Acts 14:23) and commanded that a plurality of them should be in every city. The Council of Nicea forbad having more than one bishop in a city (*Canon 8, as found in Disciplinary Decrees of the General Councils,* Schroeder, 34).

Catholic authorities deliberately mistranslated presbuteros (old man) as "priest" in the *Douay Bible.* Practically all priests are made of boys in their early twenties. It would be impossible to have an old young man! This has been admitted in later versions where *presbuteros,* the Greek word, is simply brought over into English as presbyter.

"But I fear, lest by any means, as the serpent beguiled Eve through his subtlely, so your minds should be corrupted from the simplicity that is in Christ" (2 Cor. 11:3).

Fantastic Claims for Priests

Catholic writers almost impoverish language of superlatives in advancing the hierarchical system. The following are examples:

". . . glorious priests. . . oracles of the Eternal Word. . . chiefs in the celestial militia. . . custodians of the Keys of heaven" (*The Priest, His Dignity and Obligations,* "St." John Eudes, XXV).

"The priest is a storm: hurricane, cyclone, tornado rolled into one. Like Christ in the temple. Like Christ before the Pharisees. Like Christ hanging on the cross. . . No. He is more than that. The Priest is not just the cross, he is Christ himself" ("Father" Brigante in the *Lone Star Catholic,* March 1, 1959).

134

Practically every scriptural title applied to Christ is appropriated to themselves by Catholic priests, such as judge, physician, and mediator. In the following quotation he is said to be the husband of the Church!

"Cultivate an ardent love for the Church which God has given to you as a spouse" (*The Priest, His Dignity,* Eudes, 21).

"To the carnal eye, the priest looks like other men, but to the eye of faith, he is exalted above angels" (*Faith of Our Fathers,* Gibbon, 442).

PRIEST ABOVE CHRIST!

"In obeying their directions she (the nun) is more certain of doing the will of God, than if an angel came down from heaven to manifest his will to her. . . It may be added, that there is more certainty of doing the will of God by obedience to superiors than by obedience to Jesus Christ, should he appear in person and give his commands" (St. Liguori's *True Spouse of Christ,* 92-93). This is from a two-hundred years old manual for cloistered nuns.

"Whenever our Lord commanded me to do one thing in prayer, and if my confessor forbade it our Lord Himself told me to obey my confessor" (*Autobiography of St. Teresa,* 187).

PRIEST EQUAL WITH GOD!

"God deigns to make prelates, His own equals. . . If then, you receive a command of one who holds the place of God, you should observe it with the same diligence as if it came from God Himself" (*True Spouse of Christ,* "St." Liguori, 93). This is referring to the priest who has charge of a house full of helpless nuns!

"Obey blindly, that is, without asking reasons. Be careful then, never to examine the directions of your confessor. . . In a word, keep before your eyes this great rule, that in obeying your confessor you obey God. Force yourself, then, to obey him in spite of all fears. And be persuaded that if you are not obedient to him it will be impossible for you to go on well; but if you obey him you are

135

secure. But you say, if I am damned in consequence of obeying my confessor, who will rescue me from hell? What you say is impossible" (*True Spouse of Christ,* "St." Liguori, 352).

PRIEST IS GOD!

"Thus, priests are gods in power. O power and dignity of the priesthood which surpasses all the powers of heaven and earth, second only to the ineffible dignity of the Mother of God" (*The Priest, His Dignity and Obligations,* John Eudes, 177).

"St. Gregory Nazianzen asserts that the priest is a 'God who makes gods'" (*The Priest, His Dignity and Obligations,* 13).

"Clement of Alexandria attributes to the priests the role of redeemers. . .You are visible gods in the world, children of God, fathers of God. In the work *the Celestial Hierarchy* (an acknowledged forgery!—O.C.L.), St. Dionysius invests you with these three attributes; you are gods because you take the place of God in this world and are clothed with His qualities, His prerogatives and powers. You are the children of gods because you are the children of your bishops who in turn are gods in yet a higher degree than you. You are fathers of gods, because you are the fathers of Christians, who likewise are gods, though in a lower degree than you" (*The Priest, His Dignity and Obligations,* 8).

"This is what the Church asks from the bishop, viz., that he would give her other Christs. She may ask from her priests to give every day the body and blood of our Lord to her children; she cannot ask them for other Christs: the bishop alone can perform such a wonder!" (*Our Priesthood,* Buneau, 147).

"The bishop imposes his hands without a word, a short prayer follows: and this wonderful prodigy, viz., the creation of a priest is accomplished" (*Our Priesthood,* Bruneau, 159).

PRIEST PRODUCES CHRIST—ALL POWER!

"To His priests He gave power to produce Christ in the Blessed Eucharist, which is indeed greater than to create an infinite number

136

of physical worlds. . . O admirable power of God's priests! Certainly each one (priest) may say with Christ, 'All power is given to me in heaven and in earth' (Matt. 28:18). In heaven for the priest opens and closes its gates" (*The Priest, His Dignity and Obligations,* 176).

"*The Priest the Teacher of Truth.* The Church of Christ, depository and infallible guardian of Divine Revelation, by means of her priests, pours out the treasures of heavenly truth" (*1937 Franciscan Almanac,* 228).

PRIESTS HAVE UNLIMITED POWER!

"Unlimited power of remitting sin was promised and conferred upon the Apostles and their successors by Jesus Christ. This power is expressed in the Sacrament of Penance" (*Catholic Dictionary, Vatican Edition,* 821).

CHRIST HUMBLY OBEYS THE PRIEST!

"The supreme power of the priestly office is the power of consecrating. 'No act is greater,' says St. Thomas, 'than the consecration of the body of Christ.' In this essential phase of the sacred ministry, the power of the priest is not surpassed by that of the bishop, the archbishop, the cardinal or the pope. Indeed it is equal to that of Jesus Christ. For in this role the priest speaks with the voice and the authority of God Himself.

"When the priest pronounces the tremendous words of consecration, he reaches up into the heavens, brings Christ down from His throne, and places Him upon our altar to be offered up again as the victim for the sins of man. It is a power greater than that of monarchs and emperors: it is greater than that of saints and angels, greater than that of Seraphim and Cherubim. Indeed it is greater even than the power of the Virgin Mary. For, while the Blessed Virgin was the human agency by which Christ became incarnate a single time, the priest brings Him down from Heaven, and renders Him present on our altar as the eternal Victim for the sins of man—

not once but a thousand times! The priest speaks and lo! Christ, the eternal and omnipotent God bows his head in humble obedience to the priest's command" (*The Faith of Millions,* John A. O'Brien, 268).

It seems to me, that of all the blasphemous quotations already given, this one is the most shocking. Just think of Jesus Christ, only son of the most high God, obeying a mere man! This brings to my mind part of a discussion between Satan and my Lord, in the wilderness.

"Then Jesus saith to him, 'Begone, Satan: for it is written, "The Lord thy God shalt thou worship and him *alone* shalt thou serve"'" (Matt. 4:10, *The New Testament in the Westminster Version*).

BLIND OBEDIENCE TO PRIESTS

"There.is only one remedy for this evil (a troubled conscience), and that remedy is absolute and blind obedience to a prudent director. Choose one, consult him as often as you desire, but do not leave him for another. Then submit punctiliously to his direction. His conscience must be yours for the time being. And if you should err in following him, God will hold him and not you responsible" (*of Catholic Morals,* Stapleton, 24).

"Let them be; they are blind guides of the blind. If a blind man lead a blind man, they shall both fall into a pit" (Matt. 15:14, *The New Testament in the Westminster Version*).

AN ALL-POWERFUL PRIEST IN HELL!

"The fires of hell cannot in all eternity burn out the sacerdotal character imprinted on our souls in ordination; but the splendors of heaven will make that sacred character shine out with so much the greater lustre" (*The Holy Sacrifice of the Mass,* Gihr, 207).

BAD PRIESTS FORGIVE SINS!

"Sometimes one has heard a priest address a young lady by her

Christian name, perhaps in a contracted form; which sounds startling; and the explanation is to be sought in the familiarity acquired in past years when she was only a child. If a proper reserve had been maintained then, the familiarity would never have reached its final state. . . Or they may be penitents, who come to discuss matters of conscience. . . There may be danger to us, or even in their weakness, to them in that which at first sight looks so proper and desirable. . . then those with whom the priests come into daily official contact, such as the schoolmistress or housekeeper, and, lastly, one who may belong to several of the above categories, who is truly motherly, and taking pity on the priest's loneliness, wants to tend him in his wants; to keep such a one with proper reserve requires no small determination" (*The Priestly Vocation,* Ward, 44-45).

"The sacraments too, which, through the cooperation of the priceless and unseen power of the Holy Spirit, are celebrated in the Church even though they are administered by a sinful priest, so long as the Church approves him—we in no way condemn. . . For the sinfulness of a bishop or a priest affects adversely neither an infant baptism nor the consecration of the Eucharist, nor those other ecclesiastical ministries which they perform on behalf of their subjects. . . A good priest accomplishes no more in consecrating than a bad priest" (*Sources of Christian Theology,* Paul F. Palmer, S.J., I, 88-89).

"Is the state of grace requisite for the validity of the sacraments?"

"No, a minister may confer a sacrament validly even if he be in a state of mortal sin" (*Manual of Christian Doctrine,* A Seminary Professor, 392-393).

In the section concerning penance you will find shocking statements officially affirming that a priest can commit adultery with a Catholic woman and immediately thereafter forgive her sins!

How Church Punishes Priests!

"*257.* (a) Irremovable Pastors (i) Their removal. (Canon 2147-2156). The Code gives as chief causes for the administrative removal of a pastor: ignorance or habitual infirmity either mental or physical, ill will of the people, *loss of reputation,* ineffectual administration of Church property. . . After the removal or resignation of a pastor, the Ordinary, with the advice of the same two examiners, provide for him by transferring him to another parish or pensioning him" (*Constitutions of the Church in the New Code,* Ayrinhac, 315-316).

Priest Must Not Work!

In Article 1 *Manual of Moral Theology,* Jone and Adelman, 299, which concerns individual excommunication: "Whoever (Priests, monks or nuns) either personally or through others engages in trading or business of any kind."

"Apostolicae Servitutis, a Bull issued by Benedict XIV, 23 February, 1741, against secular pursuits on the part of the clergy. In spite of many prohibitive laws of the Church, some ecclesiastics had drifted into the habit of occupying themselves with worldly business and pursuits. The object was to check that abuse among the clergy" (*Catholic Encyclopedia,* 1, 646).

Here it is characterized as an abuse for priests to work. The following quotation speaks of such as "sordid occupations"!

"As to the clause prohibiting alienation of pensions, it should be remembered that a pension is supposed to afford a decent livelihood, thus preserving the cleric from indecent begging or engaging in sordid occupation" (*Canonical and Civil Status of Catholic Parishes,* Augustine, 222).

Paul was a tentmaker and Jesus was a carpenter. Paul also admonished Christians to "be at pains to find honorable employment. . . It would be well if our brethren would learn to find honorable employment, so as to meet what necessity demands of them" (Tit. 3:8-14, Ronald Knox *Catholic Translation*).

IMPOSSIBLE FOR CATHOLICS TO DO
AS NEW TESTAMENT CHRISTIANS!

"It is impossible for a man to be both a priest and a worker. . . The Holy Father made this decision for doctrinal reasons. To be a priest and to be a priest-worker are different functions, two different states of life, and it is not possible to write them in the same person without changing the idea of the priesthood" (*Pope Pius* XII, as reported in the *Brooklyn Tablet,* Jan. 16, 1954).

Pope Pius' statement was called forth because,

"To support themselves the priests took jobs in factories, on docks and in other industries, wearing the same clothes as other workmen.

"Through such activities the priests hoped to overcome the French workers' traditional distrust of priests and the Church" (*The Brooklyn Tablet,* Jan. 16, 1954). The same article said that for priests to work "was harmful to seminarians."

ANGUISHES POPE FOR PRIEST TO DO AS PAUL AND JESUS!

"The preamble to their statement noted that the Holy Father had expressed his anguish, also shared by Cardinals, at the formidable difficulties and dangers inherent in the apostolate of the priest-workers" (Ibid).

This pope must have died of "anguish" if he learned that both Paul and Jesus worked!

PRIEST-WORKERS DISCIPLINED!

"The three Provincials have been replaced and the four priests—all prominent writers—have been told to move from the Paris area and give up their journalistic activities. All have accepted the disciplinary measures according to a reliable source" (*Brooklyn Tablet,* Feb. 18, 1954).

A priest can get drunk, commit adultery, lie, and do almost anything else that the devil wants him to do, but he must not work.

Should he work, he is "disciplined" for so doing!

THE REASON FOR THIS

I have been told, by several ex-priests, that thousands of priests would leave the priesthood if it were possible for them to earn a livelihood and be able to maintain a family, as God intended for man to do. It is very apparent that men preparing for the Catholic priesthood are forbidden to learn any gainful trade, so when they get to middle age, and realize that God is right they are helpless.

"And the Lord God said: It is not good for man to be alone" (Gen 2:18, *Douay*). He feels imprisoned. The life of a priest is designed to force this cruel, unnatural and unscriptural arrangement on men. All these *stipulations* are parts of a diabolical system and one could not be maintained without the other.

Later, while dealing with the Confessional, you will see why God said that it was not good for reasons other than being alone.

Ordination

We have already learned, from the Bible, that all Christians are on an equality as brethren (Matt. 23:8), and it is admitted that this unscriptural priesthood and laity is human, and was brought in at a much later date. All Christians preached (Acts 8:1-4). Because there was no clergy in the *New Testament* church it follows that there was no ceremony of ordination such as the Catholic Church has developed. This being true we will now examine Catholic ordination.

FORCED ORDINATION

"History furnishes several instances in early times of men ordained, and supposed to be validly ordained, in spite of their struggles and resistance. . . Augustine speaks of those who were made bishops after being imprisoned and severely handled, until they consented to 'undertake a good work'. . . (Macedonius) was ordained priest by the celebrated Flavian without the least

142

knowledge of what was going on, and was furious when he learnt what had occurred" (*Catholic Dictionary,* Addis and Arnold, 739).

This began about the time men began to "baptize" babies against their will or without their knowledge. Since both actions are of human origin, one would actually be as worthless as the other!

ORDAIN INFANTS

"Hence the ordination of children before the use of reason is valid, so also the ordination of those who are forced into receiving Orders by grave fear" (*Moral Theology,* Jone and Aldeman, 451-452).

To show how widespread this sort of thing has been for fifteen hundred years, the reader is reminded that John XI was made pope at twenty years of age (*Chevalier Artand de Montor,* I, 247; *Catholic Encyclopedia,* VIII, 426), Benedict IX at twelve (*Catholic Encyclopedia,* 11, 428-429; IV, 17). He, who was later made Pope John X, became Archbishop at the ripe old age of five years (*Catholic Encyclopedia,* VIII, 425)!

The monster, called "His Holiness" Alexander VI, made his vile, illegitimate son Archbishop two weeks after he became pope when the boy was only eighteen years old. The next year he elevated him to be a Cardinal! (*Catholic Encyclopedia,* 1, 289-293).

Vestments

"During the first four or five centuries the dress of clerics did not differ from that of the laity either in form or color" (*General Legislation in the New Code of Canon Law,* Ayrinhac, 290).

VESTMENTS BORROWED FROM PAGANS!

"We need not shrink from admitting that candles, like incense and lustral water, were commonly employed in pagan worship and the rites paid to the dead. But the Church from a very early period took them into her service, just as she adopted many other things indifferent in themselves, which seemed proper *to enhance the splendour* of religious ceremonial. We must not forget that most of these adjuncts to worship, like music, lights, perfumes, ablutions, floral decorations, canopies, fans, screens, bells, *vestments, etc.,* were not identified with any idolatrous cult in particular; but they were common to almost all cults" (*Catholic Encyclopedia,* III, 246).

"In like manner certain ceremonies, for instance, the mystical blessings, the use of light, incense, *Vestments* and many things of that nature, she employs by Apostolic (papal) prescription and tradition, in order both to manifest thereby the majesty of the great Sacrifice, as well as to animate the minds of the faithful!" (*The Holy Sacrifice of the Mass,* Gihr, 339).

"The assistants, with their noble *vestments,* the chant, the incense, the more varied ceremonies which belong to the solemn Mass, are all calculated to increase veneration and admiration" (*Holy Sacrifice of the Mass,* Gihr, 337).

"The placing over his shoulders a long silk scarf, called the humeral veil, the priests takes up the monstrance, and with it makes the sign of the cross over the people; and thus the Eucharist Christ (a piece of bread—O.C.L.) blesses the people.

"There is no more beautiful or impressive ceremony in the Catholic Church, as many non-Catholics who have witnessed it have testified" (*Question Box,* 1913 Edition, 448).

Jesus said that they do these things to be seen of men;—

"And all their works they do in order to be seen by men. They widen their phylacteries and enlarge their tassels; they love the first couch at suppers and the first seats in the synagogues and the salutations in the market-places, and to be called by men, "Rabbi." Be not ye called "Rabbi," for one is your master and all ye are brethren. And call ye father no man upon earth, for one only is your father, who is in heaven" (Matt, 23:5-9).

144

PRIESTS MAGICALLY PROTECTED BY ROBES

"The blessing is imparted to the vestments by means of prayer, the sign of the cross and sprinkling of holy water, and, at the same time, special graces are invoked for the wearers of the blessed garments; for the Church petitions not only, that the Lord may 'with the dew of His grace and abundant blessings cleanse, sanctify and consecrate these sacerdotal vestments, to the end that they may become fit for the service of God and the holy mysteries', but also that the priests 'robed in them may be protected against all the assaults or temptations of evil spirits'" (*The Holy Sacrifice of the Mass,* Gihr, 270-271).

Let us observe again that if this is so, why did our Lord not think of it, and put it in the Bible? If it is true, the Apostle Paul was wrong. He said: "I have never shrunk from declaring to you aught that was profitable" (Acts 20:20, *The New Testament in the Westminster Version*).

And again: "I have not shrunk from declaring to you the *whole* counsel of God" (Matt. 20:27, *Westminster Version*). If vestments are a good and protective thing, then God has withheld something good from us. This he said that He would not do (Ps. 84:11). God cannot lie!

NEW TESTAMENT PRACTICE NOW
WOULD BE A GREAT SIN!

"But it must be borne in mind that the vestments did not originate with the idea of carrying symbolism. The vestments are in the plain, every day garb of the days of the Apostles and early Christians" (*New Interpretation of the Mass,* Borgmann, 20).

"Gradually the custom was introduced of making them of rich and costly materials, *to add greater beauty to the rites of religion*" (*Externals of the Catholic Church,* Sullivan, 163).

"As a more effective separation from the rest of the world, and as a safe guard to the honor of the ministry, they are enjoined to wear a long black garment, different from the Common Mantle. Such is the origin of the present ecclesiastical costume" (*General History of the Catholic Church,* Darras, 11, 328-329).

NOW PRIESTS MUST WEAR THEM

"Theologians pronounce it a grave sin to give Communion without the stole and surplice and a light one to omit either" (*Legislation on the Sacraments in the New Code of Canon Law,* Ayrinhac, 157-158).

OVERCOAT BECAME SACRED!

"The word surplice is derived from the Latin word, *superpelicium,* which means over-furs. In medieval times the Cathedrals and Churches were not heated, yet the clerics entered, Winter and Summer, day and night, to chant the divine hours. In cold weather they kept themselves warm by wearing furlined cassocks" (*New Interpretation of the Mass,* Borgmann, 135).

Lights in the Early Church

"In the Christian Church they (lights) were first employed to dispel darkness when the faithful met before dawn or in the gloom of the catacombs; but their beautiful symbolic meaning was soon recognized and the custom of blessing them for Church services and private use is traceable back to an early period" (*Catholic Dictionary, Vatican Edition,* 162).

If the "faithful" in the early Church, only used lights to dispel darkness, then it would follow that the faithful, in the Church today, would be pleasing the Lord in using them for the same purpose and nothing else.

As early as the fourth century certain writers strongly condemned burning candles in the daytime, and thereby adopting a pagan practice. (*Catholic Encyclopedia,* IX, 244-246).

Disinfectant Evolved into Incense

"Moreover, the use of holy water and incense (the latter originally used as a sort of disinfectant) was also no doubt suggested by similar custom among pagans around them" (*Catholic Encyclopedia,* III, 76).

It was also during this time that the "holy saints" never bathed, changed clothes or washed their feet!

So it was that the vestments "evolved" into something sacred, along with "lights" and "incense," filling the ignorant and superstitious with awe.

"The monks first introduced the tonsure, i.e., the practice of shaving the head, and during the seventh century this was adopted by the clergy generally" (*Short History of the Catholic Church,* Wedewer and McSorley, 69).

". . . the tonsure was not in use in the primitive church" (*Catholic Encyclopedia,* XIV, 779).

Celibacy

One of the most prominent features of Catholicism, celibacy, is in direct contradiction to the Bible and to the practice of the New Testament Church.

"Clerical celibacy is not a precept of divine or natural law" (*Question Box,* Conway, 311).

"Turning now to the historical development of the present law of celibacy, we must necessarily begin with Saint Paul's directions (1 Tim. 3:2, 12 and Tit. 1:16) that a bishop or deacon should be 'the husband of one wife'. These passages seem fatal to any contention that celibacy was made obligatory upon clergy from the beginning" (*Catholic Encyclopedia,* III, 486).

The Catholic Bible does not say that a bishop *should be* the husband of one wife, but says that he *must* be! Their Bible also gives other qualifications that a bishop *must* have. Besides a wife,

147

he is to have children and be able to rule well his own house, having *his* children in subjection with all gravity.

"Virginity possesses a higher sanctity than marriage" (*Catholic Encyclopedia,* III, 481-483).

"The Council of Trent (about A.D. 1550) affirmed as a matter of faith that it is holier than marriage" (*Externals of the Catholic Church,* Sullivan, 305).

With monks, nuns and priests the vow never to marry is called "The Vow of Chastity"! Every Catholic who uses such language not only blasphemes God's institution of marriage, but reflects on his own mother!

"In fact the Church has ever spoken with no uncertain voice on the excellence of the celibate over the married state" (*The Priestly Vocation,* Ward, 35).

"Is it not becoming that a chaste Lord should be served by chaste ministers?" (*Faith of Our Fathers,* Gibbons, 459).

"In fact it would seem that the married state . . . is hardly compatible with the highest sanctity" (*The Priestly Vocation,* Ward, 35).

CATHOLIC CHURCH NOT CHANGING

"Stories eminating from news magazines and pictorial weeklies purporting to show that the Church is weakening on her law of celibacy have no foundation in fact or sound theology, a consensus of noted theologians revealed" (*Green Bay Register,* Sept. 4, 1964).

MARRIAGE OF PRIEST A CRIME!

"While Carroll was still Vicar-Apostolic a relative of his, an ex-Jesuit named Wharton, had left the Church, and married. But he committed his crime in a fairly gentlemanly sort of a way and showed no special bitterness toward the Church" (*The Story of American Catholicism,* Maynard, 244).

". . . the priest who marries commits not only a grievous sin in itself, but incurs the additional guilt of sacrilege" (*Catholic Encyclopedia,* III, 481).

CATHOLICS HAVE CHANGED

The Catholic Church was not mentioned in history for centuries after the *New Testament,* but Catholic authorities admit, without hesitation that until the eleventh and twelfth centuries Catholic priests married. After the Lateran Council held in A.D. 1123 it is said:

". . . henceforth all conjugal relations on the part of the clergy . . . were reduced in the eyes of Canon Law to mere concubinage" (*Catholic Encyclopedia,* III, 486).

"Father Gagarin, S.J., in his book *'Le Clerge' Russe'* gives such a picture of the degradation of the married Russian clergy, and its utter lack of influence over the people, that no ones for an instant would desire to introduce such a state of affairs into the vigorous, strong clergy of Western Christendom" (*Question Box* 1913 Edition, Conway, 497).

The implication of their doctrine is that the Lord introduced a practice demonstrated to be wrong, and what the Lord ordained cannot possibly be tolerated in the Roman Catholic Church!

We are not born married but acquire that state later. If the unmarried state is holier, as the Catholics teach, then a person takes a step down from holiness by getting married!

Not only does the Lord say: "It is not good that man should be alone" (Gen. 2:18), but that "marriage is honorable in all" (Heb. 13:4).

So, you see marriage is not only good *for all,* but it is also honorable in the sight of the Lord. No one denies that there were no monks, nuns and priests in the *New Testament* Church and celibacy was outlawed!

149

ANOTHER CATHOLIC CHANGE

"Pope Siricius authorized (in the fourth century) penitents and bigamists to exercise the functions of orders which they had received unlawfully" (*General Legislation in the New Code,* Ayrinhac, 79).

MARRIED PRIESTS POLLUTE THEIR WORSHIP

"Virginal chastity is the most precious pearl, the brightest jewel in the crown of sacerdotal virtues. Nothing equals in value and dignity a pure soul resplendant with the brilliance of chastity . . . It is for a virginally pure priesthood to offer the all-pure sacrifice of the virginal body of Christ" (*The Holy Sacrifice of the Mass,* Gihr, 282-283).

At the present time Catholic law allows priests to keep women. The Catholic Bible (1 Cor. 9:5) mistranslates the Greek word *gune* as "woman" instead of "wife." It teaches that all the Apostles, including Cephas, or Peter were taking women with them. Presently I will give quotations which affirm that Peter, a married man, had to permanently separate from his wife. He could not take his wife with him, but was taking a woman! Priests, bishops, archbishops, cardinals and popes have their women. "Mother Pasqualine" was "housekeeper" for Pope Pius XII for more than 40 years" (*Green Bay Register*).

HOUSEKEEPERS DANGEROUS!

". . . then those with whom the priest come into daily official contact, such as the schoolmistress or housekeeper, and lastly, one who may belong to several of the above categories, who is truly motherly, and taking pity on a priest's loneliness, wants to tend him in his wants; to keep such a one with proper reserve requires no small determination" (*The Priestly Vocation,* Ward, 45).

There are hundreds of thousands of monks, virtual slaves of the Catholic Church. Why could not these men "keep house" for the priests? Why does it have to be women? Especially since the best

150

chefs in the world are men, and so far as I know, butlers are always men.

". . . what a difficult task for the priest to preserve and defend this delicate virtue (chastity)! The day after his ordination he is just the same man as before, subject to the same temptations" (*Our Priesthood*, Bruneau, 89).

"However, the greatest danger is not to be met in the confession of great sinners; it is more likely to come from those candid and confiding souls that come to us so innocently, especially if they are afflicted and if we have to console them" (*Our Priesthood*, Bruneau, 89).

"All celebates are not chaste: celibacy is not necessarily chastity; by a large majority. Unless something other than selfishness suggests this choice of life, the word is apt to be a misnomer for profligacy. And one who fakes the vow of *celibacy* does not break it by sinning against the sixth commandment (adultery), he is true to it until he weds" (*Explanation of Catholic Morals*. Stapleton, 149).

The reader is probably as shocked as I was when I first learned that such a doctrine is taught and practiced among those religious leaders. People usually practice the things that they have been taught. Surely they have not read: "Know ye not that your bodies are the members of Christ? shall I then take the members of Christ, and make them the members of a harlot? God forbid" (1 Cor. 6:15).

Later on, in dealing with the confessional, we will have many official Catholic acknowledgements of the gross immoral results of this unnatural life, and at the same time allowing such close and familiar association with the nuns, the wives and daughters of the subservient laity. It is admitted that unmentionable sins are produced in armies, penitentiaries, boys schools and monasteries, such as:

MASOCHISM AND SADISM

"Masochism is the opposite of Sadism in that it is the experience of pleasure in one's own suffering in connection with sexual activity. We find this form of abberation mostly among sensitive neurotics and psychopaths, more among men than women. The source of such changes and deviations of the sex instinct may lie in fixations of childhood or adolescent experiences, *ascetic discipline,* revelry in humiliations and sentiments of inferiority. Since passivity is the very essence of Masochism, there is great probability (more than in the case of Sadism) that it works itself out only in desires and imaginations. It is generally true for both types of sexual aberration that they find their fulfillment much more in the mental world than in external actions. The knowledge of *this fact is particularly important for priests and educators.* Sadism and Masochism may be present in one and the same person, and the one may quickly pass into the other in the fantasies of day-dreams or real dreams. In persons with neuropathic inclinations, whose normal sex development was retarded or repressed by the psychological influence of fear, Masochistic fixations may take place and continue under harmless or even pious guises, although their sexual basis is not realized. *Hence, from the scientific point of view, all ascetical disciplines such as scourging and the like are very much to be dissuaded,* especially before the time of complete sexual maturity. *It is hardly any longer doubtful that there was a sexual element, at least unconsciously, in such phenomena as the Flagellants of the Middle Ages and other exaggerated forms of asceticism"* (Italics supplied) (*Pastoral Medicine,* Ruland-Rattler, 284).

HOMOSEXUALITY

"Where adolescents are kept strictly away from every contact with persons of the other sex, there is a possibility of occasional homosexual excesses. . . For lack of other opportunities, homosexual excesses may occur among persons of complete sexual maturity (for instance, among sailors or prisoners)" (*Pastoral Medicine*, Ruland-Rattler, 279).

BESTIALITY IN MONASTERIES

"By *sodomy* is meant the complete sin with persons of the same sex by actions resembling sexual intercourse, and also the sexual act of a man in *vas praeposterum*. We need not lose any words about the abominable and grave character of this sin. The same is true of *bestiality*, which is sexual commerce with animals. Under ordinary conditions, this sin is very rare, but may occur among persons of low mentality, who are much occupied with the care of animals. In countries where many people live the lonesome life of shepherds out in the fields (Southern Europe, the East), however, bestiality is much more frequent, the favorite animal being the goat. *In Oriental monasteries of men the law of clausura since olden times extends* also to female beasts" (Italics supplied) (*Pastoral Medicine*, Ruland-Rattler, 322).

CATHOLIC HAIR-SPLITTING!

"The attempt of some casuists to limit venial sin in sexual matters down to not quite one-eighth of complete delectation, seems to be but a result of the scholastic delight in defining and determining everything to a hair's breadth. This would be the same as allowing the starting of an avalanche which at the foot of the mountain would reach only one-eighth of the size of an ordinary destructive avalanche. The one who could determine for practical purposes one-eighth of full sexual pleasure ought to be listed at once for the Nobel prize" (*Pastoral Medicine*, Ruland-Rattler, 297).

How strange and unnatural a mental state is created by thus reversing the divine arrangement. The following is almost inconceivable to Protestants. The writer is speaking of "St." Francis of Assisi, one of Catholicism's most honored "saints":

"The care with which he watched over himself to preserve the

153

virtue of purity, ought not to be passed over. In the beginning of his conversion, finding himself assailed with violent temptations of concupiscence, he often cast himself into ditches full of snow: after this, having made seven great heaps of snow, he said to himself, 'Imagine these were my wife and children ready to die of cold; thou must then take great pains to maintain them'. Whereupon he set himself again to labor in the cold. By the vigor and fervor with which he on that occasion subdued his domestic enemy, he obtained so complete a victory that he never felt any more assaults. Yet he continued always most wary in shunning every occasion of danger; and, in treating with women, kept so strict a watch over his eyes, that he scarce knew any woman by sight" (*Butler's Lives of the Saints,* X, 81).

MENTAL ILLNESS MARK OF TRULY RELIGIOUS!

"St." Peter of Alcantara:

"He ate constantly for three years in the same reflectory, without seeing any other part of it than a part of the table where he sat, and the ground on which he trod. He told St. Teresa, that he once lived in a house (Monastery) three years, without knowing any of his religious brethren but by their voices. From the time that he put on the religious habit to his death, he never looked any woman in the face. *These were the mark of a true religious man"* (*Butlers' Lives of the Saints,* X, 416).

"St." Charles Barromeo:

"Out of the most scrupulous love of purity he would never suffer any servant to see his arm or foot, or any other part of his body that was usually covered, bare; neither would he speak to any woman, not even his pious aunt, or sisters, or any nun, but in the sight of at least two persons, and in as few words as possible" (*Butler's Lives of the Saints,* XI, 97).

"St." Jerome:

"All baths displease me in a grown up virgin, though she be alone: she ought to blush at herself and not bear to see any part of

154

her own body naked" (*Butlers Lives of the Saints,* IX, 372).

"St." Francis Borgia:

"One of his servants discovered, that on the days on which he was obliged to visit company in which ladies made a part, he wore a hair shirt" (*Butlers Lives of the Saints,* X, 188).

"St." Francis of Assisi:

"To converse too frequently with women and not suffer by it, is as hard as to take fire into one's bosom, and not to be burnt" (*Butlers Lives of the Saints,* X, 81).

"St." Bernard:

"Once he happened to fix his eyes on the face of a woman; but immediately reflecting that this was a temptation, he ran to a pond, and leaped up to his neck into the water, which was then as cold as ice, to punish himself, and he vanquished the enemy" (*Butlers Lives of the Saints,* VIII, 229).

"St." Hugh:

"Women he would never look in the face, so that he knew not the features of his own mother" (*Butlers Lives of the Saints,* IV, 5-6).

"St." Felix:

"He never looked any woman in the face" (*Butler's Lives of the Saints,* V, 286).

"St." Pachomius:

"The former says that they ate (in the Monastery) with their cowls drawn so as to hide the greatest part of their faces and with their eyes cast down, never looking at one another" (*Butler's Lives of the Saints,* V, 201-202).

"St." Benedict:

"After this by the artifice of this restless enemy, the remembrance of a woman whom the saint had formerly seen at Rome, occurred to his mind, and so strongly affected his imagination, that

155

he was tempted to leave his desert. But blushing at so base a suggestion of the enemy, he threw himself upon some briers and nettles which grew in the place where he was, and rolled himself a long time till his body was covered with blood. The wounds of his body stifled all inordinate inclinations, and their smart extinguished the flame of concupicence" (*Butler's Lives of the Saints,* III, 229).

"St." Francis of Assisi:

"St. Francis was so devout to St. Benedict, that he made a pilgrimage to Subiaca to visit his tomb; and whilst viewing the briers where the ancient Patriarch had rolled himself naked, and meditating, enraptured on his virtues, he kissed them, they instantly blossomed into most beautiful roses" (*St. Francis of Assisi,* Magliano, 618).

MOTHER AND SISTER DANGEROUS!

"The very fact of the sensible sympathy being so strong between mother and son, or between brother and sister, is one of the reasons—not the least of them—why the Synods of Westminster prohibited a priest's female relatives from living in his house, without special circumstances to justify it, lest such close intercourse might draw the heart away from that higher kind of sympathy which we seek from Almighty God in prayer" (*The Priestly Vocation,* Ward, 39).

DANGER OF INCEST!

"*Periculum incestuosi concubinatus,* when near relatives live under the same roof, and in imminent danger of concubinage" (*Commentary on Canon Law,* Augustine, V, 127).

"St." Aloysius:

"He never looked at any woman, kept his eyes strictly guarded, and generally cast down, would never stay with his mother alone in her chamber; and if she sent any message to him by some lady in her company, he received it, and gave his answer in a few words,

156

with his eyes shut, and his chamber door only half open, and when bantered on that score, he ascribed such behavour to his bashfulness (an untruth—O.C.L.). It was owing to his virginal modesty, that he did not know by their faces many ladies among his own relations with whom he had frequently conversed, and that he was afraid and ashamed to let a footman see so much as his foot uncovered" (*Butlers Lives of the Saints,* VI, 277).

How can they account for Jesus being entertained by Mary, Martha, and their brother Lazarus? These three made their home together, in the same house, and Jesus was often a guest there. Jesus washed the disciples feet and a woman washed the feet of Jesus with her tears and dried them with her hair. How is it possible for human minds to become so twisted?

Mother M. Margaret, a Catholic author says she never saw other nuns in the monastery except twice in sixteen years, and then she felt terribly guilty!

"In sixteen years she could only twice accuse herself of lifting up her eyes in the refectory" (Carmel, Official Story of Discalced (barefooted) Carmelite Nuns, 90).

These are but a few of the evidences of mental illness, which I feel sure are a product of their unnatural sort of life!

CATHOLICS ADMIT LORD'S WAY BEST!
CELIBACY SHORTENS LIFE!

"Statistics are pressed into service against the vow. They show that married people of both sexes live longer than unmarried.

"According to Dr. Casper, a husband enjoys the prospect of reaching the age of sixty years; a bachelor must be content with forty-five years. Whereas one-fourth of husbands attain an age of seventy years, it is only the twentieth part of bachelors that reach that age. Among lunatics and suicides two-thirds to three-fourths are single. The orderly and regular way of living, incident to matrimony, is taken to be the explanation of the above figures" (*Pastoral Medicine,* Sanford, 103-104).

"In some Cloisters (Monasteries) the average age amounted even to only 30 and 28 years, and was, therefore, lower than in the case in any other profession" (*Pastorial Medicine,* Sanford, 105).

HOW TITLE SISTER EVOLVED!

"Under Cover Women!"

"At that time a dangerous custom prevailed since a certain class of Christian women, virgins and widows, dwelled with unmarried men and ecclesiastic *'sub praetextu caritate's et dilectionis',* i.e., for mutual spiritual advancement, a sort of spiritual marriage, exclusive, of course, of any lawful relationship. The women were called sisters (*sorores*) or adopted (*adoptivae*). Later on, as abuses crept in, they were scornfully called *agapetae* (loved ones) and *subintroductae* (the undercover women)" (*The Sacred Canons,* I, Abbo and Hannan, 191).

"Ancient Councils often refer to a class of women called *agapetae, subintroductae,* or sisters, usually consecrated virgins who resided in the house of Clerics" (*General Legislation in the New Code of Canon Law,* Ayrinhac, 279).

PAY FOR KEEPING WOMEN!

"With some hesitation at first, ecclesiastics were authorized to have women, other than their near relations, do the housework for them, provided they would be of blameless character and mature age. A special permission was required for this in some places, in others a tax had to be paid" (*General Legislation in the New Code of Canon Law,* Ayrinhac, 280).

CHAPTER XII

Worship of Mary and the Saints

Because a colored man gave the Bible answer on the $64,000 Question, a television show, a mighty protest went up from the entire Catholic Church, and the following week, the show, sponsored by a leading cosmetics firm, reversed the statement and stated that it was mistaken about Mary having other children than our Lord. If this reversal had not been made, millions of Catholics would have boycotted this concern. Why make such a point of this? The reason is that the Catholic Church has a doctrine of the "perpetual virginity of Mary." Marriage is thought of as so unchaste that Mary would not be fit to be the mother of Jesus if she was Joseph's wife and had other children. Let us remember that "marriage is honorable in all and the bed undefiled" (Heb. 13:4). This includes Mary.

"While he yet talked to the people behold his mother and his brethren stood without, desiring to speak with him. Then one said unto him, Behold, thy mother and thy brethren stand without, desiring to speak with thee. But he answered and said unto him that told him, Who is my mother? And who are my brethren? And he stretched forth his hand toward his disciples, and said, Behold my mother and my brethren! For whosoever shall do the will of my Father which is in heaven, the same is my brother, and sister, and mother" (Matt. 12:46-50, King James).

"Is not this the carpenter's son? Is not his mother called Mary? And his brethren, James and Joses, and Simon, and Judas? And his sisters, are they not all with us?" (Matt. 13:55-56, *Westminster Version*).

The first definition Thayer gives of *adelphos,* brother, is "from the same womb." Indeed these were Mary's children and it was no disgrace, the Catholic Church notwithstanding!

159

The Saints and Mary

The entire superstitions cult of the saints is simply a continuation of the pagan doctrine concerning gods.

All Christians are called saints in the *New Testament,* because by obeying the gospel a man's sins are pardoned, and he is set apart as belonging to the Lord.

"But Ananias answered, 'Lord, I have heard from many about this man, how much evil he has done to thy saints in Jerusalem' " (Acts 9:13, *Confraternity*). The footnote to this passage gives a scriptural definition of the word: "Saints: those separated from other men and united to Christ."

"And it came to pass that Peter, while visiting all the saints, came to those living at Lydda. . . Then Peter gave her his hand and raised her up; and calling the saints and the widows, he gave her back to them alive" (Acts 9:32,41, *Confraternity'*).

"And this I (Paul) did in Jerusalem; and many of the saints I shut up in prison, having received authority from the chief priests to do so; and when they were put to death, I cast my vote against them; and oftentimes in all the synagogues I punished them and tried to force them to blaspheme; and in my extreme rage against them I even pursued them to foreign cities" (Acts 26:10-11, *Confraternity*).

"Greet Philologus and Julia, Nereus and his sister, and Olympias, and all the saints who are with thee" (Rom. 16:15, *Confraternity*).

"Now concerning the collection being made for the saints" (1 Cor. 16:1, *Confraternity*).

A footnote to this passage is as follows: "The collection for the poor Christians of Jerusalem was requested by the other Apostles."

"Paul, an Apostle of Jesus Christ by the will of God, to all the saints who are at Ephesus" (Eph. 1:1, *Confraternity*).

"Paul and Timothy, servants of Jesus Christ, to all the saints in

Christ Jesus that are at Philippi" (Phil. 1:1, *Confraternity*).

"Let a widow who is selected be not less than sixty years old, having been married but once, with a reputation for her good works in bringing up children, in practicing hospitality, in washing the saints' feet, in helping those in trouble, in carefully pursuing every good work" (1 Tim. 5:9-10, *Confraternity*).

There is no need for misunderstanding the Scriptural use of the word "saint," it is simply another way of referring to members of the Lord's church.

Catholics always refer to perfect people who are dead as "saints." In the Scriptures the saints were living weak, needy Christians (Rom. 8:27).

CATHOLIC 'SAINTS' IN PLACE OF PAGAN GODS!

"Further research has shown the origin of these fanciful details (in the lives of the saints—O.C.L.) to be pagan rather than Christian, being drawn from the tales of the pagan deities and heroes. After the age of the martyrs, the original truthful Acts were gradually incrusted with these details, so that, with the popular credulity, the romantic elements have quite buried the truthful facts. The fact that the honoring of the Christian saints took the place of the honoring and adoring of the local pagan gods and demigods, offering an opportunity for the abuse of attributing to the saints the deeds of the pagan demigods" (*Catholic Dictionary, Vatican Edition*, 552).

"In every temple, at every cross road, paganism was displaying the image of some goddess. The Christian liturgy knew nothing of the cult of saints" (*The Virgin Mary*, Jean Guitton, 84).

"But the ancient stories were much more probably nothing but the fabrication of some monastic dreamer, who after pouring over manuscripts that told of Fortunate Isles, retold them with an Irish twist. A romancer, in days where there was hardly any line drawn between sober fact and shining fable, was not necessarily a liar" (*The Story of American Catholicism*, Maynard, 2).

Pagans had thousands of imaginary deities, each had his separate sphere of power. The Catholic Church claims more than nine thousand "saints," each one appealed to as possessing special miraculous powers. The following is a list of a few, specifying their special "field of operation"!

SAINTS SUBSTITUTES FOR PAGAN GODS

(All page numbers are from *Catholic Dictionary,* Vatican Edition)

- Adalard—invoked against fever and typhus, 11
- Agapetus—colic, 17
- Agatha—nurses, 17
- Aldegundis—cancer, 24
- Alexander—charcoal burners, 25
- Aloysius—sore eyes and pestilence, 29
- Amalberga—bruises and fever, 34
- Amand—inn-keepers, wine merchants, brewers, boy scouts, 34
- Anastasius—goldsmiths, headaches, 41
- Andrew—fishermen, old maids, gout and sore throat, 43
- Andrew Avelino—apoplexy and sudden death, 43
- Anne—housewives, women in labor, cabinet makers, miners—48
- Anthony—invoked for nearly everything, 50
- Anthony of Padua—poor, barren, pregnant women, travelers, lost articles, shipwreck, 50
- Appolonia—toothache, diseases of the teeth, 55
- Arnulf of Metz—brewers, millers, lost articles, 69
- Augustine of Hippo—theologians, brewers, printers, sore eyes (p. 80), impenitence, sudden death, firearms, 95, 176
- Benedict of Nursia—poisoning, 110
- Blaise—sore throats, 124
- Camillias Lellis—hospitals and the sick, 160

- Margaret—pregnant women, 593
- Martha—cooks, 597
- Maurus—coppersmiths, charcoal burners, gout, hoarseness, 614
- Nicolas of Myra—mariners, merchants, coopers, brewers, pawnbrokers, travelers, bakers, 680
- Nicholas of Tolantina—mariners, sailors, merchants, 680
- Ouen—innkeepers, cooks, deafness, 715
- Panteleon—physicians, midwives, consumption, 724
- Peter of Alcantara—nightwatchmen, 751
- Raymond Nonnatus—midwives, falsely accused, 812
- Roch—invalids, 830
- Silvia—pregnant women, 890
- Stanislas Kostka—palpitation of the heart, severe illness, 920
- Tryphon—evil spirits, insects, 975
- Vincent—vine growers, 1003
- Vitus—epilepsy, nervousness, 1008

CATHOLIC SAINTS NOT AUTHENTIC!

"The legend considers the saint as a kind of lord of the elements, who commands the water, rain, fire, mountain, and rock; he changes, enlarges, or diminishes objects; flies through the air; delivers from dungeon and gallows; takes part in battles, and even in martyrdom is invulnerable; animals, the wildest and the most timid, serve him (e.g., the stories of the bear as a beast of burden; the ring in the fish; the frogs becoming silent, etc.); his birth is glorified by a miracle; a voice or letters from Heaven proclaim his identity; bells ring of themselves; the heavenly ones enter into personal intercourse with him (betrothal of Mary); he speaks with the dead and beholds heaven, hell, and purgatory; forces the devil to release people from compacts; he is victorious over dragons; etc. Of all this the authentic Christian narratives know nothing. But whence then does this world of fantastic concept arise? A glance at the pre-Christian religious narratives will dispel every doubt . . . In this way popular illusions found their way from Hellenism (Greek pagans) to Christianity. . . . This explains the great number of similarities between gods and saints. . . If Mary considers herself as betrothed to the priest who serves her the meaning of this is not far to seek; . . . And if in this legend of Mary, the blessed Virgin puts a ring on the hand of her betrothed under quite characteristic circumstances, that is nothing else than the Roman local legend of the betrothal of Venus" (*Catholic Encyclopedia,* IX, 129-130).

NO PERSON AS GOOD AS CATHOLIC SAINTS

Catholic *saints* who are represented as having all the goodness they themselves need, and also a "super-abundance" which is placed in the "Treasury of Merit," from which the priest is said to draw and place to the credit of one who has no merit!

"But the Scripture hath concluded all under sin" (Gal. 3:22, *Douay*).

"All have sinned" (Rom. 3:23, *Douay*).

"If we say we have no sin, we deceive ourselves and the truth is not in us . . . If we say that we have not sinned we make him a liar, and his word is not in us" (1 John 1:8, 10, *Douay*),

". . . there is no man who sinneth not" (3 Kings (1 Kings) 8:46, *Douay*).

"For there is no just man upon earth, that doeth good, and sinneth not" (Eccl. 1:21 (20), *Douay*).

So no man has one hundred percent goodness, and no man can possibly have more, or a "superabundance"!

"Even so also, when ye shall have done everything that was commanded you, say, 'We are unprofitable servants; we have done what was our duty to do'" (Luke 17:10, *Confraternity*).

"The Church which has received from Christ the power to forgive sins, both as to the guilt and the penalty, and who has the distribution of the spiritual treasures accumulated by our Lord and members of his mystical body, can satisfy the claims of divine justice by taking from the superabundant satisfactions of Christ and His saints and applying them to sinners" (*Legislation on the Sacraments in the New Code,* Ayrinhac, 273; also *Catholic Encyclopedia,* XII, 579).

"His perfect followers, the saints" (*Question Box,* 1913 Edition, Conway, 154).

No one can fail to see how Catholic teaching contradicts the Catholic Bible!

INVENTED TREASURY IN ELEVENTH CENTURY!

"This common use of indulgences led theologians to draw out more fully the theory on which the doctrine of indulgences rests, and thus, just at the beginning of the eleventh century, the phrase 'Treasury of Merit' occurs" (*Catholic Dictionary,* Addis and Arnold, 443).

INVENTED SEVEN YEARS AFTER CANONIZING STARTED

"At a Roman synod held in the Lateran on 31 January, 993, Bishop Ulric of Augsburg was solemnly canonized, an event which the pope announced to the French and German bishops in a Bull dated 3 February. This was the first time that a solemn canonization had been made by a pope" (*Catholic Encyclopedia,* VIII, 428).

UNKNOWN IN NEW TESTAMENT!

"The painstaking investigation of the life of a candidate for sainthood and the formal process of canonization, such as exists today, were unknown in the early centuries" (John A. O'Brien, Ph.D. University of Notre Dame, in *Our Sunday Visitor,* 8/11/63).

Catholic "saints" are said to have used forgeries (*Catholic Encyclopedia,* V, 778;. IX, 224; *General Legislation in the New Code,* Ayrinhac, 34). "Saint" Jerome said that "St." Liberius was a heretic (*Catholic Encyclopedia,* IX, 220, 222). "St." Siricius made priests out of bigamists (*General Legislation in the New Code,* Ayrinhac, 179). Pope "Saint" Hormisdos was father of "Saint" Silverius (*Catholic Encyclopedia,* VII, 470).

"Saints" Francis and Dominic were inquisitors and murdered thousands. So did other "saints."

"History shows us how far the inquisitors answered to this ideal. Far from being inhuman, they, as a rule, were men of spotless character and sometimes of truly admirable sanctity and not a few of them have been canonized by the Church" (*Catholic Encyclopedia,* VIII, 31).

"We know the names of many of the inquisitors, monks and bishops. There are some whose memory is beyond reproach, in fact, the Church honors them as saints, because they died for the faith" (*The Inquisition,* Vacandard, 133). This same learned work tells us how these "saints" lied to cover up their cruel and bloodthirsty work (*The Inquisition,* 128-130).

Some of the *saints* were liars, cruel murderers and heretics. It is clear to see they had a "super-abundance" of wickedness!

STILL CATHOLICS BOAST OF THEM.

"The heroic sanctity that characterized Catholic saints is nowhere to be found outside the Catholic Church. We would advise our questioners to read the lives of some of the saints" (*Question Box,* Conway, 124).

RELICS OF THE CATHOLIC 'SAINTS' SPURIOUS!

"Nevertheless it remains true that many of the more ancient relics duly exhibited for veneration in the great sanctuaries of Christendom or even at Rome itself must now be pronounced to be either certainly spurious or open to grave suspicion" (*Catholic Encyclopedia,* XII, 737).

But this ugly fact must be kept from the trusting laity who are encouraged to worship them devoutly, expecting miracles from them.

"... he bows and kisses the altar praying to God to forgive his sins through the merits of the saints whose relics are there" (*Teaching of the Catholic Church,* Smith, 58).

"A Catholic never has the slightest doubt" (*Question Box,* 1913 Edition, 204).

NOT ALLOWED TO UNDECEIVE THEM!

"But they should not permit the public discussion of these questions and let anyone raise doubt about the authenticity of the sacred relics" (*Administrative Legislation in the New Code,* Ayrinhac, 158).

"A Catholic knows there is no danger of deception, because he believes in the authority of God, voiced to him by the living, infallible witness of Christ's mouth-piece, the Church of God" (*Question Box,* 1913 edition, 19).

We learned that all the *saints* are supposed to be endowed with miraculous powers and these powers are inherent in these relics. I wonder what miracles might be expected if they had a petticoat of "St." Zacherias who for eight hundred years before her "transformation" by Clement VIII, was Popess Joan?

FICTITIOUS 'SAINTS' DON'T MATTER!

"And it is a poor Catholic that leaves devotions entirely alone, and a rare one. He may not feel enclined to enlist in favor of this or that particular saint, but he usually has a Rosary hidden away somewhere in his vest pocket and a scapular around his neck, or in his pocket, as a last extreme. If he scorns this, then the chances are that he is a Catholic only in name, for the tree of faith is such a fertile one that it rarely fails to yield fruit and flowers of such exquisite fragrance.

"Of course the lives of all the saints are not history in the strictest sense of the word. But what has that to do with the Communion of Saints? If simplicity and naivety have woven around some names an unlikely tale, a fable or a myth, it requires some effort to

168

see how that could effect their standing with God, or their disposition to help us in our needs.

"Devotions are not based on historical facts, although in certain facts, events or happenings, real or alleged, they may have been furnished with occasions for coming into existence. The authenticity of these facts is not guaranteed by the doctrinal authority of the Church, but she may, and does, approve the devotions that springs therefrom. Independently of the truth of private and individual revelations, visions and miracles, which she investigates as to their probability, she makes sure that there is nothing contrary to the deposit of faith and morals, and then she gives these devotions the stamp of her approval as a security to the faithful who wish to practice them. A Catholic or a non-Catholic may think what he likes concerning the apparitions of the Virgin at Lourdes; if he is dense enough he may refuse to believe that miracles have been performed there" (*Explanation of Catholic Morals,* Sullivan, 115-116).

The "saints" are fictitious and the "relics" are spurious!

Extravagant Claims for Mary

The most extravagant claims are made for Mary, too numerous to mention, but here are a few:

She is the ". . . gate of heaven" (*Glories of Mary,* Liguori, 177).

"Whoever asks and wishes to obtain graces without the intercession of Mary, attempts to fly without wings" (*Glories of Mary,* 189).

"Very glorious, oh Mary, and wonderful, exclaims St. Bonaventure, is thy great name. Those who are mindful to utter it at the hour of death, have nothing to fear from hell, for the devils at once abandon the soul when they hear the name of Mary" (*Glories of Mary,* 163).

MARY SAVES FROM GOD AND THE DEVILS!

"The devils have presented my sins before the tribunal of the Lord, and already they were dragging me to hell, but the holy Virgin came and said to them: 'Where are you taking this youth? What have you to do with one of my servant who has so long served me in the congregation?' The devils fled, and thus I have been saved from their hands" (*Glories of Mary*, 667).

BIRD SAID AVE MARIA—HAWK FELL DEAD!

"Father Bernardine de Bustis relates that a hawk darted upon a bird which had been taught to say *Ave Maria;* the bird said *Ave Maria,* and the Hawk fell dead" (*Glories of Mary*, 96).

"Wherefore those who are servants of Mary, and for whom Mary intercedes, are as secure of paradise as if they were already there" (*Glories of Mary*, 280).

PREVENTS GOD AND CHRIST!

"What poor sinners we should be if we had not this advocate, so powerful and so merciful, and at the same time so prudent and so wise, that the judge, her Son, cannot condemn the guilty, if she defends them. . . Precisely the same thing does Mary continually in heaven, in behalf of innumerable sinners: she knows so well how to appease the divine justice with her tender and wise entreaties, that God himself blesses her for it, and as it were thanks her, that thus she restrains him from abandoning and punishing them as they deserve" (*Glories of Mary*, 220).

Several centuries after the New Testament period Catholics began to call Mary "Mother of God." Their whole system is now built around this.

Liguori asserts that mothers can never become subject to their children, meaning that Mary was not subject to Christ (*Glories of Mary*, 200). He also says "God was also subject to her will" (p. 201).

Mary Has All Power!

"And therefore, says St. Peter Damian, the Virgin has all power in heaven as on earth" (*Glories of Mary,* 201).

"She seems to command rather than request" (*Glories of Mary,* 202).

"Thou, then oh Mary, being the Mother of God, canst save all men by thy prayers, which are enforced by a mother's authority" (*Glories of Mary,* 211).

"Command thy son" (*Catholic Prayer Book* according to *Question Box,* 1913 edition, 520).

Overrules God and Christ!

"But now, if God is offended with any sinner, and Mary undertakes to protect him, she restrains the Son from punishing him and saves him" (*Glories of Mary,* 133).

More Merciful than Christ!

"Because it belongs to Christ, as our judge, to punish, but to Mary, as our advocate, to pity. By this he would give us to understand, that we sooner find salvation by recurring to the mother than the Son" (*Glories of Mary,* 149-150).

"Oh my queen, be my advocate with thy Son, whom I dare not approach" (*Glories of Mary,* 153).

". . . the judge, her Son, cannot condemn the guilty, if she defends them" (*Glories of Mary,* 220).

". . . less fear and more confidence" (*Glories of Mary,* 221).

". . . Mary is omnipotent" (*Glories of Mary,* 203).

"We ask many things of God and do not obtain them; we ask them from Mary and obtain them" (*Glories of Mary,* 150).

Mary More Merciful!

"'I will make him richer than before; but in the first place, he must renounce God.' 'But this is not sufficient,' said the demon;

171

'he must also renounce Mary; for it is to her that we attribute our greatest losses. Oh, how many souls she has snatched from us, and led back to God and saved'; 'Oh, this I will not do,' exclaimed the youth; 'Deny Mary! why she is my only hope. I had rather be a beggar all my life.' With these words he left the place. On his way he happened to pass a church dedicated to Mary. The unhappy youth entered it, and kneeling before her altar, he began to weep and implore the most holy Virgin that she would obtain the pardon of his sins. Mary immediately began to intercede with the Son for that miserable being. Jesus at first said: 'But that ungrateful youth, my mother, has denied me.' But seeing that his mother still continued to intreat him, he at last said: 'Oh, my mother, I have never refused thee anything; he shall be pardoned, since thou dost ask it'" (*Glories of Mary,* 183).

"Oh lady, since thou art the dispenser of all graces, and we must receive the grace of salvation through thy hand alone, then our salvation depends on thee" (*Glories of Mary,* 190).

DETHRONES CHRIST—MARY NOW HAS CHRIST'S KINGDOM!

"She possesses, by right, the whole kingdom of her son" (*Glories of Mary,* 280).

DEMOTES CHRIST TO MARY'S SUB-DEACON!

"Now He lifts His eyes to her, knowing that she is His mother. At every nod of her eyes He plays the part of the 'subdeacon' and grants her every wish" (*New Interpretation of the Mass,* Borgmann, 57).

GOD OBEYS MARY!

"St. Bernardine of Sienna does not hesitate to say that all obey the commands of Mary, even God himself" (*Glories of Mary,* 202).

DEIFIED AS IT WERE!

"Holy Virgin, Mother of God, succor those who implore thy assistance. Turn to us. But, having been deified, as it were, hast thou forgotten men?" (*Glories of Mary,* 331).

". . . Mary whom he has made sovereign of heaven and earth, general of His armies, treasurer of his treasures, dispenser of His graces, worker of His greatest marvels, restorer of the human race, mediatrix of men, exterminator of the enemies of God, and the faithful companion of His grandeurs and His triumphs" (*True Devotion to the Blessed Virgin,* DeMontfort, 15).

"This beautiful and singular title of *Immaculate* given to Mary, began to appear gradually in some of the Fathers of the primitive age of the Church: admitted then by all nations, it passed from age to age, like a river, which is scarcely visible as it leaves the fountain head, increases as time goes on, and, as it winds through the fields, attains such magnitude as to be taken for the sea itself" (*Life of the Blessed Virgin,* Gentilucci, 103).

With all this blasphemy in mind, we are now prepared for this the ultimate in blasphemies;

MARY 'DIVINE'

"The divine Mary is the terrestrial Paradise of the New Adam" (*True Devotion to the Blessed Virgin,* DeMontfort, 2-3; also on pages 40-41, 59, 117, 129).

This amazing, God dishonoring fable is merely an adaptation of pagan myths, as the following quotations admit:

"Juno (supposed wife of Jupiter—O.C.L.) might also be taken as a type of Mary because she was called Queen of Heaven, was the patroness of chastity, marriage and childbirth" (*Apocryphal and Legendary Life of Christ,* Donehoo, 65).

NO MARY WORSHIP IN EARLY CHURCH!

"But in the primitive Church all feelings of love were solely for the service of the divine. The love sentiment could have been born—all the elements were there—but the right atmosphere was still lacking. Before a religious element could be introduced into the subject of womanhood, it was necessary for woman not merely to be conceived of as an equal, but to be placed in a sphere apart, to be dreamed of rather than known. This implies the existence of a fairly complex civilization, one in which *woman occupies the summit of a hierarchy,* separated from those nearest her by stages and grades—as in a Byzantine court. There had been famous and powerful queens in the East. . . But just as a hive needs only one queen for the multitude of workers and drones, so in those days there had been only one ruling queen, a woman unapproachable, with no personal relationship to the mass of her subjects. . . And this was the moment when the Virgin became 'Our Lady,' when the popular feeling for her became crystalized in the West (Roman Catholic territory— O.C.L.). It retains to this day the marks of its period of origin; for sentiments are as dateable as inventions, and they preserve, like them, their original coloring.

"We have gone carefully into this medieval cult of the woman conceived as initiating element in religion" (*The Virgin Mary,* Guitton, 89).

"First of all it should be noted that without the idea of religious development Catholic thought on the Blessed Virgin is incomprehensible. No one can pretend that the Mariology of the present day—in liturgy, in worship, in devotion and in theology—is the Mariology of the primitive age" (*The Virgin Mary,* Guitton, 105).

"It is undeniable that the cult of Mary, like everything else of a delicate nature, has been subject to numerous exaggerations and corruptions. Yet Mariology, in spite of this, is bound up with the whole system of Catholic truths.

"If I might add a final characteristic, I should say that this aspect of Catholicism has the distinctive mark of freedom. According to the faith and discipline of the Church, devotions to Mary is not necessary for the winning of God's love; otherwise, the first

174

six centuries would stand condemned. The creeds hardly speak at all of the Virgin. The liturgy of the sacraments does not mention her. The prayers of the Mass rarely name her" (*The Virgin Mary,* Guitton, 178-179).

"For these first generations, it was the honour of Christ that was at issue, not the honour of Mary" (*The Virgin Mary,* Guitton, 83).

Quite a number of ideas built in the fables concerning Mary will have to be passed over because of lack of space, such as Mary's "Virginity" and her other children, the sinlessness of Mary, "The Immaculate Conception" and the "Assumption of Mary," but we have presented enough to demonstrate that it is all unknown in the Scriptures and to the early centuries.

CHAPTER XIII

The Popes

There are a number of officially issued lists of the popes which differ widely as to their names and numbers. We will now take one of these lists, pointing out their inconsistencies and other damaging Catholic statements, concerning them. The first five hundred years of this pretended "history" is a huge fiction, and it is not until a thousand years after Christ and the Apostles that Catholic authorities can definitely state the time of their becoming popes. The dates here assigned in this list are given with this understanding.

"St." Peter
"St." Linus (67-79)
"St." Anacletus (79-90)
"St." Clement (90-99)
"St." Evaristus (99-107)
"St." Alexander I (107-116)
"St." Sixturs I (116-125)
"St." Telesphorus (125-136)
"St." Hyginus (136-140)
"St." Pius (140-154)
"St." Anicetus (154-165)
"St." Soter (165-174)
"St." Eleutherius (174-189)
"St." Victor (189-198)
"St." Zephyrinus (198-217)

A "shamefully corrupt man" (*Hippolytus,* 157).

"He (Callistus) obtained great influence over the ignorant, illiterate and grasping Zephyrinus by bribes" (*Catholic Encyclopedia,* III, 184).

"St." Callistus (217-222)
"St." Urban (222-230)

His existence is improbable (*Catholic Encyclopedia*, XV, 209).

"St." Pontian (230-235)

Resigned (*Catholic Encyclopedia*, XII, 230).

"St." Anterus (235-236)
"St." Fabian (236-250)
"St." Cornelius (251-253)
"St." Lucius (253-254)
"St." Stephen I (254-257)
"St." Sixtus II (257-258)
"St." Dionysius (259-268)
"St." Felix I (269-274)
"St." Eutychian (275-283)

"We know of no detail of his pontificate" (*Catholic Encyclopedia*, V, 639).

"St." Caius (283-296)

"Nothing whatever is known of his life" (*Catholic Encyclopedia*, III, 144).

"St." Marcellinus (296-304)

"Nothing has been handed down concerning the activities of this pope in his reign of eight years." His name is left out of some of the lists (*Catholic Encyclopedia*, IX, 637-638).

At this point there was no pope for four years (*Pageant of the Popes*, Farrow, 20). According to the foregoing statements there is no record from A.D. 275 to 308!

"St." Marcellus I (308-309)
"St." Eusebius (309 or 310)
"St." Melchiades (311-314)
"St." Sylvester I (314-335)

"It is therefore to be regretted that there is so little authoritative information concerning Sylvester's pontificate" (*Catholic Encyclopedia*, XV, 370).

Catholic writers claim that all Ecumenical councils have to be called by a pope in order to be legal, but the following quotation states that until A.D. 859 all councils were called by civil rulers. This shows how present day writers say what they think will be most convincing, without regard for the truth in the matter.

Emperors Convoked First Eight Councils!

"The first eight general councils, that is, all those held in the Orient, were convoked by the emperors. Whether this was done in each case with the approval of the Pope, is a matter that is much debated. In the case of the present council (Nicaea, 325) there is nothing to indicate that the Pope was consulted in the matter. . . Nowhere is mention made of the Pope. . . Then, too, it must be remembered that nearly all the emperors looked upon the convocation of a council as a matter that belonged entirely in their sphere of jurisdiction, even if they seek the advice of some bishops. . . Indeed Constantine the Great stated expressly that in external affairs of the Church he was a bishop *a Deo constitutus. . .* Being a bishop himself, he did not consider it necessary to consult the Bishop of Rome. . . It is true, the Sixth General Council (Third of Constantinople, 680) in its eighteenth session declared that the Nicene Council was convoked conjointly by Constantine and Pope Sylvester. But this testimony comes too late to be trustworthy; and if that declaration, made, as it was, in open session, did not provoke dissent or the slightest suggestion of controversy, it was because the bishops were ignorant of the facts and simply took for granted

178

that the speaker knew what he was talking about. That same council also said that the Second General Council (381) was summoned by St. Gregory of Nazienzus and Nectarius (a layman at the time), while as a matter of fact it was convoked by Theodosius the Great" (*Disciplinary Degrees of the General Councils,* Schroeder, 11-12).

"It is not known that Constantine ever said anything to Sylvester about convening the Nicene Council" (*Catholic Encyclopedia,* XIV, 371).

Constantine, and not the Bishop of Rome called the Nicene Council (*Pageant of the Popes,* Farrow, 24).

The bishops of Rome for centuries used the *"Donation of Constantine"* in support of their temporal pretensions. I think that no one would be naive enough to believe the hierarchy did not forge this document. They now admit it to be a forgery. Would a holy institution practice forgery? Could an infallible institution use forgeries for centuries without suspecting them?

"There is now no longer any controversy about the pretended *Donation of Constantine"* (Chevalier Artaud de Montor, in *Lives and Times of the Roman Pontiffs,* I, 73).

Catholic authorities now pretend that the church at Rome always had precedence over all other churches. This is certainly not true.

DECREES OF THE NICENE COUNCIL

Canon 7: The Bishop of Jerusalem was to have precedence, and not Rome! (*Disciplinary Decrees of the General Councils,* Schroeder, 33-34).

Canon 8: It was ruled that hereafter there could not be more than one bishop in a city (page 34).

"St." Marcus (336)

Catholic writers now claim that all controversies are to be settled by the Bishop of Rome, but this was certainly not true in the

179

fourth century.

Bishop of Rome Did Not Settle Troubles Elsewhere

"Concerning the interposition of the Pope in the Arian troubles, which were then so actively affecting the Church in the East, nothing has been handed down" (*Catholic Encyclopedia*, IX, 674).

UNCERTAINTY ABOUT COUNCILS
"St." Julius (337-352)

Sardica (A.D. 343-344): "By some historians and critics, *viz.,* Baronius, Natalis, Alexander, the Ballerini, and Palma, the Council of Sardica has been considered oecumenical. No doubt it was convoked as an oecumenical council. Moreover its canons were approved by the Council of Trullo, and received according to Pope Nicholas I by the whole Church" (*Catholic Dictionary,* Addis and Arnold, 946).

"St." Liberius (352-366)

The history of this "pope" is interesting because he has been declared, by the highest authorities, to have been a heretic, yet he appears in every list of the popes as one of the "Holy Fathers"!

"St. Jerome said that Liberius subscribed to heretical wickedness" (*Catholic Encyclopedia,* IX, 220).

Baronins said of the condemnation of Liberius that "no truer history can be found" (Chevalier Artaud de Montor, *Lives and Times of the Roman Pontiffs, 1,79*).

"It is certainly remarkable that many of the Fathers and Popes of the fourth century speak of Liberius in the highest terms, praising both his holiness and his orthodoxy" (*Question Box,* 1929 Edition, 172).

"Liberius never erred in faith" (Bishop Purcell in the *Campbell-Purcell Debate,* 165).

"The pope himself, if notoriously guilty of heresy, would cease to be pope because he would cease to be a member of the Church" (*Catholic Encyclopedia,* VII, 261).

About A.D. 360 Pontus was declared to be a heretic because he taught what Catholics now admit to be *New Testament* teaching, that there was no difference between a *presbyter* and a *bishop.* Catholic scholars admit that Catholic teaching on this point is now different from the *New Testament!* So to the Catholic Church the Bible teaching is heresy! (*Catholic Encyclopedia,* XII, 416).

"St." Damasus (366-384)

"The election of St. Damasus gave occasion to grave disorders and even battles in the streets of Rome. . . Civil rulers had often to intervene to maintain order" (*Constitution of the Church,* Ayrinhac, 28).

ROMAN SUPREMACY NOT CLAIMED BEFORE FOURTH CENTURY!

"During the same century (fourth) Roman supremacy BEGAN to be emphasized as a factor of unity" (*Catholic Encyclopedia,* XIII, 531). Caps used for emphasis—O.C.L.

Bishop of Rome was not called pope before fourth century (*Catholic Encyclopedia,* XII, 270).

Damasus was the "first to call himself pope" (Chevalier Artaud de Montor, *Lives of the Roman Pontiffs,* I, 89-90).

NO INFALLIBILITY DOCTRINE BEFORE FOURTH CENTURY

"It would of course be a monstrous anachronism were we to attribute a belief in papal infallibility to the ante-Nicene Fathers" (*Catholic Dictionary,* Addis and Arnold, 674).

"Writers of the fourth century were prone to describe many practices as apostolic institutions which certainly had no claim to be so regarded" (*Catholic Encyclopedia,* III, 484).

Damasus was the first to call himself *pope,* and was also the first to appeal to Matthew 16:18 to bolster his claim of ascendency over all churches (*Catholic Encyclopedia,* IV, 614).

"St." Anastasius I (398-401)
"St." Innocent I (402-417)
GOTHS CAPTURE ROME (408-410)

"St." Zozimus (417-418)

Deceived and misinformed (*Catholic Encyclopedia,* XV, 765).

". . . hotheaded" (*Catholic Encyclopedia,* VI, 9).

"He was the first who, to the title of bishop or pope, added the words *of Rome"* (*Lives and Times of the Roman Pontiffs,* Chevalier Artaud de Montor, I, 95).

"St." Boniface I (418-422)
"St." Celestine I (422432)

First to call Mary "Mother of God" (*Lives and Times of the Roman Pontiffs,* Chevalier Artaud de Montor, I, 98).

Council of Ephesus, 431, convoked by Theodosius without the knowledge of Celestine (Pius XI, in Encyclical, *Light of Truth,* 9).

"St." Sixtus III (432440)
"St." Leo "The Great" (440461)

Forbad public confession (*Lives and Times of the Roman Pontiffs,* Chevalier Artaud de Montor, I, 103).

DECREED THE DEATH PENALTY

"It seemed to him natural that temporal rulers should punish such sacrilegious madness, and should put to death the founder (Priscillian) of the sect, and some of his followers" (*Catholic Encyclopedia,* VIII, 27).

Priscillian, Bishop of Avila, Spain, was accused of heresy and sorcery, but the writer of this article speaks of his innocence.

ROME NOT SUPREME IN A.D. 415

The Council of Chalcedon made the following declaration in Canon 28:

"The Bishop of New Rome (Constantinople) shall enjoy the same honor as the Bishop of Old Rome, for the former possesses the same privileges" (*Disciplinary Decrees of the General Councils,* Schroeder, 125).

LEO CLAIMED THAT LENT WAS APOSTOLIC—FALSE!

"Some of the Fathers as early as the fifth century supported the view that this forty days' fast was of Apostolic institution. For example, St. Leo exhorts his hearers to abstain that they may 'fulfil with their fasts the Apostolic institution of the forty days'. . . But the best modern scholars are almost unanimous in rejecting this view, for in the existing remains of the first three centuries we find both considerable diversity of practice regarding the fast before Easter and also a gradual process of development in the matter of its duration. . . there could have been no Apostolic tradition on the subject" (*Catholic Encyclopedia,* IX, 152).

"St." Hilarius (461-468)
"St." Simplicius (468-483)
   WESTERN EMPIRE COMES TO AN END

"St." Felix II (III?) (483-492)
"St." Gelasius I (492496)
   "For a long time the fixing of the Canon of the Scriptures was attributed to Gelasius, but it seems now more probably the work of Damasus" (*Catholic Encyclopedia,* VI, 406).

   Gelasius pronounced it a sacrilege to "deny the cup to the laity"

(*Campbell-Purcell Debate,* 224, 232-233; *Catholic Encyclopedia,* VI, 406; *Campaigner's Hand Book,* Goldstein, 240; *Question Box,* 1913 Edition, 446).

HISTORY OF POPES AN ADMITTED FORGERY TO THIS POINT!

"St." Anastasius II (496-498)

"A great many of the biographies of the predecessors of Anastasius II are full of errors and historically untenable" (*Catholic Encyclopedia,* IX 224. This is from the article on *Liber Pontificalis,* or *Book of the Popes.* So away goes about fifty popes!).

"St." Symmachus (498-514)

This is a very important point in Catholic history.

"The people who were so easily aroused by all dogmatic disputes were divided into two formidable parties, and their fierce encounters often stained the streets with blood" (*General History of the Catholic Church,* Darras, II, 85).

"He died on the 19th of July, A.D. 514, after a pontificate of fifteen years, every step of which had been embittered by a new strife" (*General History of the Church,* Darras, II, 90).

He was tried, and an attempt was made to depose him, but he seems to have overcome his enemies by forgeries!

"During the dispute the adherents of Symmachus drew up four apocryphal writings called the 'Symmachian Forgeries'. . . The object of these forgeries was to produce alleged instances from earlier times to support the whole procedure of the adherents of Symmachus, and in particular, the position that the Roman Bishop could not be judged by any court composed of other bishops. Still these forgeries are not the first documents to maintain this latter tenet" (*Catholic Encyclopedia,* XIV, 378).

This was "His Holiness St. Symmachus," whose name is in all

lists of popes!

"St." Hormisdas (514-523)

His son become "Pope St. Silverius" (*Catholic Encyclopedia,* VII, 470).

Ignorance was so prevalent at this time that Emperor Leo could not read and write (*General History of the Catholic Church,* Darras, II, 97). This made Catholic forgery easy!

"St." John I (523-526)
"St." Felix III or IV (526-530)

He was son of a priest (Chevalier Artaud de Montor, *Lives and Times of the Roman Pontiffs,* I, 109).

ALL POPES ARE CALLED SAINTS TO THIS POINT!

Dioscarus (left out of *Cath. Ency.* list) was pope twenty-two days, and was anathematized by Boniface II after his death. This would lead us to believe he was murdered. Five years later "St." Agapetus burned Boniface's anathema (*Catholic Encyclopedia,* II, 660).

Boniface II (530-532)

Appointed by Felix IV (*Constitutions of the Church,* Ayrinhac, 28; also *Catholic Encyclopedia,* II, 660).

"At this period simony in the election of popes was rife among clergy and laity" (*Catholic Encyclopedia,* VIII, 421).

Boniface appointed Vigilius his successor "in direct opposition to the traditions of the Church and to the numerous canons which forbid the pope, during his lifetime to bequeath his dignity as an inheritance" (*General History of the Church,* Darras, II, 118).

John II (533-535)

185

"He censured the acts, already revoked by the Council, by which Boniface had chosen his successor" (*Lives and Times of the Roman Pontiffs,* Chevalier Artaud de Montor, I, 123).

"St." Agapetus (535-536)

Son of a priest (*Catholic Encyclopedia,* I, 203).

Burned Boniface's anathema (*Catholic Encyclopedia,* II, 660).

Denied "laymen" the right to teach (*Catholic Encyclopedia,* I, 203).

"St." Silverius (536-538)

Son of "St." Pope Hormisdas (*Catholic Encyclopedia,* VII, 470; *Lives and Times of the Roman Pontiffs*, I, 125).

Was forcibly made pope (*General Church History,* Darras, II, 143).

Forcibly taken from Rome and Vigilius made Pope instead. Was starved to death by Vigilius (*Lives and Times of the Roman Pontiffs,* I, 125; *General History of the Church,* Darras, II, 143-147; *Catholic Encyclopedia,* XIII, 793).

Vigilius (538-555)

"Vigilius and Pelagius I were forced on the Church at the imperial dictation. In the case of the latter there seems to have been no election" (*Catholic Encyclopedia,* XII, 271).

SECOND COUNCIL OF CONSTANTINOPLE (A.D. 533)

"The Council was convoked by the Emperor to be held in Constantinople. . . The Pope was invited to attend, but refused" (*Disciplinary Decrees of the General Councils,* Schroeder, 132).

Catholic writers now claim that the popes always convened the councils. This, like so many present day Catholic claims is false.

"Vigilius, the deacon, had contracted engagements which Vigilius the Pope spurned with indignation—a striking example of the ever watchful care exercised over the Church by Divine Providence, which will never suffer the gates of hell to prevail against the indefectible chair of Peter" (*General History of the Church,* Darras, II, 144).

Pelagius I (556-561)

Forced on the church—no election (*Catholic Encyclopedia,* XII, 271).

Approved the council Vigilius had condemned (*Catholic Encyclopedia,* XI, 603).

John III (561-574)

Approved the council Pelagius I had condemned (*Catholic Encyclopedia,* XIII, 793).

Benedict I (575-579)
Pelagius II (579-590)

"At this time there appeared an extraordinary plague, as sudden as it was violent. The patient frequently died in the act of sneezing or yawning" (*Lives and Times of the Roman Pontiffs,* I, 135).

Died of the plague (*Catholic Encyclopedia,* X, 604).

Before the Pope was stricken he ordered the people to say, when someone sneezed, "God bless you." It did not seem to help much, for the Pope soon died himself! (*Lives and Times of the Roman Pontiffs,* 128). This is still practiced by Catholics.

Many scourges of the plague are recorded: (*Catholic Encyclopedia,* XI, 604; *Lives and Times of the Roman Pontiffs,* I, 135, 138; *Catholic Encyclopedia,* IV, 74; XV, 715, 418; XII, 558; Crusaders died, *Catholic Encyclopedia,* IV, 546, 552).

Like the superstitious pagans around them, the popes resorted to magic words, medals, processions, etc., but in spite of this, popes, cardinals, archbishops, bishops, priests, saints and nuns continued to die. Of the "saints" they now revere, most never bathed, never changed clothes, nor washed their feet. Some of these "saints" most honored today defied every law of sanitation and health, and are praised for their humility in kissing the sores of the afflicted. They were not infallible; they were ignorant like all other people. They lived on bread and water, denied themselves sleep, and in many ways punished their bodies. The wonder is that all did not die. There was one year in the fifteenth century when about fifty percent of the inhabitants of Europe succumbed. Much of this ignorant and unsanitary superstition is still a part of Catholicism today: the priest putting the bread in their mouths, Catholics dipping their hands in the filthy "Holy Water" basin, kissing relics and crucifixes that thousands have kissed, etc.

A sample of the many foolish superstitions still practiced by Catholics is the "Agnus Dei."

"So the purpose of these consecrated medallions is to protect those who wear or possess them from all malign influences. In the prayer of blessing, a special mention of the peril from storm and pestilence, from fire and flood, and also from the dangers to which women are exposed in childbirth." This author further speaks of "its many virtues," and later that "fires are said to have been extinguished, and floods stayed" (*Catholic Encyclopedia,* I, 220).

"The Agnus Dei is a cake of wax, bearing on it an image of a lamb surmounted by the cross. It is blessed by the Pope on the low Sunday after his elevation to the See of Peter, and on every seventh low Sunday. The use of it among the faithful, is very ancient. The blessings attached to the Agnus Dei are enumerated in the prayer of the Pope: 'O God, Author of all sanctity, Lord and ruler, whose fatherly love and care we ever experience, deign to bless, sanctify, and consecrate, by the implication of the Holy Name, these cakes of wax, stamped with the image of the most innocent lamb, that by seeing and touching them, the faithful may be invited to praise

188

Thee, that they may escape the fury of whirlwinds and tempests, and danger from hail and thunder; that the evil spirits may tremble and fly when they behold the standard of the sacred cross impressed on the wax.' And he prays that all who devoutly use the Agnus Dei may be freed from pestilence, shipwreck, fire, from the dangers of childbirth, and sudden death. It should be worn devoutly, in the belief that the prayer of the Vicar of Our Lord avails much" (*Teachings of Our Lord,* Smith, 165-166).

In spite of all this, and hundreds more, Catholics need insurance like other poor mortals. More Catholic church buildings burn than all other religious groups put together. Catholic cities are destroyed by tidal waves and earthquakes. A few years ago a part of the Vatican, the building where the pope resides, fell, killing several people. Why will people, in this enlightened age, believe such superstition? The ceiling of Pope John XXI's apartment fell, killing him! (*Catholic Encyclopedia,* VIII, 431). More than two hundred pilgrims were killed in Rome by a falling bridge, and even councils have been stricken by plague and the "prelates" killed or scattered.

"An epidemic now broke out at Trent; a bishop and a general of the Franciscans died of it; the alarm was so great that ten or twelve bishops went home. The legates deemed it expedient to transfer the assembly to Bologna, and this view was adopted by the majority of the bishops, a minority being chiefly those who were devoted to the Emperor, voted to remain at Trent" (*Catholic Dictionary,* Addis and Arnold, 806).

The following quotation shows what "magic" Catholic writers attribute to the Mass:

"The Mass, moreover, wards off calamities, scourges, evils of all sorts, as well as the spiritual miseries which God would have justly inflicted on us, if the eucharistic sacrifice had not appeased his anger" (*Eucharistic Law and Practice,* 25).

Pope Pelagius II also justifies killing heretics in the following language:

189

"Pay no attention to the vain speeches of people who charge the Church with exciting persecution when she represses crime and labors for the salvation of souls. To persecute is to compel one to do evil; otherwise all laws, divine and human, which order the punishment of crime, would be deserving of abolition. Now the Scriptures and the canons teach us that schism is an evil, and that it ought to be suppressed, even by the secular power; and all who separate themselves from the Apostolic See, sin and undoubtedly are schismatics" (*Lives and Times of the Roman Pontiffs,* I, 131).

"St." Gregory' I, the Great (590-604)
"He was not a man of profound learning, not a philosopher, not a controversialist, hardly even a theologian in the constructive sense of the term" (*Catholic Encyclopedia,* VI, 786).

The *Liber Pontificate* was forged during his reign "in the seventh" century (*Catholic Encyclopedia,* IX, 224).

He was the first to use the phrase "to speak *ex cathedra'* (*Lives and Times of the Roman Pontiffs,* I 139).

He was the "father of medieval papacy" (*Catholic Encyclopedia,* VI, 786).

"Almost all the leading principles of later Catholicism are found, at any rate in germ, in Gregory the Great" (*Catholic Encyclopedia,* VI, 780).

Catholic authorities tell us that Gregory was in error in his interpretation of Scripture concerning Paul's "thorn in the flesh" (*Westminster Version of the New Testament,* 98), and "his clear expectation of a speedy end of the world" (*Catholic Encyclopedia,* VI, 780). That was over fourteen hundred years ago, and the world has not come to an end yet! He was not an infallible interpreter!

He rejected the *Apocrypha,* which is now a part of the Catholic Bible! (*A Catholic Commentary,* 18).

He rejected the title "universal bishop" (*Question Box,* 1913 Edition, 292).

190

Gregory probably instituted "processions," now such an important part of Catholic practice:

"About the time of Gregory the Great, and possibly earlier, two forms of procession played a great part in papal ceremonial" (*Catholic Encyclopedia,* VII, 447).

He is given credit for developing the doctrine of purgatory (*Catholic Dictionary,* Addis and Arnold, 706).

Sabinianus (604-606)
Boniface III (607-608)

"The See of Blessed Peter, the Apostle, should be the head of all the churches, and that the title of Universal Bishop belonged exclusively to the Bishop of Rome" (Emperor Phocas for Boniface III, *Catholic Encyclopedia,* II, 660). He advocated what Gregory rejected: one or the other was not infallible!

Boniface IV (608-615)

The heathen Pantheon (all gods) was appropriated as a church building dedicated to Mary and all martyrs. Twenty-eight cart loads of bones were removed from the catacombs and deposited under the altar (*Catholic Encyclopedia,* II, 661).

This is the origin of "All Saints Day." All saints is a substitute for Pantheon (all gods) (*Lives and Times of the Roman Pontiffs,* I, 145).

Deusdedit (615-625)

First to use leaden seals—"Bulla" (*Catholic Encyclopedia,* IV, 760).

"False Decretals of Isadora" forged about this time.

Boniface V (619-625)
Honorius (625-638)

Honorius, a condemned "heretic" is the second of a long list who are so condemned, and yet they are in all the lists of popes. Imagine "His Holiness" a heretic! The others are Liberius, Gregory XII, John XXII, Paul V, Marcellus, Vigilius, Benedict XIII and Formosus.

Honorius was a Monothelite while his protagonist, Pope "Saint" Agatho was a Diothelite!!!

"No Catholic has the right to defend Honorius" (*Catholic Encyclopedia,* VII, 455).

Honorius was first condemned as a heretic forty years after he was dead, by the Council of Constantinople (680), and by the next two councils (*Catholic Encyclopedia,* VII, 455).

HONORIUS AN UNCONSCIOUS HERETIC!

"A pope is not infallible in such proceedings as those of Honorius, who contributed unintentionally to the increase of heresy" (*Question Box,* 1929 Edition, 173).

"*Pope Honorius Deceived.*—In A.D. 630 Heraclius placed Cyrus in the Patriarchial See of Alexandria, with the instructions to announce the terms of their compromise. Many Eutychians accepted the new formula of faith, and Cyrus wrote of his success to Sergius. Sophronius, a learned monk and afterwards patriarch of Jerusalem, detected the fundamental error contained in the new teaching, and took steps to refute it and inform the Pope of the real nature of the question. Sergius, however, by a letter which will ever remain a monument of cunning duplicity, had already induced Pope Honorius (625-638) to command the cessation of all discussion on the question of the two wills of Christ" (*History of the Catholic Church,* Spalding, 374).

Catholic authorities inform us that from the time of his death until the Council of Constantinople, forty two years, eight "infallible popes" never suspected his heresy! When two popes, Leo II and Agatho declared him a heretic, somebody among these popes was not infallible! After this, for about two hundred years all the

192

popes, when they were installed, were required to swear that Pope Honorius was a heretic!

The Sixth "oecumenical" Council of Constantinople said of him:

". . . that he was altogether alien from the Apostolic dogmas" "anathema to Honorius, the heretic" "a tool in the hands of the devil" "unholy betrayal" (*Catholic Dictionary,* Addis and Arnold, 409).

Pope Agatho said:

"And in addition to these we decide that Honorius also, who was the Pope of elder Rome be with them cast out of the Holy Church of God, and be anathematized with them, because that we have found by his letter to Sergius that he followed his opinions in all things and confirmed his wicked dogmas" (*Catholic Encyclopedia,* VII, 452, 455-456).

Honorius' letter was condemned to be burned, yet of Honorius our author says:

"He was undoubtedly of excellent intentions. . . died with an untarnished reputation." What further need could there be for refuting the claim of papal infallibility?

"This council was composed almost entirely of Greek bishops, whose bosoms were already swayed by a rising jealousy of Rome; which feeling, a little later, led them into open schism; and there is no evidence that the incidental charge against Honorius was ever approved by the Western (Roman Catholic—O.C.L.) Church (Archbishop Spalding, in *Miscellanae,* 29).

This is an excellent example of the Catholic squirming in an effort to deny what the Catholic Church affirmed for centuries. By this statement Spalding rejected the Sixth, Seventh, and Eighth Councils, which the Catholic Church claims as genuine "oecumenical" councils! There is evidently no infallibility anywhere in the Catholic Church, either in councils or popes!

Severinus (638-640)
John IV (640-642)
Theodore I (642-649)

"He was the first pope officially styled *Sovereign Pontiff,* and the last whom the bishops called brother. The preeminence of the first See and the extension of the pontifical authority were becoming more necessary in proportion as the Church spread farther her conquests" (*General History of the Church,* Darras, II, 232).

"St." Martin I (649-655)

Martin authorized making slaves of the Turks (*Lives and Times of the Roman Pontiffs,* I, 157).

"One of the noblest and most tragic figures in the catalogue of the Roman Pontiffs" (*Disciplinary Decrees of the General Councils,* Schroeder, 157).

"St." Eugene I (654-657)

He was put in office by the Emperor while "St." Martin was lying in prison. He was "forcibly placed in the Chair of Peter" (*Catholic Encyclopedia, N,* 598).

"St." Vitalian (657-672)

During the time he was pope instrumental music was introduced in the Catholic Church (*Lives and Times of the Roman Pontiffs,* I, 162).

"While we are on the subject, we may remark, that organs were either invented in Italy, or at least introduced into Europe by the Italians, in the eighth century" (Archbishop Spalding, in *Miscellanae,* 90).

Adeodatus (672-676)
Donus (676-678)
"St." Agatho (678-681)

194

Agatho condemned Pope Honorius as a heretic (*Catholic Encyclopedia*, VII, 452, 455-456).

COUNCIL OF CONSTANCE A.D. 680

"St." Leo II (682-683)

He "instituted the Kiss of Peace in the Mass and the sprinkling of Holy Water upon the people" (*Lives and Times of the Roman Pontiffs*, I, 168).

"St." Benedict II (684-685)
John V (685-686)
Conon (686-687)

Condemned Pope Honorius as a heretic (*Catholic Dictionary*, Addis and Arnold, 409).

Condemned Pascal to death for "magic" (*Catholic Encyclopedia*, XIII, 7280).

Died in prison (*Catholic Encyclopedia*, XIII, 728).

COUNCIL OF TRULLO A.D. 692

This council was approved by the Second Nicene Council A.D. 787 (*Catholic Dictionary*, Addis and Arnold, 609).

Pope Hadrian I recognized this council "as a continuation of the Sixth General Council" (*Catholic Dictionary*, Addis and Arnold, 821).

"The decrees betray strong animus against Rome" (*Catholic Dictionary*, Addis and Arnold, 220).

This council was "all Eastern" (*Catholic Dictionary*, Addis and Arnold, 821).

The Council of Trullo approved the Council of Sardica (*Catholic Dictionary*, Addis and Arnold, 926).

Though Catholics boast of certainty, they are not only uncertain about their line of popes, but also as to how many general councils they have had!

John VI (701-705)
John VII (705-707)

Not well liked by historians (Lives and Times of the Roman Pontiffs, I, 175).

Sisinnius (708)

Died of gout after twenty days (*Lives and Times of the Roman Pontiffs,* I, 176).

Constantine (708-715)
"St." Gregory II (715-731)

". . . independent authority of the popes which in fact began with Gregory II" (*Catholic Encyclopedia,* VI, 788).

"By such circumstances, did the popes gradually become temporal sovereigns of Rome and part of Italy; indeed they held that power *de facto* long before it was granted *de jure*" (*General History of the Church,* Darras, II, 295).

"Providence was plainly opening the way for the temporal sovereignty and independence of the popes, and Charlemagne but gave the finishing strokes to the work" (*General History of the Church,* Darras, II, 297).

Emperor Leo began his one hundred and eighteen year war on images in A.D. 726 (*Lives and Times of the Roman Pontiffs,* II, 310).

Gregory III (731-741)

"The Iconoclast heresy was by far the most unpopular of all in Italy. Pagan Rome, after the Grecian conquest, had hailed the arts with enthusiasm: Christian Rome now earnestly defended the same arts which were likewise to prove her glory. Gregory III adorned

196

the interior of St. Peter's, on one side the images of the Savior and the Apostles, on the other with those of the Blessed Virgin and the most illustrious martyrs" (*General, History of the Church,* Darras, II, 317-318).

Along about this time the kissing of the pope's foot was instituted (*Catholic Encyclopedia,* XII, 270). Also carrying the pope in "sedia gestatoria" (*General History,* Darras, II, 339).

The Woman Pope Transformed into a Man!

"St." Zacherias (Joan) (741-752)

"In the fourteenth and fifteenth centuries this popess was already counted as an historical personage, whose existence no one doubted. She had her place among the carved busts which stood in the Siena Cathedral. Under Clement VIII (eight hundred and forty years after she was dead!), and at his request, she was transformed into Pope Zacherias. The heretic Huss in the defence of his false doctrine before the council of Constance, referred to the popess and no one offered to question her existence. . . Since the sixteenth century (after Clement VIII changed her into a man in 1592) Catholic historians BEGAN to deny her existence" (*Catholic Encyclopedia,* VIII, 407).

"Nay aquiescence in the fable induced John XX to style himself John XXI" (*Catholic Dictionary,* Addis and Arnold, 870). This was more than three hundred years before she was changed into a man! There was a John XXII A.D. 1328, and a John XXIII in A.D. 1410. All three of these Johns were a long time before she became a man! That accounts for the fact that we have another John XXIII recently! They will insist that they simply did not know what John they were!

Stephen II (752-757)

He ". . . became practically the first pope-king" (*Catholic Encyclopedia,* XIV, 288).

197

'Sedia Gestatoria'

The crowds carried Stephen on their shoulders (*Lives and Times of the Roman Pontiffs,* I, 195; *General History of the Church,* Darras, II, 339).

Stephen was the brother of the next Pope, Paul I (*Catholic Encyclopedia,* XI, 577).

Paul I (757-767)

Brother of his predecessor, Stephen II.

Using the Civil Power to Destroy Their Enemies!

Paul to Pepin:

"Rejoice most happy prince. By the power of your arms, your spiritual mother, the Catholic Church, has triumphed ever her enemies" (*General History of the* Cherek Parras, II, 254).

Ferocious Paul I!

The antipopes eyes were put out and be was imprisoned in a monastery (*General History of the Church,* Darras, II. 359-300).

Try to Excuse Fraud and Superstition

"If, notwithstanding the precepts of sound doctrine explained by the Church, ignorance and fraud have introduced some superstitious ideas to alter its purity, was that a reason for abolishing a received, popular, reasonable and consoling institution (images)?" (*Lives and Times of the Roman Pontiffs,* I, 197).

Stephen III or IV (768-772)
Adrian I (772-795)

Adrian is said to be the "real founder" of the pope's sovereignty (*Catholic Encyclopedia,* I, 156). ". . . founder of a new dynasty."

"It was in no slight degree owing to Adrian's political sagacity, vigilance and activity, that the temporal power of the Papacy did not remain a fiction of the imagination" (*Catholic Encyclopedia*, I, 155).

SECOND COUNCIL NICAEA CONCERNING IMAGES

"The council uses the word *proskunei* of the veneration due to images" (*Catholic Dictionary*, Addis and Arnold, 423).

This is the word used with reference to Cornelius who attempted to worship Peter (Acts 10:25).

Pope Hadrian (Adrian) sent a very unfortunate translation of the Acts of the Nicene Council to Charlemagne." Charlemagne rejected it as sacrilegious (*Catholic Dictionary*, Addis and Arnold, 423).

"The great council at Frankfort, in 794 rejected the Nicene decree, evidently misled, as Charlemagne had been, by the faulty translation which made no distinction between supreme worship (latria) and secondary veneration" (*Catholic Dictionary*, Addis and Arnold, 423).

This author speaks of it further as a "grossly erroneous translation" (*Catholic Dictionary*, Addis and Arnold, 357).

Catholic writers now speak of the Pope as "infallible with reference to faith and morals." Pope Adrian was not!

This Council Endorsed a Forgery!

"The Second Nicene Council, the Seventh General, met in 787 under Tarasius. Besides defining the veneration due to holy images, the Council published the twenty-two canons in which the so-called *Apostolic Canons,* (admitted forgeries) and the oecumenical character of the Council of Trullo were recognized" (*Catholic Dictionary*, Addis and Arnold, 609).

"St." Leo III (795-816)

Leo crowned Charlemagne on Christmas day A.D. 800.

Charlemagne waged fifty-three campaigns as "protector of the Church," and gave the people the alternative of baptism or death. He was married several times, but he is now almost deified by Catholics.

"With all the irregularity of his frequent marriages, it is Charlemagne's glory that he was truly a Christian hero" (*General History of the Church,* Darras, II, 364).

Stephen IV or V (816-817)
"St" Pascal I (817-824)
Eugene II (824-827)
Valentine (827)

Pope only forty days (*Campaigners Handbook,* Goldstein, 122).

Gregory IV (827-844)

The *"False Decretals of Isadora,"* one of the colossal forgeries, was produced by the Catholic hierarchy during Gregory's time, or soon thereafter, is in substance incorporated into Canon Law. This is admitted to have been forged to bolster papal claims. See *Catholicism Against Itself,* volume I, pages 95-99.

Sergius II (844-847)
Leo IV (847-855)
Benedict III (855-858)
"St" Nicholas I (855-867)

"It was to his interest to quote the authority of the *False Decretals,* and he did not fail to do so" (*Catholic Encyclopedia,* V, 778).

Other popes who used them are: "St." Leo IX (*Catholic Encyclopedia,* V, 778), "St." Gregory VII (*Catholic Encyclopedia,* V, 778), Stephen V (*Catholic Encyclopedia,* V. 778).

Nicholas claimed absolute power (*Catholic Encyclopedia*, V, 779), and Catholics now repeat the fable that the "Emperor led his horse" (*Catholic Encyclopedia*, XI, 54).

"St." Nicholas Lied!

"Yet what is our surprise to find him claiming in support thereof the canons of the Council of Sardica, which say nothing of the sort" (*Catholic Encyclopedia*, V, 779).

Adrian II (867-872)

Adrian had been married and *Catholic Encyclopedia* speaks of a "domestic tragedy in his old age" (I, 56).

He used forgeries (*Catholic Encyclopedia*, V, 778).

John VIII (872-882)

"When he mounted the throne of Peter he found many of the chief offices in the hands of disreputable nobles, most of them connected with one another, and with a number of women as bad as themselves" (*Catholic Encyclopedia*, VIII, 424; III, 729; VI, 140). Among them was Formosas who fled and was excommunicated.

He "excommunicated Formosus from jealousy and a party spirit. . . saw in Formosus a rival whom he gravely suspected" (*Catholic Encyclopedia*, VI, 140).

"His election was opposed by Formosus, who remained in opposition to him throughout the whole of his pontificate" (*Catholic Encyclopedia*, VIII, 423).

Marinus I (882-884)

"Reversed the action of his predecessor regarding Formosus of Porto, whom he absolved from all censure, and permitted to return to Rome" (*Catholic Encyclopedia*, IX, 670).

Adrian III (884-885)

"After the destruction of the Frankish supremacy under Charles the Fat (A.D. 884-887) the neighboring princes took forcible possession of Rome and placed on the pontifical throne men favorable to their personal interests and ambitions" (*History of the Church of God,* B.J. Spalding, 411).

Magic Sacramentals Evidently Did Not Work!

Stephen V or VI (885-891)

". . . famine caused by drought and locusts" (*Catholic Encyclopedia,* XIV, 289).

". . . exposing (at Ravenna) the sandals of Christ to the veneration of the faithful" (*Catholic Encyclopedia,* XIV, 289).

Formosus (891-896)

He had already been excommunicated as a heretic by John VIII, and this action had been reversed by Marinus!

"From Formosus (881-896) to John XIII (965-972) a few Italian despots and corrupt and influential women made a monopoly of the highest dignity of the Church, placed on the pontifical throne their children and their favorites, and plunged the Church of Rome into an abyss of miseries. Of the popes during this period two or three disgraced the Chair of Peter by their personal hatreds and passions, while others, unworthy of the exalted position, were timid and weak; and weakness in high places has been for the Church the most pernicious of crimes" (*History of the Church of God,* B.J. Spalding, 412).

"At one time two notorious women, Theodora and Morozia, seemed influential enough to elevate, remove, and even murder popes at will. Several vicious men occupied the papal throne, notably John XII (955- 965), elevated at the age of eighteen, and Benedict IX (1032-1044), elected at the age of twelve" (*Short History of the Church,* Wedewer and McSorley, 87).

Consensus now favors Formosus (*Catholic Encyclopedia,* VIII, 426).

Boniface VI (896)

Was pope for only fifteen days (*Catholic Encyclopedia,* II, 661).

Stephen VI or VII (896-897)

"Under Stephen VI, the successor of Boniface VI, Emperor Lambert and Agiltrude recovered the authority in Rome at the beginning of 897, having renounced their claim to the greater part of Upper and Central Italy. Agiltrude being determined to wreak vengeance on her opponent even after his death, Stephen VI lent himself to the revolting scene by sitting in judgment on his predecessor Formosus. At the synod convened for that purpose, he occupied the chair; the corpse (of Formosus), clad in papal vestments, was withdrawn from the sacrophagas and seated on a throne; close by stood a deacon to answer in its name, all the old charges formulated against Formosus under John VIII being revived. The decision was that the deceased had been unworthy of the pontificate, which he could not have validly received since he was bishop of another See. All his measures and acts were annulled, and all the orders conferred by him were declared invalid. The papal vestments were torn from his body; the three fingers which the dead pope had used in consecrations were severed from his right hand; and the corpse was cast into a grave in the cemetery for strangers, to be removed after a few days and consigned to the Tiber. In 897 the second successor of Stephen had the body, which a monk had withdrawn from the Tiber, reinterred in St. Peter's. He furthermore annulled at a synod, the decisions of the court of Stephen VI, and declared all orders conferred by Formosus valid" (*Catholic Encyclopedia,* VI, 141).

"Stephen was a Roman, and the son of John, a priest. . .

Whether induced by evil passion, or perhaps more probably compelled by the Emperor Lambert, and his mother Agiltrude, he caused the body of Formosus to be exhumed, and in January, 897, to be placed before an unwilling synod of Roman clergy. A deacon was appointed to answer for the deceased pontiff, who was condemned for performing functions of a bishop when he had been deposed, and for passing from the See of Porto to that of Rome. The corpse was then stripped of its sacred vestments, deprived of two fingers of its right hand, clad in the garb of a layman, and ultimately thrown into the Tiber. Fortunately it was not granted to Stephen to have time to do much else besides this atrocious deed. Before he was put to death by strangulation, he forced several of those who had been ordained by Formosus to resign their offices and granted a few privileges to churches" (*Catholic Encyclopedia,* IV, 289-290).

"Stephen was strangled in prison in the Summer of 897, and the six following popes (to May 904) owed their elevation to the struggles of the political parties. Christopherus, the last of them, was overthrown by Sergius III (May 904-August 911). Sergius had been a partizan of Stephen VI, and like the latter regarded the elevation of Formosus to the papacy as illegal and the orders conferred by him null and void" (*Catholic Encyclopedia,* II, 147).

Romanus (897)

Annulled the excommunication of Formosus by Stephen VI, and recovered the body of Formosus (*Catholic Encyclopedia,* VI, 141).

Romanus was Pope for only four months (*Catholic Encyclopedia,* XIII, 163).

He was deposed and died a monk (*Catholic Encyclopedia,* XIII, 164).

Theodore II (897)

204

"He reinstated in synod the clerics who had been degraded by Stephen VI. . . and formally recognized the validity of the orders conferred by Pope Formosus. He caused the body of the last named pope, which had been thrown into the Tiber and cast ashore by a flood to be reburied in St. Peter's" (*Catholic Encyclopedia*, XIV, 570).

Theodore was pope only twenty days (*Catholic Encyclopedia*, XIV, 570).

John IX (898-900)

John was pope for only a year (*Catholic Encyclopedia*, VIII, 425).

He approved Formosus (*Catholic Encyclopedia*, VIII, 425), pronounced the election of Boniface VI null (*Catholic Encyclopedia*, II, 661) and excommunicated Sergius who later became Pope Sergius III (*Catholic Encyclopedia*, VIII, 425).

Benedict IV (900-903)

"The popes Benedict from the fourth to the ninth inclusive belong to the darkest period of papal history" (*Catholic Encyclopedia*, II, 428).

Benedict IV supported Formosus (*Catholic Encyclopedia*, II, 428).

Leo V (903)

Leo was forcibly dethroned (*Catholic Encyclopedia*, III, 729), and was imprisoned in a monastery where he died (*Catholic Encyclopedia*, IX, 159).

"At this period, however, the darkest ever known in papal Rome, when its barons were making and unmaking popes at their pleasure. . . We can scarcely tell fact from fiction. . . Christopher was driven from the Chair of Peter by his successor Sergius III" (*Catholic Encyclopedia*, III, 719).

How Bad Were the Catholic People?

". . . the monks and the clergy were at all times better than other people" (*Question Box,* 1913 Edition, 150).

Christopher (903-904)

Driven from the popedom and killed by Sergius III (*Catholic Encyclopedia,* III, 729; IX, 159; XIII, 729).

Sergius III (904-911)

Sergius had been excommunicated by John IX (*Catholic Encyclopedia,* VIII, 425).

"According to one authority Sergius took pity on the two imprisoned pontiffs (Leo V and Christopher) and caused them to be put to death" (*Catholic Encyclopedia,* IX, 159; III, 729).

Annulled the acts of Romanus and Formosus (*Catholic Encyclopedia,* VI, 141; III, 729).

Sergius III was father of John XI by illegitimate union with Morozia, one of the most wicked women who ever lived (*Catholic Encyclopedia,* VIII, 426).

Sergius Approved a Fourth Marriage of Emperor, Leo VI!

". . . showed his good sense in declaring valid the fourth marriage of the Greek Emperor, Leo VI" (*Catholic Encyclopedia,* XIII, 729).

Anastasius III (911-913)
Lando (913-914)
John X (914-928)

He was made an archbishop at the age of five years (*Catholic Encyclopedia,* VIII, 425).

He was related to Theodora's family, so she "supported John's election in order to cover more easily her relations with him" (*Catholic Encyclopedia,* VIII, 425).

"But John remained true to the discipline of the Western Church (Roman Catholic—O.C.L.), which permitted as valid even a fourth marriage" (*Catholic Encyclopedia*, VIII, 426).

"The pontiff himself was seized and cast into prison where he died shortly after" (*Catholic Encyclopedia*, VIII, 426).

Leo VI (928)
Stephen VII or VIII (928-931)
John XI (931-936)

Made pope at twenty years of age (*Lives and Times of the Roman Pontiffs*, I, 247).

Illegitimate son of Pope Sergius III and Morozia.

"Through the intrigues of his mother, who ruled at the time in Rome, he was raised to the Chair of Peter and was completely under the influence of the *Senatrix et Patricia* of Rome (Morozia)" (*Catholic Encyclopedia*, VIII, 426).

Leo VIII (936-939)

He expelled the Jews from Rome because they would not embrace Catholicism (*Catholic Encyclopedia*, IX, 160).

Stephen VIII or IX (939-942)
Marinus II (Martin III) (942-946)
Agapetus II (945-955)
John XII (955-964)

He became pope at eighteen (*Catholic Encyclopedia*, VIII, 426).

"A coarse, immoral man, whose life was such that the Lateran was spoken of as a brothel" (*Catholic Encyclopedia*, VIII, 426). He is said to have been perfidious, and was stricken with paralysis in the act of adultery!

"Leo VIII fled, while John XII re-entered Rome, and took bloody vengeance on the leaders of the opposite party. Cardinal Deacon John had his right hand struck off, Bishop Otgar, of Speyer, was scourged, a high Palatine official lost nose and ears" (*Catholic Encyclopedia,* VIII, 427).

The *Catholic Encyclopedia* speaks of the "perfect union of Church and State" during his reign (III, 13).

Leo VIII (963-965)
Benedict V (964)
John XIII (965-972)

John XIII hanged his conspiring enemies (*Catholic Encyclopedia,* VIII, 427).

Benedict VI (973-974)
Benedict VII (974-983)
John XIV (983-984)
Boniface VII (984-985)

He was antipope during the reign of Benedict VII, and about a year later became Pope! (*Catholic Encyclopedia,* H, 661).

Robbed the Catholic treasury (*Catholic Encyclopedia,* II, 661).

Killed Two Popes!

"For more than a year Rome endured this monster, *steeped in the blood of his predecessors.* But the vengeance was terrible. After his sudden death in July 985, due in all probability to violence, the body of Boniface was exposed to the insults of the populace, dragged through the streets of the city, and finally naked and covered with wounds, flung under the statue of Marcus Aurelius, which at that time stood in the Lateran Place. The following morning compassionate clerics removed the corpse and gave it Christian burial" (*Catholic Encyclopedia,* II, 661-662).

He evidently killed Benedict VII and John XIV!

208

Some lists have a John between Boniface VII and John XV, but *Catholic Encyclopedia* says he "never existed" (VIII, 428).

John XV (985-996)

He is first to "canonize" saints (*Catholic Encyclopedia*, VIII, 428), and this is significant, for it was more than nine hundred and fifty years after the Lord's church was established!

Gregory V (996-999)

Gregory was the first German pope (*Catholic Encyclopedia*, VI, 790).

The antipope was deprived "of his nose, ears, eyes and tongue" (*Catholic Encyclopedia*, VI, 790).

John XVI (997-998)
Sylvester II (999-1003)

He was first to introduce Arabic numbers to Europe (Archbishop Spalding's *Miscellanae*, 112). This is disputed by the *New Standard Dictionary of the English language.*

"One of the greatest literati of the Middle Ages was the monk Gerbert, afterwards Pope Sylvester II (Archbishop Spalding's *Miscellanae*, 109).

"He was the first French pope" (*Catholic Encyclopedia*, XIV, 371), and condemned Gregory V, the first German pope (*Catholic Encyclopedia*, VI, 790).

John XVII (1003)

He had been married and had three sons (*Catholic Encyclopedia*, VIII, 429).

John XVIII (1003-1009)

He was the son of a priest and died a monk (*Catholic Encyclopedia,* VIII, 429).

Sergius IV (1009-1012)
Benedict VIII (1012-1024)

He was made pope by force (*Catholic Encyclopedia,* II, 428), and was a brother of his successor (*Catholic Encyclopedia,* VIII, 429).

John XIX (1024-1032)

He was the brother to his predecessor and was elected while still a "layman" (*Catholic Encyclopedia,* VIII, 429).

SOLD INDULGENCES

"He seems to have been the first pope to grant an indulgence in return for alms bestowed" (*Catholic Encyclopedia,* VIII, 429).

Benedict IX (1032-1049)

He was a nephew of the two preceding popes and the succeeding one, and "He was a disgrace to the Chair of Peter . . . of dissolute life" (*Catholic Encyclopedia,* II, 429; IV, 17). He was a "youthful libertine" (*Catholic Encyclopedia,* VI, 791), and was made pope by force (*Catholic Encyclopedia,* II, 428), renounced the popedom and sold it to his uncle, Gregory VI, because he expected to marry. Failing to win the hand of the lady of his choice, he again became a contender, still claiming to be pope. So Benedict IX, Gregory VI and Sylvester III, all claimed to be popes at the same time. All three were deposed and Clement II was elected. Now there were four! (*Catholic Encyclopedia,* IV, 17).

"In 1046, the scandals of preceding elections, in which the Supreme Pontiff had become a prize for rival factions, regardless of what means they employed, led the clergy and the people to leave the nomination to Henry III. Three popes were chosen in this manner" (*Catholic Encyclopedia,* XII, 271).

". . . that stripling" (*Catholic Encyclopedia,* IV, 17).

Sylvester III was "stripped of his sacerdotal rank and shut up in a monastery" (*Catholic Encyclopedia,* IV, 18).

Gregory VI (1045-1046)

"Gregory showed himself to be, if not an *idiota,* at least a man *mirae simplicitatis,* by explaining in straightforward speech his compact with Benedict, and he made no other defence than his good intentions" (*Catholic Encyclopedia,* IV, 18). If he was not an idiot, he was, at least, a simpleton!

He bought the popedom from his nephew, Benedict IX (*Catholic Encyclopedia,* IV, 17-18; VI, 791-793).

Clement II (1046-1047)

He was "unceremoniously appointed by Emperor, Henry III" (*Catholic Encyclopedia,* IV, 18). On the same page, our author speaks of the "tyranny of the Roman Factions." The property of the papacy was "diverted into the hands of the Roman nobility" (*Catholic Encyclopedia,* VI, 792).

At this time "monks were attended in their refectory by women" (*Catholic Encyclopedia,* VI, 792).

Damasus II (1048)

A German, he was pope only twenty-three days, dying of malaria, and was one of the few popes of this era who died a natural death. He used the colossal forgery, *"The False Decretals"* (*Catholic Encyclopedia,* V, 778).

A Warrior Pope!

"St" Leo IX (1049-1054)

"He knew how to make peace, and if necessary, to wield the sword in self defence" (*Catholic Encyclopedia,* IX, 161).

"Before Leo could do anything in the matter of the reform of the Church on which his heart was set, he had first to put down another attempt on the part of the ex-pope, Benedict IX to seize the papal throne. . . he condemned the two notorious evils of the day, simony and clerical incontinence" (*Catholic Encyclopedia,* IX, 161)." . . . vast throngs of simonical and immoral clerics" (*Catholic Encyclopedia,* VI, 790).

Miracle Worker Defeated in War!

Leo "declared war on the Normans" and was defeated. "After the battle of Civitella Leo never recovered his spirits. . . was a broken hearted man." The writer insists, though, that he "was a worker of miracles, both in life and in death" (*Catholic Encyclopedia,* IX, 162).

AT THIS POINT THERE WAS A NOTABLE SCHISM

Victor II (1055-1057)
Stephen IX or X (1057-1058)

Cousin of Leo IX (*Catholic Encyclopedia,* XIV, 290).

Benedict X (1058-1059)

Catholic Encyclopedia skips a Benedict X, except to say that there was an antipope by that name (2, 429).

Nicholas II (1059-1061)

"His elevation was due to violence and corruption" (*Catholic Encyclopedia,* XI, 55).

Alexander II (1061-1073)

Catholic Encyclopedia commends "his helpfulness amid the Roman factions" (I, 286).

Gregory VII (1073-1085)

Hildebrand, before he was made Pope Gregory VII, was a pope-maker for twenty years (*Catholic Encyclopedia,* VI, 792).

"Gregory VII finally prescribed that it (the title Pope) should be confined to the successors of Peter" (*Catholic Encyclopedia,* XII, 270).

He used forgeries (The *"False Decretals"*) freely in support of his presumptuous claims (*Catholic Encyclopedia,* V, 778).

"Gregory VII was the first Roman Pontiff who ever attempted to depose a temporal prince" (Archbishop Spalding in *Miscellanae,* 151).

Medieval Papacy In Action, by Baldwin speaks of the "unheard of step of excommunicating an emperor" (18).

"He (Gregory VII) lived in a gross age, an age of iron, which had nothing in common with our age. So the acts of that age cannot be judged according to our principles and our manners" (*Lives and Times of the Roman Pontiffs,* I, 309).

That is a poor excuse, seeing that Catholics claim the same powers today. The only difference is that the popes are unable to carry out these principles right now. Another important principle is that it is claimed all popes have always been infallible. If it was infallibly right then, it ought to be so now.

Gregory VII Humiliates the Emperor

"Stript of his royal robes; and clad as a penitent, Henry had to come barefooted mid ice and snow, and crave for admission to the presence of the pope. All day he remained at the door of the citadel, fasting and exposed to the inclemency of the wintry weather, but was refused admission. A second and third day he thus humiliated

213

and disciplined himself, and finally on 28 January, 1077, he was received by the Pontiff and absolved from censure, but only on condition that he would appear at the proposed council and submit himself to its decisions" (*Catholic Encyclopedia,* VI, 794).

Gregory then released Henry's subjects from their oath of allegiance to him (*Catholic Encyclopedia,* VI, 794).

Henry got his revenge when four years later he marched on Rome. Gregory fled and died in exile (*Catholic Encyclopedia,* VI, 794).

In demanding that Henry appear before a council, he thus admitted that a council was above a pope!

"He (the Pope) can dispense with any vow, no matter how solemn or sacred" (*Externals of the Catholic Church,* Sullivan, 51).

Victor III (1087)

"Four days after he was elected he fled to his monastery, Monte Cassino, after he put off his pontifical habit. . . it was necessary to pursue him, force him to resume his sacred vestments, and take him back to Rome, where he was kept under guard and consecrated. . . at length attacked while celebrating the council, by a new disease. . . He died at Monte Cassino of a dysentery, caused, it is said, by poison administered by order of king Henry, that malignant enemy of Gregory VII" (*Lives and Times of the Roman Pontiffs,* I, 317).

This story is strikingly similar to another two hundred years later, concerning Celestine V.

Victor III was pope only from May until September (*Catholic Encyclopedia,* XII, 274).

Urban II (1088-1099)

Urban organized the first Crusade (*Catholic Encyclopedia,* IV, 544).

"Preachers of the Crusade appeared everywhere, and on all sides sprang up disorganized, undisciplined, penniless hordes, almost destitute of equipment, who, surging Eastward through the valley of the Danube, plundered as they went along and murdered the Jews in the German cities. . . in Asia Minor they turned to pillage and were nearly all slain by the Turks" (*Catholic Encyclopedia*, IV, 546).

"Christians entered Jerusalem from all sides and slew the inhabitants regardless of age or sex" (*Catholic Encyclopedia*, IV, 547).

The Pope "granted a plenary indulgence to all Crusaders" (*Lives and Times of the Roman Pontiffs*, I, 319).

Urban bolstered his pretended authority with an immense forgery, *"The Donation of Constantine"* (*Catholic Encyclopedia*, V, 121).

Pascal II (1099-1118)
He had a "stormy pontificate" (*Catholic Encyclopedia*, VI, 407).

Gelasius II (1118-1119)
Also stormy, "leaving fifty years of war to his successor" (*Catholic Encyclopedia*, VI, 407).

Callistus II (1119-1124)
Married priests until twelfth century (*Catholic Encyclopedia*, III, 486).

LATERAN COUNCIL 1123

"Henceforth all conjugal relations on the part of the clergy. . . were reduced in the eyes of Canon Law to mere concubinage" (*Catholic Encyclopedia*, III, 486).

Celibacy Not Divine!

"Strange to say, it would be legally possible to select even a married man (to be pope) for *the law of celibacy of the clergy is not of divine institution,* but is a rule of the Church which developed gradually and was finally made a part of the legal code for the greater part of the world" (*Externals of the Catholic Church,* Sullivan, 6).

Honorius II (1124-1130)

His name was Lambert (*Catholic Encyclopedia,* VII, 456; III, 186).

Innocent II (1130-1143)

LATERAN COUNCIL 1139

Effort to destroy the Albigenses

Celestine II (1143-1144)

He was Pope only seven months.

Lucius II (1144-1145)

He was Pope only eleven months.

Eugene III (1145-1153)
Anastasius IV (1153-1154)

He was Pope for a little more than a year.

Adrian IV (1154-1159)

He was an Englishman (*Catholic Encyclopedia,* I, 157).

Granted Indulgences for Killing!

"The Pope granted indulgences to all who carried on this pious work" (*The Inquisition,* Vacandard, 43).

Alexander III (1159-1181)

"Romans pursued his remains with curses and stones" (*Catholic Encyclopedia,* I, 287).

Similar treatment was accorded to Pius IX, seven hundred years later (*Catholic Encyclopedia,* I, 287).

Released the subjects of Otto from their oath of allegiance (*Catholic Encyclopedia,* I, 287).

Approved as authentic the great forgery, "The False Decretals" (*General Legislation in the New Code*, Ayrinhac, 34).

He passed 3,939 decrees (*General Legislation in the New Code,* Ayrinhac, 42).

"The Third Council of Lateran (1179) was convened by Alexander III, one of the greatest pontiffs of the Middle Ages" (Archbishop Spalding's *Miscellanae,* 121).

Made war on the Waldenses.

Lucius III (1181-1185)

First burning of heretics (Synod of Verona, 1184). "Heretics" handed over to the secular power (*Catholic Encyclopedia,* VII, 260; *The Inquisition,* Vacandard, 83).

Urban III (1185-1187)

". . . inherited a legacy of feud" (*Catholic Encyclopedia,* XV, 211).

Gregory VIII (1187)

Was Pope only two months.

Clement III (1187-1191)
Celestine II (1191-1198)

Was deceived (*Catholic Encyclopedia,* III, 479).

Innocent III (1198-1216)

Most powerful pope, who claimed that conferring the imperial crown belonged to the pope alone. His "decretals" were later incorporated into Canon Law (*Catholic Encyclopedia,* VIII, 14-15).

Caused many bloody wars against "heretics," and declared the "Magna Charta" null, and excommunicated the barons who forced King John to sign the "Magna Charta" (*Catholic Encyclopedia,* VIII, 15).

"He called upon France for an army to suppress the Albigenses. Under the leadership of Simon de Montfort a cruel campaign ensued, which despite the protests of Innocent, soon turned into a war of conquest. The culminating point of the glorious reign of Innocent III was the convocation of the Fourth Lateran Council A.D. 1215" (*Catholic Encyclopedia,* VIII, 15).

This council decreed the burning of heretics (*Catholic Encyclopedia,* VII, 260).

Cardinal's red hat means that he will shed blood (*Teachings of the Catholic Church,* Smith, 138).

From the time of Innocent III the popes style themselves "The Vicar of Christ" (*Catholic Encyclopedia,* XV, 403).

"Alexander III is said to have issued thirty-nine hundred and thirty-nine decrees, and Innocent III over five thousand" (*General Legislation in the New Code,* Ayrinhac, 42).

Innocent III also used the great forgery *"The Donation of Constantine"* (*Catholic Encyclopedia,* V, 121).

Decreed annual confession and communion for Catholics.

Innocent admits that Crusaders spared neither age nor sex, and that they were adulterers with wives, widows and nuns (*Lives and Times of the Roman Pontiffs,* I, 383).

Arnold of Bressia.

"The date before us prove that the Church forgot her early tradition of toleration, and borrowed from Roman jurisprudence (pagan), revived by the legalists, laws and practices which remind one of the cruelty of ancient paganism" (*The Inquisition,* Vacandard, 113).

"It is therefore proved beyond question that the Church, in the person of the popes, used every means at her disposal, especially excommunication, to compel the state to enforce the infliction of the death penalty upon heretics. The excommunication, moreover, was all the more dreaded, because, according to the Canons, the one excommunicated (civil ruler) unless absolved from the censure, was regarded as a heretic himself within a year's time, and was liable therefore to the death penalty" (*The Inquisition,* Vacandard, 105).

Disrespect for Innocent III After Death!

"On the night he died Innocent's body was left through carelessness unwatched, and thieves broke in and robbed the dead man of the vestments that clothed him, so that on the next morning the corpse of the chief shepherd of Christendom was found almost naked" (*Pope Innocent III and His Times,* 192).

A National Disgrace!

A plaque of Innocent III, and another for his nephew, Gregory IX, are in the House Chamber in the Capitol in Washington! These are two of the most un-democratic, the most blood-thirsty and tyrannical of all the popes!

Honorius III (1216-1227)
Gregory IX (1227-1241)

He was nephew of Innocent III (*Catholic Encyclopedia,* VI, 796).

219

He used the forgery, "The Donation of Constantine" (*Catholic Encyclopedia,* V, 121).

He substituted the penalty of death at the stake for banishment (*The Inquisition,* Vacandard, 77).

"Finally in the fourth year of his pontificate, and undoubtedly after mature deliberation, he decided to compel princes and podesta to enforce the law condemning heretics to the stake" (*The Inquisition,* Vacandard, 133).

He made Dominicans and Franciscans inquisitors (*The Inquisition,* 121).

"Gregory IX had maintained (1232, 1236), in the conflict with the Greeks and with Frederick II, that Constantine the Great had given temporal power to the popes (an admitted forgery) and that emperors and kings were only auxiliaries bound to use the material sword at his direction" (*Catholic Encyclopedia,* II, 667).

The Council of Toulouse (1229) forbad the laity to read the Bible (*Catholic Dictionary,* Addis and Arnold, 82).

Pius IV more than three hundred years later re-affirmed the same.

Celestine IV (1241)

He was Pope only a few days.

Innocent IV (1243-1254)

"The Church is also responsible for having introduced torture (of witnesses) into the proceedings of the Inquisition. This cruel practice was introduced by Innocent IV in 1252" (*The Inquisition,* 147).

The "Bull Extirpanda" condemned "heretics" to death, and "was to be inscribed in perpetuity in all the local statute books. Any attempt to modify it was a crime, which condemned the offender to perpetual infamy, and a fine enforced by the ban" (*The*

Inquisition, 145).

Alexander IV (1254-1261)

"The unity of Christendom was a thing of the past" (*Catholic Encyclopedia,* I, 288.)

Urban IV (1261-1264)

"He (the pope) can dispense with any vow, no matter how solemn or sacred" (Externals of the Catholic Church, 5).

"He absolved the king from his promise to observe the provisions of Oxford" (*Catholic Encyclopedia,* XV, 214).

Two Parties—Guelphs and Ghibellines

"He aroused dissensions between rival Ghibelline cities, and, by an adroit use of the then generally acknowledged right of the Holy See to declare null all obligations toward persons excommunicated, was able to throw their commercial affairs into confusion" (*Catholic Encyclopedia,* XV, 213).

"Popes were found on the side of the Guelphs" (Archbishop Spalding's *Miscellanae,* 144).

Clement IV (1265-1268)

He was a Bishop of Rome who never saw Rome (*Catholic Encyclopedia,* IV, 19).

Clement was married and had two daughters (*Catholic Encyclpedia,* IV, 19).

"Papal legates and mendicant friars appeared on the scene, preaching the formal crusade, with the amplest indulgences and most lavish promises" (*Catholic Encyclopedia,* IV, 19).

Quarrels among Cardinals delayed the selection of Clement's successor for nearly three years (*Catholic Encyclopedia,* II, 650; IV, 20).

Catholic Church was headless for nearly three years. But that is no more strange than having four heads at the same time!

"St." Thomas and "St." Bonaventure Contemporaries
"St." Gregory X (1271-1276)

Thomas Aquinas died in 1274.

COUNCIL OF LYONS 1274

"St." Bonaventure was poisoned and died during the Council. Catholic writers claim he was exhumed one hundred and sixty years later and that his head was "in a perfect state of preservation, his tongue being as red as in life" (*Catholic Encyclopedia,* II, 650).

Innocent V (1276)

He was Pope only six months (*Catholic Encyclopedia,* XII, 274).

". . . his policy was peaceable" (*Catholic Encyclopedia,* VIII, 18).

Adrian V (1276)

He was Pope only one month (*Catholic Encyclopedia,* XII, 274).

John XXI (1276-1277)

"Nay acquiescence in the fable (Popess Joan) induced John XX to style himself John XXI" (*Catholic Dictionary,* Addis and Arnold, 870).

He was Pope only eight months (*Catholic Encyclopedia,* XII, 274).

Before he was elected disturbance broke out in the town" (*Catholic Encyclopedia,* VIII, 430).

The One Hundred and Twenty-five =
Sacramentals Didn't Work!

"On 14 May, 1277, while the Pope was alone in his apartment, it collapsed; John was buried under the ruins, and died on 20 May in consequence of the serious injuries he had received" (*Catholic Encyclopedia,* VIII, 431).

Nicholas III (1277-1280)
First to call himself "Vicar of God" (*Catholic Encyclopedia,* XV, 403).

Martin IV (1281-1285)
"The awful massacre of 31 March, 1282, known as the *Sicilian Vespers,* had precluded every possibility of coming to an amicable understanding with Martin IV, a Frenchman who owed the tiara to Charles of Anjou. Pope Martin. . . demanded unconditional submission to Charles of Anjou and the Apostolic See and, when this was refused, put Sicily and Pedro III under the ban, deprived Pedro of the kingdom of Aragon, and gave it to Charles of Valois, the son of King Philip III of France" (*Catholic Encyclopedia,* VII, 459).

Honorius IV (1285-1287)
"Removed the interdict which had been imprudently placed upon Venice by Martin IV" (*Catholic Encyclopedia,* VII, 460).

Nicholas IV (1288-1292)
After his demise the Catholic Church was headless for nearly three years.

"St." Celestine V (1294)
He was Pope only five months (*Catholic Encyclopedia,* XII, 274).

His was very similar case to that of Victor III 1087 (See p. 150).

He was said to be a "simple old man" (*Catholic Encyclopedia,* III, 480).

"Saintly, but wholly incompetent hermit-pope Celestine V. . . inexperienced and simple-minded" (*Catholic Encyclopedia,* II, 662).

"It is wonderful how many serious mistakes the simple old man crowded into five short months. We have no full register of them, because his official acts were annulled by his successor" (*Catholic Encyclopedia,* III, 480).

One mistake, so *Catholic Encyclopedia* states, was by "renewing the rigorous laws of Gregory X regulating the conclave, which Adrian V had suspended. . . He granted the same place or benefice to three or four rival suitors" (*Catholic Encyclopedia,* III, 480).

He was deceived (*Catholic Encyclopedia,* III, 479).

"Boniface VIII, therefore before leaving Naples, ordered Celestine V to be taken to Rome in the custody of the Abbot of Monte Cassino. On their way thither the saint escaped and returned to his hermitage near Sulmona. Apprehended again, he fled a second time, and after weary weeks of roaming through the woods of Apulia reached the sea and embarked on board a vessel about to sail for Dalmatia. But a storm cast the luckless fugitive ashore at Viesta in Capatanata, where the authorities recognized and detained him. He was brought before Boniface in his palace at Anagni, kept in custody there for some time, and finally transferred to the strong castle of Fumore at Ferentino. Here he remained until his death ten months later, 19 May, 1296. The detention of Celestine was a simple measure of prudence for which Boniface deserves no censure; but the rigorous treatment to which the old man of over eighty years was subjected—whoever may have been responsible for it— will not be easily condoned. Of this treatment there can now no longer be any question. The place wherein Celestine was confined was so narrow 'that the spot whereon the saint stood when saying Mass was the same whereon his head lay when he reclined'" (*Catholic Encyclopedia*, II, 662).

All his misfortunes may have been due to "the designing Cardinal Gaetani" (Boniface VIII) (*Catholic Encyclopedia*, II, 662).

Boniface VIII (1294-1303)

He is said to have been "designing" (*Catholic Encyclopedia*, II, 662).

". . . the boldest asserter of papal supremacy" (*Catholic Encyclopedia*, III, 703).

Bull Unam Sanctam Represented Intolerable Arrogance

"Boniface VIII seemed exceptionally well qualified to maintain inviolate the rights and privileges of the papacy as they had been handed down to him. But he failed either to recognize the altered temper of the times, or to gauge accurately the strength of the forces arrayed against him; and when he attempted to exercise his supreme authority in temporal affairs as in spiritual, over princes and people, he met almost everywhere with a determined resistance. His aim of universal peace and Christian coalition against the Turks were not realized; and during the nine years of his troubled reign he scarcely ever achieved a decisive triumph. Though certainly one of the most remarkable pontiffs that ever occupied the papal throne, Boniface VIII was also one of the most unfortunate. His pontificate marks in history the decline of the Medieval power and glory of the papacy" (*Catholic Encyclopedia*, II, 663).

"The second crown in the papal tiara, indicative of the temporal power, is said to date from the reign of Boniface, and may have been added at this time" (*Catholic Encyclopedia*, II, 666).

Bonifaces Infamous Bull Ausculta Fili (Listen O Son!)

". . . he stood forth as the mouthpiece of the medieval papacy, and as the genuine successor of the Gregories and the Innocents. In it he appeals to the king to listen to the Vicar of Christ, who is *placed over kings and kingdoms* (cf. Jer. 1:10). He is *the keeper of the keys, the judge of the living and the dead,* and sits on the throne of justice, with *power to extirpate all iniquity.* He is the head of the Church, which is one and stainless, and not a many-headed monster, and *has full divine authority* to pluck out and tear down, to build up and plant. Let not the king imagine that he has no superior, is not subject to the highest authority in the Church" (*Catholic Encyclopedia,* II, 666).

". . . with the approval of the Cardinals, the new Pope immediately revoked (Dec. 27, 1294) all the extraordinary favors and privileges which in the fulness of simplicity Celestine V had had distributed with such reckless prodigality" (*Catholic Encyclopedia,* II, 662).

UNAM SANCTAM
All of Us under the Pope NOW!

"The dogmatic definition contained in the Bull IS THE DOCTRINE NECESSARILY HELD BY EVERY CATHOLIC, namely, that BY DIVINE LAW ALL MEN ARE SUBJECT TO THE JURISDICTION OF ST. PETER AND HIS SUCCESSORS THE ROMAN PONTIFFS" (Capitals for emphasis—O.C.L.) (*Short History of the Catholic Church,* Wedewer and McSorley, 103.) This is from a book copyrighted in 1916 and used to teach Catholic children in the United States that the offensive doctrine of Boniface VIII is still universally held by all Catholics!

"As the Church went on scattering broadcast her blessings, grateful nations gradually clothed her with an almost unlimited power, even in temporal matters; and thus the Middle Ages show us the papacy controlling kings and people, not by any usurpation of power, but by a necessary consequence, and as if by the very logic of events" (*General History of the Church,* Darras, II, 2).

Benedict XI (1303-1304)

He was poisoned (*Catholic Encyclopedia,* II, 429).

Clement V (1305-1314)

It took the conclave eleven months to elect him (*Catholic Encyclopedia,* IV, 20).

"Confusion and anarchy were prevalent, owing to the implacable mutual hatred of the Colonna and the Orsini, the traditional turbulence of the Romans, and the frequent angry conflicts between the people and the nobles, conditions that had been growing worse all through the thirteenth century and had eventually driven even the Italian popes to such outside strongholds as Viterbo, Anagne, Orvieto, and Perugia" (*Catholic Encyclopedia,* IV, 20).

"Clement V freed King Edward of England of the obligation of keeping his promise" (*Catholic Encyclopedia,* IV, 23).

He burned many Knights Templars (*Catholic Encyclopedia,* V, 22).

"His reign was an uninterrupted secession of blunders" (*History of the Church of God,* B.J. Spalding, 435).

"Clement V himself and the ecclesiastical judges were both unfortunately guilty of truckling in the whole affair. But their unjust condemnation was due chiefly to the king's desire to confiscate their great possessions" (*The Inquisition,* 136).

COUNCIL OF VIENNA 1311

Made immersion "obsolete" and substituted pouring.

The Pope Advocated Marriage for Priests

"A memoir drawn up at the pope's request (Clement V) by

William Durand, Bishop of Mende gives an appalling picture of the state of the Church. He mentions particularly the want of all observance in monastic orders, the immorality of the monks and clergy, the veniality of the Roman Court, the way in which benefices were kept vacant, etc. He pleads for reform in the Curia and among the clergy, and proposes that priests should be allowed to marry" (*Catholic Dictionary,* Addis and Arnold, 822).

"All celibates are not chaste; celibacy is not necessarily chastity, by a large majority. Unless something other than selfishness suggests this sort of life, the word is apt to be a misnomer for profligacy. And one who takes the vow of celibacy does not break it by sinning against the sixth commandment (adultery); he is true to it until he weds" (*Explanation of Catholic Morals,* Sullivan, 149).

John XXII (1316-1334)

There were two violent factions. "For this reason he found himself involved in grievous disputes which lasted throughout the greater portion of his pontificate. Great difficulties were also raised for the Pope by the controversies among the Franciscans, which Clement V had tried in vain to settle. . . much disorder" (*Catholic Encyclopedia,* VIII, 431).

A straw image of the pope was publicly burned in Rome (*Catholic Encyclopedia,* VIII, 432).

He lied about the *Clementines* (decrees) of Clement V, pretending that they were decrees of the Council of Vienna (*Disciplinary Decrees of the General Councils,* Schroeder, 372).

"Political conditions in Germany and Italy moved the Pope to assert over the latter far reaching political claims, and similarly with regard to the German crown, because of the latter's union with the imperial office. On this score a violent quarrel broke out between the Pope and King Louis of Bavaria" (*Catholic Encyclopedia,* VIII, 431).

JOHN XXII A HERETIC

"In the last years of John's pontificate there arose a dogmatic conflict about the 'Beatific Vision,' which was brought on by himself, and which his enemies made use of to discredit him. Before his elevation to the Holy See, he had written a book on the question, in which he stated that the souls of the blessed departed do not see God until after the Last Judgment. After becoming Pope he advanced the same teaching in his sermons. In this he met with strong opposition, many theologians, who adhered to the usual opinion that the blessed departed did see God before the resurrection of the body and the Last Judgment, even calling his views heretical. A great commotion was aroused in the University of Paris when the General of the Minorities, and a Dominican tried to disseminate there the Pope's view. Pope John wrote to King Philip IV on the matter (Nov., 1333), and emphasized the fact that as long as the Holy See had not given a decision, the theologians enjoyed perfect freedom in the matter. In December 1333, the theologians of Paris, after a consultation on the question, decided in favor of the doctrine that the souls of the blessed departed saw God immediately after death, or after the complete purification; at the same time they pointed out that the Pope had given no decision on the question but only his personal opinion, and now petitioned the Pope to confirm their decision. John appointed a commission at Avignon to study the writings of the fathers, and to discuss further the disputed question. In a consistory held on 3 January, 1334, the Pope explicitly declared that he had never meant to teach aught contrary to the Holy Scriptures or the rule of faith, and in fact had not intended to give any decision whatever. Before his death he withdrew his former opinion and declared his belief that souls separated from their bodies enjoyed in heaven the Beatific Vision" (*Catholic Encyclopedia,* VIII, 432-433).

". . . revenues grew very meager. . . Pope John on the other hand, had need of large revenues, not only for the maintenance for his court, but particularly for the wars in Italy" (*Catholic Encyclopedia,* VIII, 433).

"Still there can be no doubt that during the fourteenth century certain Papal Constitutions of John XXII and Benedict XII did very much to stimulate the persecution by the Inquisition of witches and others engaged in magical practice especially in the South of France" (*Catholic Encyclopedia,* XV, 676).

He published the "Clementines" as the official Corpus Juris Canonici (*Catholic Encyclopedia,* VIII, 433).

Benedict XII (1334-1342)

"He revoked the scandalous 'expectancies' granted by his predecessor (*Catholic Encyclopedia,* II, 430).

Benedict "distracted Italy" but was "no match for the kings and their allies" (*Catholic Encyclopedia,* II, 430-431).

The Pope's Three Crowns

"The original tiara consisting of a plain, helmet-like cap, of white material, and was provided with its first circlet about 1130, the second being added during the pontificate of Boniface VIII (1294-1303), while the earlier representation of the tiara with three crowns is found on the effigy of Benedict XII (died 1342). The first circlet symbolizes the pope's universal episcopate, second his supremacy or jurisdiction, and the third his temporal influence. . . father of princes and kings, ruler of the world, Vicar of Our Saviour Jesus Christ" (*New Catholic Dictionary,* Vatican Edition, 955).

Clement VI (1342-1352)

He lived in France.

Black death, or the "Great Pestilence" killed one third of the people of Europe, in spite of the hundreds of "magical" things invented by the popes (*Catholic Encyclopedia,* IV, 24).

Clement VI practiced "gross nepotism" (*Catholic Encyclopedia*, IV, 24).

He allowed the King of France to have communion with both bread and wine (*Catholic Encyclopedia*, IV, 23).

Innocent VI (1352-1362)
He also lived in France.

Urban V (1362-1370)
THE GREAT WESTERN SCHISM

Bishops of Rome lived in France from 1316 to 1375. The head for a long time was a considerable distance from the body!

Gregory XI (1370-1378)
He was nephew of Clement VI, and made Cardinal at Eighteen (*Catholic Encyclopedia*, VI, 799).

This was a period of "turbulent affairs in Italy" (*Catholic Encyclopedia*, VI, 799).

Catholics Do Not Know Who Was Pope!

Urban VI (1378-1389)
"It is very different in the Great Schism of the fourteenth century. For forty years, two and even three pretenders to the papacy claimed the allegiance of the Catholics: whole countries, learned men and canonized saints, ranged themselves on different sides, and even now it is not perhaps absolutely certain who was pope and who was anti-pope" (*Catholic Dictionary*, Addis and Arnold, 869).

"A final and quite recent argument comes from Rome. In 1904 'Gerarchia Cattolica,' basing its arguments on the date of the *Liber Pontificalia*, compiled a new and corrected list of the sovereign pontiffs. Ten names have disappeared from the list of the legitimate popes, neither the popes of Avignon nor those of Pisa being ranked in the true lineage of St. Peter. If this deliberate omission is not proof positive, it is at least a very strong presumption in favor of the legitimacy of the Roman popes Urban VI, Boniface IX, Innocent VII and Gregory XII (*Catholic Encyclopedia*, XIII, 541).

". . . his whole reign was a series of misadventures. . . his capricious ways. . . Urban's inconsiderate behaviour. . . he acted very unwisely. . . he insulted the ambassadors. . . However the tempest which broke out at Fondi in September of the same year, was already brewing at Rome a few weeks after his election. . . Soon he quarreled with the sacred college. . . Cardinals. . . put to death. . . inconsistent and quarrelsome" (*Catholic Encyclopedia*, XV, 216-217).

He was poisoned by the Romans (*Catholic Encyclopedia*, XV, 216).

"Unfortunately Pope Urban did not realize the hopes to which his election had given rise. He showed himself whimsical, haughty, suspicious and sometimes choleric in his relations with the Cardinals who had elected him. Too obvious roughness and blamable extravagance seemed to show that his unexpected election had altered his character" (*Catholic Encyclopedia*, XIII, 539).

"Christendom was quickly divided into two almost equal parties. Everywhere the faithful faced the anxious problem: where is the true pope? Saints themselves were divided" (*Catholic Encyclopedia*, XIII, 539).

"So great was the confusion that saints and theologians are to be found on either side" (*Short History of the Catholic Church*, Wedewer and McSorley, 123).

"Men's minds and consciences were unsettled, and their faith sought in vain to determine with certainty which of the two contestants was the successor of Peter" (*History of the Church of God*, Spalding, 480).

"All were ready to admit the authority of the legitimate pope if they could only be certain which one had the lawful succession" (*Question Box,* 1913 Edition, 147).

"After many conferences, projects, discussions (oftentimes violent), interventions of the civil powers, catastrophes of all kinds, the Council of Constance (1414) deposed the suspicious John XXIII, received the abdication of the gentle and timid Gregory XII, and finally dismissed the obstinate Benedict XIII. On 11 November, 1417, the assembly elected Odo Colonna who took the name of Martin V. This ended the Great Schism of the West" (*Catholic Encyclopedia,* XIII, 540).

Boniface IX (1389-1404)

He had been excommunicated by Clement VII (*Catholic Encyclopedia,* II, 671).

He lacked good theological training (*Catholic Encyclopedia,* II, 670). He was deposed.

Burning at the Stake Not Cruel!

". . . there was nothing exceptionally cruel or intolerant about the statute *'De haeretico comburendo'* of 1401, which provided that heretics convicted before a spiritual court, and refusing to recant were to be handed over to the secular arm and burnt" (*Catholic Encyclopedia,* V, 441).

Innocent VII (1404-1406)
Gregory XII (1406-1416)

His successor, Alexander V helped to declare him a heretic (*Catholic Encyclopedia,* I, 28).

He lied (*Catholic Encyclopedia,* VII, I) and perjured himself (*Catholic Encyclopedia,* VII, 1).

Deposed by the Council of Constance (*Catholic Encyclopedia,* VII, 1; VIII, 434).

Alexander V (1409-1410)

It is not known if he were a true pope (*Catholic Encyclopedia,* I, 289).

COUNCIL OF PISA 1409

Bellarmine declared it oecumenical (*Catholic Dictionary,* Addis and Arnold, 663).

Archbishop Spalding uncertain (*Miscellanae,* 182).

The Council of Constance (1414-1418) condemned Wycliffe and Huss as heretics, deposed three popes and elected another!

John XXIII listed as a true pope in *Catholic Encyclopedia* list of popes. He called the Council of Constance.

Martin V (1417-1431)

Martin V and Eugene IV approved these councils which made the council superior to the pope! (*Constitutions of the Church,* Ayrinhac, 39-40). So did Pius II (Ibid.).

Eugene IV (1431-1447)

COUNCIL OF BASLE 1431

COUNCIL OF FLORENCE 1439

Declared the supremacy of the Roman bishop over the whole world (*Catholic Facts,* 54).

Nicholas V (1447-1455)

Nicholas was a humanist (*Catholic Encyclopedia,* VII, 539).

PRINTING PRESS INVENTED

"His (Nicholas V) immediate predecessor had held the humanists in suspicion; Nicholas welcomed them to the Vatican as friends. Carried away by his enthusiasm for the New Learning, he overlooked any irregularities in their morals and opinions. He accepted the dedication of a work by Poggio, in which Eugene was assailed as a hypocrite; Valla, the Voltaire of the Renaissance, was made an Apostolic Notary" (*Catholic Encyclopedia*, XI, 59).

"Vast multitudes flocked to Rome (1450) in the first part of the year; but when the hot weather began, the plague which had been ravaging the countries North of the Alps wrought fearful havoc among the pilgrims. Nicholas was seized with a panic; he hurried away from the doomed city and fled from castle to castle in hope of escaping infection. As soon as the pestilence abated he returned to Rome" (*Catholic Encyclopedia*, XI, 59).

"More than two hundred pilgrims lost their lives in a crush which occurred on the bridge of "Saint" Angelo a few days before Christmas" (*Catholic Encyclopedia*, XI, 59).

Nicholas "founded the Vatican Library" (*Catholic Encyclopedia*, XII, 766).

Callistus III (1455-1458)

He was the uncle of Alexander VI (*Catholic Encyclopedia*, I, 289).

Pius II (1458-1464)

He was a humanist and prepared the way for humanism before becoming pope (*Catholic Encyclopedia*, VI, 499).

Before becoming pope he was "the apostle of the new movement" (humanism) in the court of Frederick III (*Catholic Encyclopedia*, VII, 540).

"It is true that Aeneas Sylvius (Pius II) was chief abreviator at the schismatical Synod of Basle, which fought Pope Eugenius IV (1431-1447) and maintained the superiority of the General Council over the pope. He also for a time entered the service of the anti-Pope Felix V. It is true that his private life as a layman, was not above reproach, and that he wrote many a page in the spirit of the

235

pagan renaissance" (*Question Box,* 1929 Edition, 163).

He approved the Council of Constance which claimed to be above the pope (*Constitutions of the Church,* Ayrinhac, 39-40).

"In the renaissance, religion, also, was subordinated to the dictation of astrology" (*Catholic Encyclopedia,* II, 22).

"The renaissance looked up to beauty, and looked away from duty" (*Catholic Encyclopedia,* XII, 767).

Paul II (1464-1471)
Sixtus IV (1471-1484)

He was the uncle of Julius II, and was an astrologer (*Catholic Encyclopedia,* II, 22).

The Rosary was invented at this time by Alan de Rupe, a Dominican, who forged documents to make it appear that "St." Dominic had been authorized by the Virgin Mary to have a Rosary, two hundred and fifty years before (*Catholic Encyclopedia,* XIII, 184).

LUTHER WAS BORN 1483

Superstitious and Ignorant

Innocent VIII (1484-1492)

By his Bull, *"Summis Desiderantes,"* Dec. 5, 1484, he declared that men and women could have immoral relations with demons, sorcerers, could injure harvests, orchards and fields (*The Inquisition,* Vacandard, 146).

He "complained of the folly of ecclesiastics and laymen who opposed the Inquisition in the prosecution of heretical sorcerers." This author states that the Catholic Church burned thirty thousand "witches" in one hundred and fifty years (*The Inquisition,* 199).

Innocent (?) had many illegitimate children and sold offices to the highest bidders (*Catholic Encyclopedia,* VIII, 19).

Alexander VI (1492-1503)

Catholic writers describe him as the worst pope. He had many illegitimate children by several women, four infamous ones by one woman. After he became pope he acknowledged this woman as his concubine and her four children as his. He made his eighteen year old son, Caesar, archbishop two weeks after becoming pope, and made him Cardinal the next year! His daughter married several times and her husbands were not dead. There was "General rejoicing" when Alexander became Pope (*Catholic Encyclopedia,* I, 289-293).

Alexander was the "nephew" of Callistus III, and great grandfather of "St." Francis Borgia (*Catholic Encyclopedia,* VI, 213, I, 289-293).

LUTHER ENTERED THE UNIVERSITY AT ERFORT 1501

Alexander VI burned Savanarola.

Pius III (1503)

He was Pope less than one month (*Catholic Encyclopedia,* XII, 274).

Julius II (1503-1513)

He had three illegitimate daughters and bribed the Cardinals for the office (*Catholic Encyclopedia,* VIII, 562).

LUTHER ENTERED THE MONASTERY 1505

LUTHER BECAME A PRIEST 1507—WENT TO ROME 1510 OR 1511

Julius II was an astrologer (*Catholic Encyclopedia,* II, 22).

LATERAN COUNCIL 1512-1517

Leo X (1513-1521)

"From Leo X his age received its title—he was 'the incarnation of Renaissance in its most brilliant form'" (*Catholic Encyclopedia,*

XII, 766).

"The pope was either unwilling or not in a position to regulate the unworthy and immoral conduct of many of the Roman courtiers" (*Catholic Encyclopedia,* IX, 165).

"Luther's attack occasioned the correction of many real abuses which he pointed out" (*Short History of the Catholic Church,* Wedewer and McSorley, 183).

"There had been for some time abuses in the form of dispensing and preaching indulgences; pious bishops had pointed them out and statesmen had protested against them. Tetzel did not altogether avoid abuses, and later the papal legate, Militz, sharply rebuked him for his indiscretions" (*History of the Church of God,* Spalding, 506).

"Various popes from Gregory VII in the eleventh century to Leo X in the sixteenth, and many councils (Second Lateran, A.D. 1139; First of Lyons, A.D. 1245; Vienna, A.D. 1311, and Trent, A.D. 1545-1563) have condemned these abuses. The Council of Trent (Sess. XXV): 'Being desirious that the abuses which have crept in, and by occasion of which the excellent name of indulgences is blasphemed by heretics, be amended and corrected ordains. . . that *all evil gains* for the obtaining thereof—whence a most prolific cause of abuses among the Christian people has been derived—be *wholly abolished*'" (*Question Box,* 1913 Edition, 412).

Of Luther the Catholic Encyclopedia says:

"The immediate cause was bound up with the odious greed for money displayed by the Roman Curia and shows how far short all efforts at reform had hitherto fallen" (IX, 166). Leo was "deceitful, dissimulating. . . double-faced methods," "double-dealing" (IX, 165-166). . . reckless extravagance. . . quite worldly" (IX, 160, 162).

Leo X was an astrologer (*Catholic Encyclopedia,* II, 22).

LUTHER STARTED HIS REVOLT IN 1517

Leo chose Cardinals on account of the large sums of money advanced (*Catholic Encyclopedia,* IX, 165).

". . . various doubtful and reprehensible methods were resorted to for raising money" (*Catholic Encyclopedia,* IX, 163).

"John Tetzel began to preach in Germany the indulgences proclaimed by Leo X" (*Catholic Encyclopedia,* VII, 258; IX, 166).

Cardinals who conspired to have Leo poisoned were executed (*Catholic Encyclopedia,* IX, 165).

"That Leo, in one of the most serious of all crises which threatened the Church, should fail to prove the proper guide for her, is clear enough from what has been related above" (*Catholic Encyclopedia,* IX, 166).

Terrible Conditions in Catholicism in Luther's Day

"There were not wanting bishops who expressed regret at the early dissolution of the Council (Fifth Lateran, 1512-1517); yet it is difficult to see what would have been the advantage of its continuance. Only a few months later (Oct. 31, 1517) Luther affixed to the castle church door his ninety-five theses. No council, certainly no council with Leo at its head and surrounded by an army of corrupt cardinals and self-interested bishops, could have stemmed the storm of revolt. The evil was too wide spread, and its roots lay too deep to be destroyed over night. Many salutary reform decrees had been enacted by this council of the Lateran, but unfortunately they were not enforced. In the highest ecclesiastical circles there does not appear to have been any real desire for reform. Leo did not hesitate to ignore repeatedly the decrees in the making of which he played a principal role. His Curia remained as worldly as ever. Many bishops instead of recognizing the urgent need of reform in themselves and in the secular clergy, thought of it only with reference to the religious orders, whose privileges were an obstacle to their increasing their sources of revenue. The custom of bestowing ecclesiastical dignities on children continued and, lastly, the curse of pluralism and commendatory benefices remained. It might be added that one of the most flagrant and crying abuses of the time, the traffic in indulgences, did not receive a word of condemnation from the council" (*Disciplinary Decrees of the General Councils,* Schroeder, 486).

Adrian VI (1522-1523)

"Appalling tasks lay before him in the darkest hour of the papacy. To extirpate inveterate abuses; to reform a court which thrived on corruption, and detested the very name of reform. . . Two days later he received the triple crown. History presents no more pathetic figure than that of this noble pontiff, struggling single-handed against insurmountable difficulties. . . His exaggerated acknowledgement that the Roman court had been the fountain head of all the corruption in the Church was eagerly seized upon by the Reformers as a justification of their apostasy" (*Catholic Encyclopedia,* I, 160).

Adrian Ignorant and Superstitious

On July 20, 1522, Adrian issued his Bull, *"Dudam"* against witches (*The Inquisition,* Vacandard, 200).

Clement VII (1523-1534)

He was the illegitimate son of Guiliano Medici (*Catholic Encyclopedia,* X, 121; IV, 24).

He is represented as a very weak and vacillating individual (*Catholic Encyclopedia,* IV, 25).

Clement VII died from eating toadstools (*Strange But True Column,* Brooklyn Tablet, Dec. 14, 1957).

Paul III (1534-1549)

An astrologer (*Catholic Encyclopedia,* II, 22) whose sister was mistress to Alexander VI, which seems to account for his being made a cardinal (*Pastor's History,* V, 416-418; XI, 17).

Paul's grandson entered a league against his grandfather! (*General History of the Church,* Darras, IV, 147-148).

Approved the Jesuits to war against the Protestants (*Externals of the Catholic Church,* 32).

Julius II (1550-1555)

Acknowledged a son and a daughter (Von Ranke, 1,165).

Marcellus II (1555)

He was Pope only twenty-two days (*Catholic Encyclopedia,* XIII, 274; XV, 34). His sister was mother of Robert Bellarmine (*Catholic Encyclopedia,* XV, 34).

Paul IV (1555-1559)

He issued a Bull reestablishing the Inquisition, Apr. 25, 1557.

He is reported to have been a heavy drinker (Von Ranke, I, 196).

Pius IV (1559-1565)

"To meet these evils (reading Protestant versions of the Bible), The Council of Toulouse (1229) and Terragona (1234) forbad the laity to read the vernacular translations of the Bible. Pius IV required the bishops to refuse lay persons leave to read even Catholic versions of the Scriptures unless their confessor or parish priests judged that such reading was likely to prove beneficial" (*Catholic Dictionary,* Addis and Arnold, 82).

"St." Pius V (1566-1572)

This is one of the most interesting periods of Catholic history. Pius was declared a saint by Clement X, one hundred and fifty years after he was Pope. He was the only "saint" in the list of popes for six hundred and nine years. The last "saint" before him was Celestine, admittedly a simpleton. This was A.D. 1294! Now there are only two "saints" among the popes for nearly seven hundred years!

What Kind of Man was Pius V?

From what we are about to reveal, he was about the most determined killer of all the popes!

"About ten years before he was made Pope "His zeal against heresy caused him to be selected as Inquisitor of the faith in Milan and Lombardy, and in 1557, Paul II (IV?) made him a Cardinal and named him Inquisitor General for all Christendom" (*Catholic Encyclopedia,* XII, 130).

"In the Bull *'In Coena Domini'* he proclaimed the traditional principles of the Roman Church and the supremacy of the Holy See over the civil power" (*Catholic Encyclopedia,* XII, 130).

"In the ardour of his faith he did not hesitate to display severity against dissidents when necessary, and to give a new impulse to the activity of the Inquisition, for which he has been blamed by certain historians who have exaggerated his conduct. . . He left the memory of a rare virtue and an unfailing and inflexible integrity" (*Catholic Encyclopedia,* XII, 130-131).

Pius planned the Massacre of St. Bartholomew which was perpetrated on August 24, 1572, but he died about three months before it was executed.

"At the time of the Massacre of St. Bartholomew, Salviati, a relative of Catherine d'Medici, was the Pope's Nuncio at Paris" (*Catholic Encyclopedia,* XIII, 337).

"St." Pius furnished Charles IX with 6,000 troops and wrote Catherine, the king's mother, who was also niece of Pope Clement VII: "If your majesty continues openly and freely to fight the enemies of the Catholic Church unto their utter destruction divine help will never fail you" (*Catholic Encyclopedia,* XIII, 336).

"To establish political peace and religious unity by the royal sword was the inexorable dream of Pius V who must not be judged by our modern standards" (*Catholic Encyclopedia,* XII, 336).

After the Massacre, when the streets ran with blood Gregory VIII said: "'And what I most commend is the resolution taken by his Majesty to exterminate this vermin'. . . Then with all the Cardinals he repaired to the Church of St. Mark for the *Te Deum,* and prayed and ordered prayers that the Most Christian King might rid and purge his entire kingdom of the Huguenot plague. . . On 8 September a procession of thanksgiving took place in Rome, and the Pope, in a prayer after Mass, thanked God for having 'granted the Catholic people a glorious triumph over a perfidious race'. . . Just as the Turks had succumbed at Lepanto, the Protestants had succumbed in France, Gregory XIII ordered a jubilee in celebration of both events and engaged Vasari to paint side by side in one of the Vatican apartments scenes commemorative of the victory of Lepanto and of the triumph of the Most Christian King over the Huguenots. Finally he had a medal struck representing an exterminating angel smiting the Huguenots with his sword, the inscription reading: *Hugonottorum Strages"* (*Catholic Encyclopedia,* XIH, 337).

Pius excommunicated Elizabeth I of England, even though she had never been a member of the Catholic Church, and "absolved" all the English from her allegiance and gave England to Phillip II of Spain. He also entered into partnership with Phillip to build the Spanish Armada, the greatest navy ever conceived up to that time for the purpose of invading England, overthrowing the government, assassinating Elizabeth and forcing the people of England back into the Catholic Church! It was sixteen years after the death of Pius that the disastrous attempt was made. The Armada was destroyed, leaving Elizabeth mistress of the seas. Elizabeth was still queen thirty-one years after Pius was dead!

Pius also sent swarms of Jesuits into England in disguise with the commission to assassinate the queen and help to overthrow the government!

Gregory XIII (1572-1585)

Gregory was an adulterer with an illegitimate son (*Catholic Encyclopedia*, VII, 2, 3).

He is praised by Catholics for having reformed the calendar, though they admit his had errors also. He it was who rejoiced so greatly over the Massacre of St. Bartholomew.

Sixtus V (1585-1590)

Pius V had used Jesuits in a tremendous way, but for some reason Gregory XIII and Sixtus V had trouble with them.

Did Jesuits Kill Sixtus V?

"Finally Sixtus V, who had always been unfriendly to the society (Jesuits), determined to change it completely. The Emperor Ferdinand implored him not to act; the College of Cardinals resisted; but the Pope was obstinate. The Bull was prepared, and Acquaviva (General of the Jesuits—the Black Pope) himself was compelled to send in a personal request to have even its name changed, when the death of the pontiff saved the situation—a coincidence which gave rise to accusations against the Society. His successor, Gregory XIV, hastened to renew all the former privileges of the Order and to confirm its previous approbations" (*Catholic Encyclopedia*, I, 109).

A great fight was being waged for and against the Jesuits. Sixtus V excommunicated Robert Bellarmine, a high ranking Jesuit, but after about two years Bellarmine became the right hand of Pope Clement VIII. A "heretic" in two years became the main support of the Pope, who was at that time a Jesuit. Nearly four hundred years later Robert Bellarmine was enrolled among the Catholic saints!

Sixtus increased the number and price of salable offices!

244

(*Catholic Encyclopedia,* II, 411).

Sixtus not only excommunicated Robert Bellarmine, but placed his books on the Index of Forbidden Books. Of his chief work, *"De Controversus" Catholic Encyclopedia* says: ". . . nor has it even yet been superseded as a classical book on the subject matter, though as was to be expected, the progress of criticism has impaired the value of some of the historical arguments" (*Catholic Encyclopedia,* II, 411).

Sixtus V issued the Bull *Coelia et Terrae* against witches Jan. 5, 1586 (*The Inquisition,* Vacandard, 200). He was also ignorant and superstitious.

He renewed the excommunication against Elizabeth and promised Philip a subsidy for the Armada (*Catholic Encyclopedia* I, 729).

He "established a new printing office for the purpose of securing an improved edition of the Church Fathers" (*Short History of the Catholic Church,* Wedewer and McSorley, 189).

Urban VII (1590)
Before he became the Pope he was a Jesuit, and Inquisitor General (*Catholic Encyclopedia,* XV, 218), but was Pope only two weeks (*Catholic Encyclopedia,* XII, 274).

Gregory XIV (1590-1591)
He was Pope ten months (*Catholic Encyclopedia,* XII, 274), and approved a commission to correct Pope Sixtus V's Vulgate! (*Catholic Encyclopedia,* VII, 4).

He was a Jesuit and approved Robert Bellarmine and his *"De Controversus"* (*Catholic Encyclopedia,* II, 412).

Excommunicated a Protestant King!

"As soon as he became Pope, he gave energetic support to the

French League, and took active measures against Henry of Navarre, whom Sixtus V had declared a heretic and excluded from the succession to the French throne" (*Catholic Encyclopedia*, VII, 4). He raised an army to overthrow him!

Innocent IX (1591)

He was Pope only two months (*Catholic Encyclopedia*, XII, 274).

Clement VIII (1592-1605)

Bellarmine the "greatest controversialist" was his chief aid (*Catholic Encyclopedia*, XIV, 593; IX, 167).

Called in and burnt all of Sixtus' Bibles he could find, and issued another under Sixtus' name, with a series of lies in the Preface, which remain to this day! (*Catholic Encyclopedia*, II, 411, 412; XIV, 110). Sixtus had made more than two thousand "corrections" in the Catholic Bible!

Clement VIII "transformed" Popess Joan into a man, Pope Zacharias, eight hundred years after she was dead! (*Catholic Encyclopedia*, VIII, 407).

FORGED PROPHECIES AT THIS TIME—CATHOLICS USE THEM!

". . . these prophecies were first published in 1595, by Arnold Wion, a Benedictine monk, four hundred and fifty years after the supposed author. The circumstances favor the belief that they were forged to further party interests in the conclave of 1590, which elected Gregory XV, for the prophecies relating to the pontiff's predecessors are remarkably clear and concise" (*General History of the Church*, Darras, III, 283).

"Most of the papal elections during the sixteenth century were influenced by political conditions" (*Catholic Encyclopedia*, VII, 5).

246

Leo XI (1605)

He was Pope twenty-seven days (*Catholic Encyclopedia,* II, 412; XII, 274).

Paul V (1605-1621)

The importance of his pontificate lies largely in the fact that he condemned Galileo and the Heliocentric theory, pronouncing it heresy. This was in 1615. Galileo was imprisoned for life, his books put on the Index of Forbidden Books (Index Expurgatorius) where they remained for two hundred and thirteen years. Since 1829 Catholics have been allowed to read them; for now, all Catholics, including the popes, believe exactly what Galileo believed. If Galileo was heretic, as Paul V said, then all the hierarchy are heretics now!

In order to prevent the priesthood from wriggling out of this dilemma I will present quotations admitting that the supposedly infallible Paul V was simply ignorant like nearly all the people were at that time. By this incident the doctrine of papal infallibility received a mortal blow!

". . . there is no doubt that he fully approved the decision, having presided at the session of the Inquisition wherein the matter was discussed and decided. In thus acting, it is undeniable that the ecclesiastical authorities committed a grave and deplorable error, and sanctioned an altogether false principle as to the proper use of the Scriptures" (*Catholic Encyclopedia,* VI, 544).

"So Tanquary in his *'Synopsis Theologica,'* published in New York, writes: We readily grant that these congregations (Index and Inquisition) were wrong in condemning Galileo. . . and that the two popes (Paul and Urban VIII) erred, not only as private persons, but as the heads of these congregations, whose decrees are valueless unless approved by the pope'" (*Question Box,* 1913 Edition, 318).

"That both these pontiffs were convinced anti-Copernicans

247

cannot be doubted, nor that they believed the Copernican system to be unscriptural and desired its suppression" (*Catholic Encyclopedia*, VI, 345).

"In the beginning of the seventeenth century the world of scientists and theologians, with some few exceptions, believed most firmly in the Ptolemaic system of astronomy, relying on the authority of Aristotle, the Scriptures, the Fathers of the Church, certain scientific arguments" (*Question Box*, 1913 Edition, 313).

The Catholic Church asks us to believe that these groups are the ones we should implicitly follow!

"He (the pope) may advocate historical and scientific views that are absolutely false. He may write books which may be full of inaccuracies and misstatements" (*Externals of the Catholic Church*, 5).

"Akin to these divine laws is the purely ecclesiastical law or law of the Church. Christ sent forth His Church clothed with His own and His Father's authority . . . To enable her to carry out this divine plan she makes laws, purely ecclesiastical, but laws that have the same binding force as the divine laws themselves . . . For Catholics, therefore, as far as obligations are concerned, there is no practical difference between God's law and the law of the Church" (*Explanation of Catholic Morals*, 26).

"Indeed even among Fathers of the Church, before certain doctrines were defined, you come across loosely worded, inaccurate and even erroneous expressions" (*Question Box*, 1929 Edition, 112).

Galileo Was Right But Disobedient!

"To take a particular example, of Galileo, who happened to be right, while the ecclesiastical tribunal which condemned him was wrong, had he really possessed convincing scientific evidence in favor of the heliocentric theory, he would have been justified in refusing his internal assent to the opposite theory, provided that in doing so he observed with thorough loyalty all the conditions involved in the duty of external obedience" (*Catholic Encyclopedia,* VII, 792).

This says that a Catholic must obey the hierarchy when he believes them to be in error!

Catholic writers similarly dispose of the case of Savanarola. Here, a man fighting for pure morals, is killed by Pope Alexander VI, one of the worst men who ever lived! He disobediently talked back to "His Holiness, Pope Alexander VI, the *infallible* head of the Church"!

Here is a clincher! The Holy Ghost guides the Catholic Church to make mistakes!

"It is true that the Church's leaders may make a mistake in placing a book upon the Index, but the one mistake in the condemnation of Copernicus and Galileo is a clear testimony of the guidance of the Holy Ghost, even when the Church is giving a non-infallible decision" (*Question Box,* 1929 Edition, 207).

Gregory XV (1621-1623)

He put his brother as head of the pontifical army (*Catholic Encyclopedia,* VII, 5).

Ignorant and Superstitious

"Before passing to the political achievements of Gregory XV, mention must be made of his constitution *'Omnipotentis Dei'* issued against magicians and witches on 20 March, 1623. It is the last papal ordinance against witchcraft. Former punishments were lessened, and the death penalty was decreed only on those who were proved to have entered into a compact with the devil, and to have committed homicide with his assistance" (*Catholic Encyclopedia,* VII, 5-6).

This is a misstatement. See the information concerning Clement X fifty years later.

Urban VIII (1623-1644)
Innocent X (1644-1655)

"The great blemish in his pontificate was his dependence on Donna Olimpia Maidalchini, the wife of his deceased brother. . . But the Pope seemed to be unable to get along without her, and at her instance Astalli was deprived of the purple and removed from the Vatican" (*Catholic Encyclopedia*, VIII, 21).

"It was the misfortune of the Pamfili Pope that the only person in his family circle possessed of the requisite qualities of such a position, was a woman, viz. his sister-in-law Olimpia Maidalchini-Pamfili, whereas all the nephews whom he successively adorned with the purple proved utter failures.

"Donna Maidalchini, born at Viterbo in 1594, was first married to Paolo Nini. She contracted a second marriage with the Pope's older brother Pamfili to whom she bore a son, Camillo, in 1622, and subsequently two daughters, Maria and Costanza."

"Olimpia, whose energetic, resolute but anything but attractive features, are admirably portrayed in Algardi's bust in the Doria Gallery, was a very gifted woman but exceedingly ambitious and domineering. She had had a rich dowry; she accordingly managed to become the most important person in the Pamfili family. Her clerical brother-in-law Giambattista, (later Innocent X) she supplied with the requisite funds to enable him to rise, thereby putting him under great obligation to her. The influence she exercised over him continued even when Giambattista had to leave Rome: both as nuncio at Naples and at Madrid he kept up a lively correspondence with his shrewd sister-in-law."

"Hence it was not surprising that on the elevation of her brother-in-law to the papacy, Olimpia should have acquired considerable importance. 'Olimpia's influence,' so the Florentine envoy wrote on Feb. 11th, 1645, 'grows daily; she visits the Pope every other day and the whole world turns to her.' But there were not wanting enemies who, by word of mouth and in writing, spread such evil reports that Olimpia lodged a complaint with the Governor of Rome, whereupon a number of arrests were made. However this did not put an end to the libel. . . She was frequently closeted for as long time as four to six hours with the Pope who did nothing of importance without consulting her."

"On January 20th it was learned that Camillo's (son of Donna Olimpia) wife had been with the Pope for three hours and had received rich presents from him, shortly before she had given birth to her second child. Thereafter she visited the Pope almost every week and won a not inconsiderable influence, whereas Camillo (her husband) had none at all. . . Thus it came about that Innocent's attachment to his sister-in-law, which had never been wholly extinct, came once more to life. . . Olimpia's influence waxed greater than ever. . . Olimpia's avarice revealed itself in a most revolting fashion after the Pope's demise (January 7th, 1655): the woman who owed to the dead man such vast sums of money refused, as did Camillo Pamfili (Donna's son) to pay for the customary wood and lead coffins so that after it had been exposed in St. Peter's, the body had to be kept for several days in a damp corner of the sacristy and to be buried in the most simple manner imaginable" (*Pastors History,* XXX, 32-46).

"The body of Innocent has been exposed at St. Peter's during three days, and no one took any measures for the interment. Olimpia was asked to order a coffin and shroud for him; her reply was, 'I am a poor widow.' The other relatives and nephews of the deceased pope did not in the least bestir themselves on the occasion. Finally the deserted corpse was carried into a room in which the masons were accustomed to deposit their tools. One of these men compassionately took a tallow candle thither and placed it at the head of the corpse. As it was said that there were many in the room, another person paid, from his own means, a man to watch over the body. On the following day, a chief majordomo, who had been discharged, purchased a coffin and paid for the interment of his late master" (*Lives and Times of the Roman Pontiffs,* Chevalier Artaud de Montor, II, 92-94).

Innocent's successor, Alexander VII, when he became sick, called in the cardinals and showed them his cypress coffin (*Lives and Times of the Roman Pontiffs,* II, 120). This author observes: "No attentive reader needs to be told why he had that coffin made. We have seen how Innocent X for want of such precautions, was left in an unworthy condition, even by his own sister-in-law."

Alexander VII (1655-1667)
Clement IX (1667-1669)
Clement X (1669-1676)
"The Roman Pontiff, Clement X, in a Bull published in 1672, enumerates offences for which persons might be proceeded against by the Inquisition, and it is remarkable, that out of the thirteen different classes of crimes only one is heresy. If our readers be inclined to smile at the prominent place assigned to witchcraft, sorcery, etc., by the Pontiff, we ask them only to remember the history of the Salem witchcraft" (Archbishop Spalding, *Miscellanae,* 227).

The Archbishop should have reminded his readers, also that the Protestants in Massachusetts were not infallible! They were rather recently out of Catholicism! The Salem witch trials were in 1692.

Innocent XI (1676-1689)
Threatened to suppress the Jesuits (*Catholic Encyclopedia,* XIV, 85).

Alexander VIII (1689-1691)
He was pope for sixteen months (*Catholic Encyclopedia,* I, 295).

Innocent XII (1691-1700)
Clement XI (1700-1721)

His Bull *"Unigenitus Dei Eilius"* condemned one hundred and one propositions, including the proposition that "the reading of the Scriptures is for all" (*Catholic Dictionary,* Addis and Arnold, 82).

This proposition Pius IV (1559) had condemned. The Councils of Toulouse (1229) and Terragona (1234) forbad laity to have or to read vernacular translations (*Catholic Dictionary,* Addis and Arnold, 82).

Innocent XIII (1721-1724)

He demanded obedience to the Bull *Unigenitus.*

Benedict XIII (1724-1730)

Demanded obedience to the Bull *Unigenitus* (*Catholic Encyclopedia,* II, 432-33).

Clement XII (1730-1740)

He issued the first papal decree against Freemasons, 1738 (*Catholic Encyclopedia,* IV, 31).

Demanded obedience to *Unigenitus* (*Ibid.*).

Benedict XIV (1740-1758)
Clement XIII (1758-1769)

Jesuit Trouble

Spanish America, Portugal, Spain and France expelled the Jesuits, so the Pope took an unusual step:

Clement Refused These Jesuits in Italy!

"Foreseeing the difficulty of so large an influx of expelled religious into his states, Clement felt compelled to refuse them permission to land, and after various wanderings they had to settle down in Corsica, where they were joined by their brethren who had been similarly sent away from Spanish America. When, a year and a half later, they were forced to move again, the Pope's compassion overcame his administrative prudence, and he permitted them to take refuge in his territory" (*Catholic Encyclopedia,* IV, 32, 34).

". . . writings of nearly one hundred Jesuits have been placed on the Index" (*Catholic Encyclopedia,* XIV, 103).

Clement XIV (1769-1774)

Catholic countries stubbornly demanded that Clement XIV suppress the Jesuits.

"An ever-recurring and almost solitary grievance against the Society (Jesuits) was that the Fathers disturbed the peace wherever they were firmly established. The accusation is not unfounded: the Jesuits did indeed disturb the peace of the enemies of the Church, for in the words of d'Alembert to Frederick II they were 'the grenadiers of the pope's guard'" (*Catholic Encyclopedia,* IV, 35).

"In 1773 Pope Clement XIV issued a Brief of suppression by which the entire Jesuit Order was suppressed throughout Christendom. He had been under pressure of the Spanish Court and the Duc de Choiseul and other strong influences. In the separate countries (Portugal, France, Spain) the Jesuits had been already expelled some years before. The suppression was due to the same causes which in further development brought about the French Revolution. . . During most of the time of the suppression the only priests in the United States were Jesuits" (*The New Catholic Dictionary, Vatican Edition,* 905).

The Jesuits have been running Catholic affairs in the United States ever since, and it is just as dangerous now as then. They would love to run the United States government now!

Pius VI (1775-1799)

During this man's time the world was rocked by one of history's greatest upheavals, the American and French Revolutions, which lasted about twenty-five years. The tidal waves of this surge for liberty has been convulsing the countries, which for so many centuries were under Catholic domination, ever since.

Pius VII (1800-1823)
Leo XII (1823-1829)

This pope removed the works of Galileo from the Index of Forbidden Books, where they had been for more than two hundred years (*Recollections of the Last Four Popes,* Wiseman, 228). The reason for this is that all the Catholic hierarchy now believe exactly what Galileo believed!

Pius VIII (1829-1830)
Gregory XVI (1831-1846)
Pius IX (1846-1878)

Pius IX was the author of one of the most undemocratic documents of history, *"The Syllabus of Errors,"* which is the condemnation of eighty propositions having to do with every aspect of liberty. This was promulgated in 1864.

He declared himself to be infallible in 1870. Immediately, Garibaldi and Victor Emanuel made war on the Pope, taking away every foot of the territory he claimed. For eight years he was "a prisoner in the Vatican."

The demands of the Italians for a greater share of liberty, made the Pope a hated man. These manifestations became evident early in his "pontificate." "Riot followed riot, the pope was denounced as a traitor to his country, his prime minister Rossi was stabbed to death while ascending the steps of the Cancelleria, whither he had gone to open the parliament, and on the following day the pope himself was besieged in the Quirinal. Palma, a papal prelate, who was standing at a window, was shot, and the pope was forced to promise a democratic ministry. With the assistance of the Bavarian ambassador, Count Spaur, and the French ambassador, Duc d'Harcourt, Pius IX escaped from the Quirinal in disguise, 24 November, and fled to Gaeta where he was joined by many of the cardinals. Meanwhile Rome was ruled by traitors and adventurers who abolished the temporal power of the pope, 9 February, 1849, and under the name of a democratic republic terrorized the people and committed untold outrages. The pope appealed to France, Austria, Spain, and Naples. On 29 June French troops under Oudinot restored order in his territory. On 12 April, 1850, Pius IX returned to Rome, no longer a political liberalist. Cardinal Antonelli, his secretary of state, exerted a paramount political influence until his death on 6 November, 1876. The temporal reign of Pius IX, up to the seizure of the last of his temporal possessions in 1870, was one continuous struggle, on the one hand against the intrigues of the revolutionaries, on the other against the Piedmontese ruler Victor Emanuel, his crafty premier Cavour, and other antipapal statesmen who aimed at a united Italy, with Rome as its capital, and the Piedmontese ruler as its king" (*Catholic Encyclopedia,* XII, 135).

The last eight years of his life he dared not go out into the city of Rome because of the great animosity of the people.

Romans Demonstrated at His Funeral!

"A glance at the Decretals shows that, as an ecclesiastical legislator (Alexander III, 1159-1181), he was scarcely second to Innocent III. Worn out by trials, he died at Civita Casteliana. When we are told that *the Romans* pursued his remains with curses and stones, the remembrance of a similar scene at the burial of Pius IX teaches us what value to attach to such demonstration" (*Catholic Encyclopedia,* I, 287).

Leo XIII (1878-1903)

Like his predecessors, Leo was bitterly undemocratic. His book, *"Great Encyclical Letters"* should be in the hands of every person who cherishes liberty, to keep him from the illusion that the

Catholic Church loves our American institutions.

Pius X (1903-1914)
   He has since his death been declared to be a saint.

Benedict XV (1914-1922)
Pius XI (1922-1939)
Pius XII (1939-1958)
John XXIII (1958-1963)
Paul VI (1963-1978)

Note: As this book was originally published in the 1960s, no notes are included on any popes since then.

CHAPTER XIV

Claim of Superior Education Fosters Ignorance Instead

"IF notwithstanding the precepts of sound doctrine explained by the Church, ignorance and fraud have introduced some superstitious ideas to alter their purity, was that a reason for abolishing a received, popular, reasonable and consoling institution?" (*Lives and Times of the Roman Pontiffs,* Chevalier Artuard de Montor, I, 197).

This statement is made in justification for encouraging pagans, who had always worshipped images, to continue to do so. The rage for image worship followed when Constantine made the already adulterated "Christianity" the state religion and gave them the heathen temples filled with pagan images. The superstition admitted in the above quotation is encouraged in the most official way, as the following quotations prove:

"Not long after his return to Assisi, whilst Francis was praying before an ancient Crucifix in a forsaken Wayside Chapel of St. Damian's below the town, he heard a voice saying: 'Go Francis, and repair my house, which you see is falling into ruin'" (*Catholic Encyclopedia,* VI, 222).

This ignorant superstition is given the highest indorsement in the following:

"The great servant of God, Brother Bernard of Corlien, a Capuchin, did not know how to read, and his fellow religious wished to teach him. He went to ask for advice from the crucifix, and Jesus answered him from the cross: 'What necessity for books of reading! I am your book—a book in which you can always read the love I have borne you'" (*Devotion of the Holy Rosary,* Muller, 96).

Compare this quotation with the following:

"Carefully study to present thyself approved unto God, a workman that needeth not to be ashamed, rightly handling the word of truth" (2 Tim. 2:15, *Douay*).

"It was by constantly saying the Rosary that she ("St. Margaret") was introduced into this happy country of the interior life—a country overflowing with milk and honey. Here she learned more of God in one moment than by reading all the books in the world; she spoke to God, and God spoke to her, in a manner inexplicable" (*Devotion of the Holy Rosary,* Muller, 102-103).

"It may also be said, without exaggeration, that the greater part of Catholics neglect reading edifying books" (*Devotion of the Holy Rosary,* Muller, 44).

"On one occasion at Naples, in 1273, after he had completed his treatise on the Eucharist, three of the brethren saw him lifted in ecstasy, and they heard a voice proceeding from the crucifix on the altar, saying 'Thou hast written well of me Thomas; what reward wilt thou have?' Thomas replied 'None other than thyself, Lord.' Similar declarations are said to have been made at Orvieto and at Paris" (*Catholic Encyclopedia,* XIV, 665).

"Going into the Church, he offered up his prayers before a great crucifix, begging with many tears and extraordinary fervor that God would mercifully grant him pardon of his sins. Whilst he continued his prayer the crucifix miraculously bowed its head to him, as it were to give a token how acceptable the sacrifice of his resentment, and his sincere repentance were" (*Butler's Lives of the Saints,* VII, 91, 92).

"A humble and changed man, he ("St." John Gaulbert) entered the Church of St. Miniato, which was near; and whilst he prayed, the figure of our crucified Lord, before which he was kneeling, bowed its head toward him as if to ratify his pardon" (*Butlers Lives of the Saints,* One Volume Edition, 247).

"An abortive attempt to kill a former Archbishop by smearing

259

poison on a crucifix he customarily kissed in Metropolitan Cathedral, Mexico City, traditionally caused it to turn black and it is venerated as 'Senor Del Veneno'" (*The Tablet,* Sept. 3, 1955).

"St. Pius (V, the pope who ordered the Massacre of St. Bartholomew—O.C.L.), was accustomed to kiss the feet of his crucifix on leaving, or entering his room. One day the feet moved away from his lips. Sorrow filled his heart, and he made acts of contrition, fearing he must have committed some secret offense but still he could not kiss the feet. It was afterwards found that they had been poisoned by an enemy" (*Butlers Lives of the Saints,* One Volume Edition, 170).

Rosary Such a Convenient Book

"What book is so convenient to carry with us as our beads? It can always be about us; in going to our work we can take it in our hands and say a decade; at night we can put it around our neck or on the arm, and before falling asleep offer to our Mother another decade of prayers" (*Devotion of the Holy Rosary,* Muller, 187).

Just think of the countless millions of fervent prayers, sent by honest hearts, that have failed to reach God's throne because they were addressed to the wrong person.

"For there is one God, and one mediator of God and men, the man Christ Jesus" (1 Tim. 2:5, *Douay*).

"All whatsoever you do in word or in work, *all* things do ye in the name of the Lord Jesus Christ, giving thanks to God and the Father by him" (Col. 3:17, *Douay*).

"You have not chosen me: but I have chosen you; and have appointed you, that you should go, and should bring forth fruit; and your fruit should remain: that whatsoever you shall ask of the Father in my name he may give it you" (John 15:16, *Douay*).

"And he (Jesus) said unto them, When ye pray, say, Our Father which art in heaven, Hallowed be thy name" (Luke 11:2, *King James Version*).

St. Bonaventure Did Not Need Bible

"Once when a great master of theology came to visit him, he inquired where he had learned so much heavenly science. St. Bonaventure pointed to his crucifix, and exclaimed, 'This is the fountain of all knowledge; for I desire no other book, save Jesus crucified'" (*Life of St. Francis Assisi,* Magliano, 334).

Bread Talked!

Said of her "Confessor":

"He used to console me out of his great compassion; and if he had trusted to his own convictions, I should not have had so much to suffer; for God revealed the whole truth to him. I believe that he received his light from the Blessed Sacrament" (St. Teresa's *Autobiography* 207).

Some Interesting Information

"One can be a very exalted mystic without knowing how to read or write" (*History of Christian Philosophy,* Gilson, 170).

"St. Angelica Merici foundress of the great teaching order, the Ursulines, never herself learned to read or write" (*Strange But True,* Column in *Brooklyn Tablet,* Aug. 4, 1962).

"This holy woman (St. Teresa), taught of our Lord perfectly understood—though she could not read" (*St. Teresa's Autobiography,* 268-269).

"The nobleman went into the church, and on seeing the figure of Mary he felt himself, as it were, invited by her to cast himself at her feet and trust. He hastens to do so, kisses her feet, and Mary, from the statue, extended her hand for him to kiss" (*Glories of Mary,* Liguori, 232).

This is the kind of idolatry indulged in by the whole Catholic Church, through the centuries. It equals, or exceeds, those pagans from whom this was borrowed. The less enlightened people are, the more readily they accept this ignorant superstition.

It is a well-known fact that the backward countries are Catholic countries. The reason is apparent.

In spite of these facts priests awe the laity and frequently intimidate others by a mystical claim to superior learning. Catholics are attempting to take over our public schools under the pretext that a Catholic school system is infinitely superior. So it seems in order, to examine this claim, to use Catholic priests themselves as witnesses. Before they are introduced, let us be reminded that a priest is made so by a bishop, who lays his hands on his head, claiming thereby to bestow the Holy Spirit. The Catholic Bible tells us that those who have the Holy Spirit know everything:

"Howbeit when he, the Spirit of truth, is come, he will guide you into all truth" (John 16:13). In the face of this truth, uttered by Jesus himself, do you think it necessary that they look to the Crucifix, statues, bread and the Rosary for information?

The hierarchy of the Roman Catholic Church has labored to create the illusion that her priests have almost an unapproachable superiority in learning and understanding. But if they had the Holy Spirit, as they claim, they would know all that they need to know without years of seminary training. The Apostles and others who wrote the *New Testament,* most of them probably had no formal schooling at all. They were called "unlearned and ignorant men" (Acts 4:13). We shall comment later on their own admissions that priests generally are poorly trained.

Holy Ghost Teaches All Things

"But the Paraclete, the Holy Ghost, whom the Father will send in my name, he will teach you all things, and bring all things to your mind, whatsoever I have said to you" (John 14:16, *Douay Version*).

This was the promise that Jesus made to his Apostles shortly before his going away. If it is true that the Apostles had successors and if the priests have, or ever had the Holy Ghost, they would have correct knowledge of all things, and the following grammatical blunders would not have been in the Catholic English Bible, in the first place, much less allowed to remain for nearly four hundred years.

"Therefore after Moses *had wrote* the words of the law in a volume and finished it" (Deut. 31:24, *Douay Version*).

"No, nor Herod neither" (Luke 23:15, *Douay*).

Other officially promulgated books, by the infallible (?) church, are not models of scholarship:

He Eat It!

"Unfortunately, he yielded to the allurements of Eve, who had been seduced by the wiles and crafty promises of the serpent, envious of the great happiness which man enjoyed. Adam imprudently stretched out his hand to receive the fatal fruit which his companion offered him, and *eat* it" (*Life of the Blessed Virgin,* by Monsignore Romuald Gentillucci, 16). This man, so the book says, was "Chamberlain of Honor to His Holiness (Pius IX), and Prebendary of the Vatican Basilica." It was printed in 1856, and contains 951 pages.

"St." Columbian *blowed upon it"* (Butler's *Lives of the Saints,* Vol. XI, 367).

"I saw that Master Lee did most of the talking and let him show more enthusiasm *than me"* (*Autobiography of a Hunted Priest,* John Gerard, 193).

"They viewed the teeming mobs *with amaze,* and saw that the Chinese were a mighty people" (*Father McShane of Maryknoll,* 57-58). This book was printed in 1932 under the Imprimatur of Cardinal Hayes.

"In fact, they were much better off now, for I left Father Brooks with them, and he was a finer man than me in every way" (Autobiography of a Hunted Priest, John Gerard, 176).

Calling attention to such errors as these may appear childish to you but coming from "Saints" and from the highest officials of the

Catholic Church, those who claim to have the Holy Ghost, they do merit our attention. There are literally hundreds of such errors that could have been cited and all from different men and ages. Errors that should prove to us that these men are not infallible or even highly educated.

Creation of Priest

"The Bishop imposes his hands, *without a word a short prayer follows*; and this wonderful prodigy, viz., the creation of a priest is accomplished" (*Our Priesthood*, Bruneau, 159).

". . . the Bishop alone can perform such a wonder" (*Our Priesthood*, 47).

Christ a Priest from Conception

"Thus ordained a priest from His conception, Jesus Christ—we may well say—began to exercise His priesthood from the very moment of His life, and will continue to do so throughout all eternity" (*Our Priesthood*, Bruneau, 22. See also *Pulpit Commentary on Catholic Teaching*, the Creed, I, 259).

"If then he were on earth, he would not be a priest" (Heb. 8:4, Douay). From this we can see that Catholic teaching contradicts the Catholic Bible!

Holy Ghost—Like Pentecost!

"The Holy Ghost descends upon them and pervades their soul. The mystery of Pentecost is enacted again" (*Our Priesthood*, 127).

Afraid To Meet the Issues!

If the Catholic priesthood were so superbly trained and had at their side the infallible guidance of the Holy Spirit, they should be more than a match for any opposition. This would be doubly true if they possessed all the truth on their side! Jesus and the early preachers met all comers (Acts 6:9-15 and 7:1-60; 19:8-10). Why will Catholic priests not do so now? Why has the Catholic Church outlawed this apostolic way of propagating the truth?

Catholic Unfairness

Having traveled extensively in many parts of the country, through many years, I have had an excellent opportunity to get an accurate measure of official Catholic reaction. On a great many occasions there have been priests in the audiences, and frequently representatives of the Catholic press. Many times reporters garbled my statements, leaving out official facts and attributed to me things that I never dreamed of saying.

But strange as it may seem, no priest, or any other qualified representative of the Catholic Church, ever denied publicly a single quotation or accusation that I have made against their system. Paul was a Christian and if the priests are carrying on his work they should do as Paul did when he said: "I am set for the defense of the gospel" (Phil. 1:16, *Douay*).

The treatment at the hands of those who are supposed to represent our free public press has been almost the same. They will print the most outrageous misrepresentations and deny me my constitutional right to the press. I can only attribute this to the apparent fact that Catholics have acquired control of most of our newspapers and magazines. Those they do not control in this way are controlled by intimidation. Sometimes I am denied a suitable auditorium in which to speak. Free speech and free press are almost a thing of the past.

Editors, radio and television managers, who claim to be Protestant, are as careful as the Catholic hierarchy to see that nothing goes out over their media except that which is complimentary to the Catholic Church. There are some exceptions, and it is almost unbelievable, that in a few rare instances, Catholic editors have defied the wrath of the hierarchy. In one instance brethren broadcasted my lectures over three different radio stations. The priests tried boycott, failing in this they threatened to dynamite the station!

I never learned whether the owner of this radio station was a member of any church or not, but this I am convinced of, he was not afraid.

In Long Beach, California three young Negro men walked up and down before the auditorium, each night, with placards. I had reason to suspect that they were influenced to do this by Catholics who hoped to discredit the lectures because I was from Alabama. During the lectures an ambulance, with motorcycle escort, with sirens screaming, rushed up to the building. Men jumped out, and with stretchers started rushing into the church building. It was with great difficulty that they were prevented from going into the audience. Even though they were told that nothing was wrong with me and they could hear me speaking they insisted that they had come for O.C. Lambert. From their commotion and insistence that they be allowed to enter the auditorium it was evident that their purpose was to break up the meeting in confusion.

A television station, owned by a large insurance company, surprised me. When more than five hundred protests came in, after my first speech, they informed the local priest that they were Americans and believed in free speech. They explained to him that I was simply exercising my constitutional right of free speech and that the station would be glad to sell him time in which to answer me at the same rate that I was paying. I instructed the station owner to tell him that we would pay for equal time for him if he would only use it. He was never heard from again concerning the matter!

It is clear that the reason why Catholic authorities do not come out openly in defense of these things is their inability to do so.

I am doing this in all humility, believing that the people have a right to hear both sides.

"Prove all things; hold fast that which is good" (1 Thess. 5:21).

I have had letters, usually anonymous, from very high authorities among the clergy to the most unlettered "laymen." Nearly al-

ways these letters are fairly dripping with bitterness, expressed, oftentimes, in unprintable language. Many times there is an effort to
intimidate with anonymous letters and telephone calls. One bishop
of a Southern city said to me over the telephone, "You are going
to keep on until someone does away with you!"

There is a brighter side to this story. The greater number of
letters are sweet and encouraging ones. They come from those who
are not Catholic any longer, after hearing my lectures and reading
my books. These compensate me a thousand times for all my efforts. I wish that space and expense would permit me to insert a
few of these wonderful letters here.

In order that you may see how the adverse type follow a pattern
I will call attention to a few of those.

Some Characteristic Letters

I was scheduled to speak in the Church building of the University Parkway Church of Christ in Baltimore, Maryland during December 1957. This building is only a few blocks from Saint Mary's
Seminary, the oldest and most renowned seminary in America. It
was established by John Carroll, the first bishop in America, Oc-
tober 3, 1791. According to *Catholic Encyclopedia* thousands of
priests have been trained there, including Cardinal Gibbons and
other important dignitaries.

The day I was to begin my lectures there, I had made a long
drive, through a great snowstorm, from Springfield, Vermont and
was practically exhausted by the time I arrived, late in the afternoon. After a few hurried preparations for the evening service I
made my way to the auditorium. Immediately after arriving there
I was handed a letter from a man who signed himself "Rev. Miles
M. McAndrews." He announced himself as "Professor of New
Testament Literature and Interpretation" in Saint Mary's Seminary. He informed me that he had before him the *Stevens-Beevers
Debate.* Knowing I had something to do with that debate, he proceeded to "challenge you and the Church of Christ through you."

I was too tired to answer him that night, and the next morning I had another letter from him. The following is one paragraph from the morning letter:

"Excuse me for saying it, Mr. Lambert, but in dealing with me, you are dealing with a man who knows his business far better than Eric Stevens does. (He evidently meant Eric Beevers). And Eric Stevens would be the first man to admit it. I have been a student and Professor of Holy Scripture for thirty years and more."

As this theological Goliath strides across the field you observe his armor and his "spear like a weaver's beam"! "And the Philistine said to David, Come to me, and I will give thy flesh unto the fowls of the air, and to the beasts of the field." Though the letter was signed, "With great respect" I thought I felt his claws beneath his furry pat!

The Challenge

As soon as possible after receiving Mr. McAndrews' letters, Brother Dean Clutter, the local preacher of the church of Christ, and I called on him at the Saint Mary's Seminary. I told him I had received his letters containing his challenge, that this was what I had been wishing for for a long time, and that I was ready. I explained, though, that I wanted it extensively advertised, and that would take some time. I wanted the debate just as soon as this could be properly done, for I was anxious for as many people as possible to hear it. He replied, "That is not what I meant. We would have to have an authorization from the Pope to do that." Catholic priests rarely ever debate, for they evidently feel that they can make a more convincing case if the other side is not presented. It has been my experience that if they are willing to meet the opposition only in the privacy of their office. Rarely will they agree to such a meeting if there are any Catholics present. I saw at once that Mr. McAndrews wanted a private correspondence. The evident reason for such reluctance is not hard to decipher. I strongly suspected that he figured I did not know much about the matter, and

268

that by a private correspondence he could find many "chinks" in my armor. I replied that if he was not prepared for a public debate he should not have mentioned a challenge, and that if he was not willing or really ready to debate I was not the least bit interested. I asked him, since he could not do it, if there were any of his superiors who could. I informed him further that if at any time in the future the Catholic hierarchy decided they wanted a debate that I would gladly make myself available.

I believe that it will be readily seen by the reader why hundreds of preachers of the church of Christ would welcome the opportunity to engage in such a discussion. After reading all the matter presented in *Catholicism Against Itself,* volumes I and II the reader will readily understand the reluctance of priests.

At the conclusion of the Stevens-Beevers Debate I announced that we had requests to repeat that debate in all the larger cities of the Southwest, and that we were prepared to sign up for a hundred such debates, that night. No one, including Mr. Beevers, volunteered.

Someone may insist that debates are ugly, and that that was the reason. The more than five-thousand people who attended that debate, from about half the states in this nation, remember that there has never been a prayer-meeting carried on more reverently. Even though more than four-thousand could not get in the building, perfect order prevailed.

This is the sort of claim Catholic priests like to make. In a recent debate, in West Texas, a priest began by boasting of how many years he had studied theology, and how many more years he had studied philosophy. It just so happened that on that same night he made a vain effort to find Second Timothy. His apparent confusion must have convinced his many members present, that he should have been studying the Bible. I have had several priests, who have had these years of Catholic training, to confess to me, before witnesses, that they did not know enough about these issues to even talk about them.

I think it well, at this point to examine this seminary training, and as is my custom, I will let Catholic priests tell us of its deficiencies.

I have before me a book, entitled, *The Training of a Priest,* by "Rev." Talbot Smith, LL.D.," published by Longman, Green and Company, in 1908. This book gives a candid look at the dreadfully inadequate educational system, just about the time "Rev. Miles M. McAndrews" enrolled and began his "thirty years and more." This man Smith was a Catholic priest, and not a prejudiced Protestant. The following are some rather extensive quotations from this book.

"As our history is just at that point where radical changes in method are necessary, it is possible that new institutions may blunder into keeping alive the routine which has already endured fifty years too long. It is admitted on all sides that the clerical training of fifty years ago is not the thing for these times as far as methods and external features are concerned" (page 4).

Seminary Training Ruins Health

"4. Physically sound. The writer admits here the temptation to say bitter things, but declines to yield to it. Instead he presents to dispassionate consideration two pictures: on this side a graduating class from any of our colleges, robust, cheerful, muscular, active, healthy men, strong enough for any tussle that life may give them; on that side the same class five years later going up for ordination after the seminary career; every man lean or worn in appearance, the little flesh left them of a flabby texture, their stomachs and nerves played out, and the pleasant certainty ahead that an ordinary attack of disease will end them, or that years of recuperation will be required, or that real health will never be theirs again. There is not one touch of exaggeration in the picture. The physical condition of seminarians for the later half of the course is inexcusable. The seminary life is peaceful and regular as the life of a garrison. It is a virtuous and lofty life. Its graduates should leave it with perfect constitutions, if they entered it with any, or should leave it

270

improved in health, for its regularity and spirit make it the truest of sanitariums. Why then should the students have difficulty in keeping body and soul together during these five years? This is the task of inquiry assumed by the writer, who holds that the second main object of a seminary should be the turning out of priests in good physical condition. Youth should be robust. Pastors need healthy assistants. Yet it would be safe to say that fifty percent of the newly ordained need nursing for months, and sometimes years, after ordination" (page 19).

"We have all seen some of the results of this false asceticism in our seminaries; where it was often regarded as a sin against the spirit to complain of cold rooms, bad food, poor hospital treatment, long kneeling at prayers, and other violation of the rules of health and common sense; and a demand for gymnasium or reasonable variety of exercise was thought to show a lack of vocation. . . It admits that certain literary exponents of asceticism lay down rules whose observance would hinder the work of charity in the church, as a matter of fact their observance in seminaries has deprived students of health and spirit, often of reason, and given the dioceses too large a percentage of invalid priests to support" (page 62).

"With the results we are familiar. What are many seminaries but homes for hypochondriacs, where dyspepsia, headache, constipation, biliousness live riotously and drive many students to the grave, or bring on scrupulousness and other forms of insanity, or send them into the world with lowered vitality and enfeebled constitutions" (page 66).

"The seminary table is severe enough, and ought to be better in details to be pointed out later; but its severity is as water to ice compared with the internal anguish caused by nature's attempts at assimilation of the food. It is incredible that our seminary educators can expect a young American to keep his health and mental powers after the sudden and cheerless change from a fair table and an active life to a poorly supplied table and a sedentary routine. It is regrettable that a student must do without physical development

271

in the seminary, yet in addition, to lose his health there, or suffer injury which takes years to repair, is an outrage. It could be tolerated only by the innocent, who have trusted too much to the supposed good qualities of an old system. . . It may look spiritual to display a certain neglect of the body, but with growing children that sort of spirituality is out of the question. There is one matter which can only be hinted at here; the relationship between health and natural chastity, between ill health and impurity. The seminarian is preparing to take the obligation of chastity. The yoke which he puts upon nature ought not to be weighted beyond endurance. There is a natural chastity, born of a healthy body and a careful training, which is found in many who have never had any stronger motive for preserving a fine purity of thought, speech, desire, and action through many years" (Pages 67-68).

"A feeble body, on the other hand, seems to be the true parent of a crotchety mind, and impotency; in many cases this physical feebleness leads to various forms of impurity, as medical men testify; even in persons who before were of pure habit, and who still hold to the standard of chastity" (page 69).

"Whereas at present too large a number of young priests enter into parish work emaciated, weak, bloodless, spend years recovering from injuries inflicted by seminary training, grow fat and shapeless in body before their youth is passed, and often mentally morbid, and drop into the grave between fifty and sixty after a physically irregular and uncomfortable life" (page 74).

"More important than either the gymnasium or the national games in keeping the student in good health, or providing him with it, is the refectory (dining-room, O.C.L.) and kitchen of the seminary. To judge from the universal experience on this point there is not a seminary on the continent where this fact has ever been recognized. . . He has yet to meet the priest who could speak in praise of his seminary refectory. . . All institutions of learning follow this simple regime nowadays; but the butter is poor, for really good butter never yet reached a seminarian's table; the coffee and tea

272

are always pure slop. . . the refectory is never too clean" (pages 77-79).

"This brings up another important subject in relation to the health of the student, the management of the infirmary. No man of sense could ever understand why this department is usually the worst managed and worst fitted of the seminary, impregnable to the assault of real invalids, wide open to the tricksters, uncomfortable to the inmates, inefficient in its methods of treatment" (page 82).

"The girl-boy learns his condition very quickly, suffers incredibly to be so comically different from other boys, and yet has no knowledge of any way to get out of his difficulty, because he cannot see the hundred minute details which mark him as the Miss Nancy of the seminary or the school" (page 97).

"The latter, especially where secular and ecclesiastical students are mixed, destroys more vocations than it conserves. A serious objection to an ecclesiastical boarding-school lies in the length of time that these young men will have to pass in the abnormal life of the seminary—five or six years in the preparatory, and six in the highest seminary, to follow out the decrees of the Third Plenary Council. The monotony wears them out" (page XXV).

Catholics Refuse To Modernize!

"In non-Catholic colleges there has been within a half century a complete revolution in methods; but our institutions march on in the same path, seemingly afraid or perhaps unwilling to make radical changes. In the opinion of many fair judges this devotion to tradition is the sole reason why colleges do not reach the standard set by their own faculties" (page 28).

Catholic Training Far Beneath Non-Catholic!

"It will be more difficult for the faculties to answer the most important charge against them, that their course of studies does not exhaust the average capacity of students. This may be attributed to poor methods or to poor professors" (page 31).

"It is not the best commentary that the graduate of the average Catholic college must spend two or three more years in non-Catholic institutions to make up for the gaps in his knowledge" (page 32).

Unending Parochial Drudgery!

"Whereas now, in the Eastern portion of the United States at least, the young priest enters upon his ecclesiastical career with the expectation of spending from ten to fifteen years as an assistant before having a house of his own and the liberty that waits on it. His ambitious aspirations are clipped as he ceases to soar high. If he be a man of more than ordinary intellectual ability, and the right opportunities have been given him, he may prefer the professor's chair to the *unending routine* of *parochial drudgery;* all the more readily if his position as professor be an honorable one, giving him standing in the diocese, with suitable treatment while filling the professor's chair" (page XXX).

Priests Learn Little English—Poor Preaching!

"Seminary sermons accomplish little; occasionally they furnish some amusement, and give opportunity to the critics to try the humility of the preacher. . . It seems absurd in striving to give a young man an all-round education to keep him from familiarity with the language in which he will have to present his ideas and knowledge to the people for whose souls he is to become responsible" (page XXXl).

All these statements from a Catholic "clergyman" dims the magnificence of the pretended superiority of seminary training.

But Mr. McAndrews may counter that this was the condition in seminaries when he began his training but that now it has outstripped all other schooling. If this were true, what of the testimony of Emmett McLoughlin, given in his book, *American Culture and Catholic Schools,* XXX? The chapter dealing with this, is entitled, *The Well-Washed Brain.*

Seminarians Not Taught the Bible

McLoughlin states that in all his Grammar and High School experience never did the priests or nuns, and even in five years in seminary, teach the use of the Bible. He asserts that never in Grammar School did he ever have a course in hygiene. He further states that throughout his Catholic training the world's greatest literature was forbidden, and that, "In short—I was not educated. I was merely indoctrinated. I had achieved the level of the *rigor mortis* of intellectual mediocrity" (page 37).

I can anticipate Mr. McAndrews' reply to this last quotation as being from a prejudiced source. He may even accuse, as they usually do, an ex-priest of lying. But the following cannot be so easily disposed of. Msgr. John Tracy Ellis, Professor of History in the Catholic University of America, Washington, D.C., ten years ago, "defended the thesis that Catholics in America had not produced the number of intellectuals proportionate to their number in education." That was in 1955, two years before my letter from Mr. McAndrews. Msgr. Ellis is much higher on the ecclesiastical ladder than Mr. McAndrews. This same Msgr. Ellis and fifty Catholic clergymen are members of "The Catholic Commission on Intellectual and Cultural Affairs," along with two hundred and eighty-three "lay" members, who "are disturbed because so few Catholic individuals are recognized by *Who's Who in America* and that Catholic colleges "are not turning out intellectuals and national leaders" (*The Brooklyn Tablet,* February 22, 1958).

Catholics Still Criticize Seminaries!

"Albany, New York—(N.C.)—Those who place too much emphasis on secular studies in seminaries would wind up by producing 'spiritual automation,' Archbishop Celestine J. Damiano has

275

warned here.

"Speaking at the dedication Mass of Our Lady of the Angels Seminary (May 6), the Bishop of Camden, New Jersey, said such courses as psychology, sociology and public relations do not necessarily produce the kind of priests the Church needs.

"Spiritual automatons are not saints no matter how perfectly they function, the Archbishop said, and he accused critics of seminaries of being swept off their feet by modern progress.

"He said too many critics have attacked obedience, the seminary rule and studies 'either as unbecoming to the free nature and dignity of man, or as inept in preparing him for the life of today.'

"But, he continued, the entire person must be educated to meet the onslaught of the times, and the changeless aspect of the priesthood cannot be set aside without endangering the very priesthood.

"'The Divine call to the priesthood concerns not only the spiritual faculties—his intelligence and free will—but also involves all his faculties, his entire being!

"'The divine call is a mystery, and the training that centers around this particular vocation borders on the mysterious.'

"'Here, as in all mysteries, the magisterium of the Church is the guiding light and the most competent to deal with it'" (*Green Bay Register,* May 15, 1964).

Think how absurd and untrue is the following, in view of these, and many other candid admissions of the inferiority of Catholic educational institutions.

"For 120 years, the University of Notre Dame has been a recognized leader in American higher education. To Our Lady's campus come students from every state and many foreign countries. In virtually every community, Notre Dame men of competence and integrity are leaders in business and the professions.

"Recognized more than ever before for the caliber of its teaching and research, Notre Dame today has the capacity for greatness. To help achieve it, the University is building a 13-story library.

276

Soon construction will begin on a residence hall for nuns—the heart of every Catholic school—who will be equipped even better as teachers with graduate degrees from Notre Dame.

"You are invited to help build this greater Notre Dame.

"Your support will speed Notre Dame toward its goal and benefit all Catholic education as well. The impact of your gift, whether large or small, will be increased 50% by a matching grant from The Ford Foundation which has singled out Notre Dame for its educational leadership.

"Your gift will be promptly and personally acknowledged.

"As a benefactor, your name will be permanently inscribed in the foyer of the Notre Dame Memorial Library—enduring testimony of your support of Catholic higher education.

"To send your gift, or for further information write: (Rev. John E. Walsh, C.S.C. Director, *The Notre Dame Foundation,* Dept. V, Notre Dame, Indiana).

Catholic Prejudice Fault of Texts

"St. Louis—(N.C.)—Catholics have had some badly prejudiced religious textbooks in the past, but most of the objectionable ones have disappeared from the market.

"This is the report of Father Trafford J. Maher, S.J., who directed a recently issued three year study of prejudice in Catholic textbooks. The study, sponsored by the American Jewish Congress, is part of a survey of prejudice in Catholic, Protestant and Jewish Textbook materials.

"The Jesuit priest, director of St. Louis University's department of education, said newer Catholic textbooks are based on much better Scriptural and historical scholarship than those available 30 or 40 years ago.

"'Too many of those in the past were the product of the rigorist mentality that was common in that era,' he said. 'But fortunately most of the poorly written and prejudicial types are rapidly phasing

277

out'.

"'The textbooks being adopted by school systems today are much more positive, religiously much more accurate, and more consonant with the reality of educating a Catholic to live in our kind of pluralistic world.'

"Martin Luther and the Jews were the subjects getting most of the unfair treatment in earlier textbooks, Father Maher said.

"'Most of the remarks about the Jews came out of a stereotype kind of nomenclature—the perfidious Jews, the hardhearted Jew,' he said.

"'In other words, the things that were being assumed in the texts were the products of very poor Biblical and historical research'" (*Green Bay Register,* May 15, 1964).

Papal Infallibility

One of the greatest claims for superiority over the laity is that of Papal Infallibility. After refuting the claim of superiority on a basis of education and school it is now time to demolish the claim of infallibility.

Fourteen Years a Jesuit

Let us hear the testimony of one who was fourteen years a Jesuit as to the "absolutely inadequate training" in Jesuit institutions. (*Fourteen Years a Jesuit,* Baron Von Hoensbroech, 228).

On page 70 he says:

"The ignorance of the author (Jesuit J. Gretser) of this Greek Grammar is so unfathomable that any attempt at sounding it, or finding a standard of comparison, is wasted labor. A schoolboy in his first year of Greek, even the stupidest, could not invent so many impossible grammatical blunders as the author of this book produces and sells to us for knowledge.

"The history of education in Austria affords an excellent illustration of the worthlessness of the Jesuit curriculum, and the stupid obstinacy with which the Order (Jesuits), regardless of the needs and progress of the age, adheres to its foolish system of instruction. I deal with this in detail, because I was myself educated at one of the Austrian schools under Jesuit direction."

"A report laid before an Imperial Commission on Education in 1840 says:

"At the present time teaching is dissipated, the desire for knowledge stifled, in spite of great efforts little is achieved, and the young people know nothing of the delight of gaining fresh knowledge. In spite of all the Latin teaching and conversation—a point on which the Jesuit Scheme of Study lays especial stress—they are incapable, at the end of seven years, of writing a Latin composition. . . At the history lesson no historical maps are used. The mathematical teaching is beneath criticism. The simplest mathematical processes are spread over six years, and yet treated in the scantiest fashion. In fact, arithmetic is unlearned by the pupils.

"Another egotistic practice is the exclusive use of Jesuit textbooks, except, indeed where compelled by the State to introduce books by non-Jesuits. No matter how much behind the modern methods such textbooks may be, or how many mistakes they contain, it makes no difference. . .

"This institution of Jesuit textbooks is closely connected with their internationalism, for Jesuits recognize only the textbooks of the Order, not those of the nation (pages 70, 71, 82, 83).

"The educational system of the Jesuits is mechanical and superficial, concerned with externals rather than what lies beneath; it polishes the surface, but penetrates no further. . . But its worst effect is spiritual bondage in the widest sense of the word.

"The Jesuit pupil never learns to stand on his own feet, but leans on the crutches of external authority—Church, confessor, spiritual director. His freedom and independence of thought are enslaved. And everywhere internationalists, though not always known openly, is present, because it springs from the innermost nature of the Order, and keeps down patriotism, that mighty instrument of education" (page 127).

Catholic Intellectual Contribution Lagging

"A spirit of complacency is a far greater danger to Catholic education than 'frank, mature criticism' of its standards, Father John J. Cavanaugh, C.S.C., said here.

"The former president of the University of Notre Dame defended the thesis that Catholics are not contributing a proportionate share to the intellectual and social leadership of this country. Improvement will come, he said, 'only through a combination of higher standards in the schools and a renaissance of respect for culture and scholarship' in Catholic homes.

"Speaking to 400 persons interested in adult education and in Kansas City's Catholic Community Library, Father Cavanaugh both defended his previously widely publicized analysis of deficiencies in Catholic education and extended it to include the less formal education conveyed through the 'atmosphere' of the Catholic home.

"At the outset, Father Cavanaugh reviewed the evidence that he and others have cited to show that Catholics are under-represented at the top levels of American leadership. He listed these indications:

"Out of a roster of 50 leaders of business compiled by *Forbes' Magazine,* only two were Catholic—and one of these was a convert. In a study of leading educational institutions carried by the *Chicago Tribune,* a 'painful absence' of Catholic schools was apparent.

"In comparison with the far smaller Jewish community, Catholics can boast of relatively few—if any—artists and scientists ranking with men like 'Salk, Oppenheimer, Einstein, Heifetz, Horowitz, and many more equally illustrious (Jewish) artists and scientists'" (*Our Sunday Visitor, Lone Star Edition,* November 2, 1958).

Catholic Scholars Discredit Catholic Schools

Some of the conditions in Catholic schools, as pointed out by Catholic writers are:

- Substandard because of poor textbooks, full of incorrect matter, poor, antiquated methods and exceedingly poor teachers. They show that these produce few excellencies.
- They ignore the laws of sanitation and health which produces immorality, physical diseases, hypochondria, and insanity!
- Instructors are so poor that after a seven year course in Latin a student is unable to write a Latin composition!
- They destroy initiative and patriotism, but are designed to promote internationalism with control in the Vatican.

Once Catholic "intellectuals" like the usual individuals believed that you could pronounce their "hocus pocus" over base metals and turn them into gold. John XXII believed that this could be done and his writings, to that effect, are still extant. "Saint" Thomas, the greatest teacher they have ever had, they say, accepted this as true, and his problem was to try to decide if it would be morally permissible to use such gold. If he were the greatest teacher that they ever had, then, he is a greater teacher than all their two-hundred and sixty-two or more Popes! This, to say the least, is not a very logical claim. Do Catholic authorities, including the Pope, now believe that Catholics can turn lead into gold?

Certainly not, because they are not as ignorant as they once were. If this had been possible Catholic priests would not have allowed any lead to remain lead. It would all now be gold and deposited in the Vatican!

281

No Perfect Bible in Any Language

If the Catholic Church were infallible, as she claims, is it reasonable that after fifteen hundred and fifty years after Jerome translated their Vulgate, or Latin Bible, it would have hundreds of faults? Especially is this interesting since innumerable revisions have been made, through the centuries, in an effort to correct its blunders. Catholic scholars still admit, without hesitation, that at the present time it is far from perfect. This was dealt with at some length in Volume I, and in earlier chapters of this book.

Bad Translations in English Bible

We have already called your attention to the fact that the hierarchy waited one hundred and sixty years before the printing press reluctantly printed an English translation of the Bible.

Let us take a look at this translation, which has been current for more than three hundred and fifty years. We will call attention to instances where they admit, either implicitly or explicitly, to have deliberately mistranslated, and where some of these mistranslations were, in 1941, corrected in the official *Confraternity New Testament* and made to conform to the Protestant versions!

Why discard their translations in favor of the Protestant Version? Is this not an admission that the Catholic Bible was wrong for three hundred and fifty years and the Protestant Bible right?

Sheen Boasts Not One "Small Blunder"!

"If one small blunder concerning the doctrine of original sin, were made in her twenty centuries of charting the course of men to God, huge blunders would have been made in human happiness. A mistranslation of a single word one thousand years ago might have smashed all the statues of Europe" (*Moods and Truth*, Bishop Sheen, 94).

Penance vs. Repentance

Since sixteen hundred and eleven, Protestant versions have read: "Repent and be baptized" (Acts 2:38).

During all this time, since sixteen hundred and nine, the *Douay version* has read: "Do penance and be baptized."

Catholics Admit Penance Not Repentance!

"Sins committed after baptism are forgiven on repentance and on doing penance" (*Pope Innocent III and His Times,* Clayton, 176).

Catholic scholars recognize that penance is not repentance. The Douay rendering "do penance" has been repudiated in favor of the Protestant Bible, in the *Confraternity.* It reads "Repent" just as the Protestant version has always read. Is this not also an admission that the Protestants have been right for three hundred and fifty years and that the Catholics wrong?

Before 1941 priests pointed triumphantly to Ephesians 5:32 as providing scriptural proof for Catholic sacraments. In the *Douay Version* it reads:

"This is a great sacrament; but I speak in Christ and in the Church." We are made to wonder just how conscientious Catholics can still keep their respect for that institution when they are shown that the New *Confraternity Version* reads:

"This is a great mystery," just as the Protestant version has always read. As long as eighty years ago, in the *Catholic Dictionary,* Addis and Arnold stated that the word here translated "sacrament" is mistranslated (546).

This author states that no one before 1609 appealed to this passage as scriptural authority for Catholic sacraments. Again it is admitted that the Protestant version is correct and the Catholic version incorrect. There were about thirty popes during this time who allowed this false translation to continue to mislead Catholics!

283

"And Aaron and the children of Israel seeing the face of Moses was *horned* were afraid to come near. . . And they saw that the face of Moses when he came was *horned,* but he covered his face again, if at any time he spoke to them" (Exodus 34:30, 35, *Douay Catholic Version*).

Pope Julius II, the warrior pope, stood over Michelangelo as he carved the great statue of Moses, and had him make the image to conform to the Catholic Bible. It is still exhibited with large horns!

CHAPTER XV

History of Infallibility

CATHOLIC AUTHORITIES now tell us that no one in the hierarchy is infallible except the pope, and in trying to trim this doctrine to fit everything, they hardly have any left. In Volume I, I gave Catholic quotations stating that the pope is not infallible with reference to physical facts, neither do they claim he is infallible when he preaches or when he writes a book.

They are very vague as to infallible decisions through the centuries, but they assure us there have not been more than nineteen! In spite of this admission they acknowledge that the Catholic authorities have been woefully and violently divided on numberless questions.

Why does the pope allow them to be uncertain when they contend that he can infallibly settle all questions? This question should be a challenge to all our reasoning faculties.

It is very clearly admitted that NO ONE believed in papal infallibility for three hundred years after the Church was established, and during the early centuries everyone read the Bible and decided all questions by measuring them by the Scriptures. The facts are that in the early centuries of the Catholic Church, they settled questions in their councils. There were no popes in those days. Long after the Bishop of Rome began to claim unusual powers, the council was thought of as above him and even down to the Reformation period bishops of Rome were deposed by the Councils. But after this period there was a tug-of-war between popes and councils. It was not until after the American Civil War that the pope began to be universally accepted in the Catholic Church as possessing infallibility. Pope Pius IX called the Vatican Council in 1869 for the express purpose of declaring himself infallible, against a very stubborn opposition in the hierarchy. More than one hundred of the prelates assembled for that council opposed the declaration and some of the most scholarly and important among them left the Catholic Church rather than to submit to it! Since that time there has arisen a generation, all of which acknowledge it. It has been an article in the Catholic creed since 1870 and all who refuse to acknowledge it are "heretics."

Why Does Pope Delegate Big Jobs?

The translating of the *Vulgate,* more than fifteen centuries ago, Catholic scholars tell us, was turned over to Jerome, evidently because he was more scholarly and therefore more capable than the Bishop of Rome.

Jerome World's Greatest Scholar

"This work was entrusted to St. Jerome, the greatest Bible scholar the world has known" (*Our Faith and the Facts,* Donovan, 349).

"To preserve for future times, and irrevocably to fix the text of Sacred Scripture, the pope had just caused St. Jerome to furnish under his personal supervision, an exact translation from the original Hebrew. This is the version which the Council of Trent afterwards called authentic. . . The pope lavished upon St. Jerome the honors due to his talents, but painful to his modesty" (*General History of the Church,* Darras, I, 522).

Jerome evidently did not "fix" "irrevocably" the Latin Bible, for it has been changed countless times since. It is not an "exact translation" for it would have needed no changes, and present-day Catholic scholars would not have to point out its many faults! The *"Vulgate"* of Jerome is not the one the Council of Trent called "authentic"!

286

"Jerome (is) the most eminent Biblical scholar" (*Our Priesthood,* Bruneau, 60).

Catholic writers now admit that this version, which was accepted by the Bishop of Rome, was quite faulty. We wonder why the bishop did not do this job in the first place. And why did he accept a faulty version in the second place? Both show that he was not, nor did he think himself to be, infallible. Numberless "corrections" were made during the centuries that followed. None of which are now affirmed by Catholic scholars to be perfect. More than twelve hundred years after Jerome, Sixtus V made more than two thousand "corrections" in it. Less than two years later Clement VIII, another "infallible pope" recalled all of Sixtus' Bibles he could find and destroyed them because he thought Sixtus V (also an "infallible pope") had just about ruined the Bible. Clement and "St." Robert Bellarmine issued another one. But for fear someone might suspect that one or the other of these "infallible popes" had blundered, they issued it surreptitiously. They placed a series of falsehoods in the preface, that have remained there until this day! This Clementine Bible is called the *Sixtine Bible,* in order to help in this deception. Catholic scholars now admit that there are forty of Sixtus' Bibles still in existence.

To make the case still stronger, against the claim of papal infallibility, Catholic scholars still point out the many faults in the *Vulgate!* It is admitted that the Catholic Church has never had a Bible, in any language, that was without fault!

What better evidence could we have that there are no perfect Catholic scholars, and that there has never been any man, nor group of men, who are infallible, in the Catholic Church or out?

One Example of Many Absurdities

"Saul was a child of one year when he began to reign" (1 Kings 13:1 in *Douay Bible*, 1 Samuel 13:1 in Protestant Bibles).

First and Second Samuel in the Protestant Bibles is called First and Second Kings in the Catholic Bibles. They have First, Second, Third and Fourth Kings.

But we are introduced to Saul in the ninth chapter. At this time he was far away from home looking for his father's donkeys. According to this translation by an "infallible Church" he was less than one year old. Just what his age was at that time, the reader is left to guess, probably about six months! Anyway, he was quite young to be so far from home on such an important mission!

Still that is not the full story according to the Catholic Bible. After telling us in First Kings Chapter thirteen and verse one that Saul was a year old when he became King, the continuing verses one and two, it says "and he reigned two years over Israel. And Saul chose him three thousand men of Israel: and two thousand were with Saul at Michmas, and in Mount Bethel: and two thousand with Jonathan in Gibaa of Benjamin." This would make him the youngest father and general on record! He, according to this story, was only three years old and at the same time had a son old enough to lead part of the army!

Catholic Bibles Contradict!

"We shall not all be changed" (1 Cor. 15:51, *Douay Version*).
"We shall all be changed" (*Westminster Version*).

"Saint" Popes were Heretics

There have been Councils against popes and popes against popes, in fact there have been a number of popes who were condemned as heretics: the most notable are Liberius, Honorius, Gregory XII, John XXII, Paul V, Marcellus, Vigilius, Benedict XIII, and Formosus. (*Catholic Encyclopedia*, VII, 455; IX, 220; I, 288; II, 430; VI, 141; VII, 798). One of the heretic popes was Saint Liberius! Popes have been deceived (*Catholic Encyclopedia*, VII, 455; XIV, 288; XV, 765; VI, 780). This does not seem consistent with the claim of infallibility.

Popes Ignorant Concerning Witches!

Not only were popes deceived but many of them were ignorant. Gregory XV was the last of many popes who decreed the death penalty against witches, March 20, 1963. (*Catholic Encyclopedia,* VII, 5, 6).

Catholic writers rather gleefully remind their readers of the Salem witch trials in Massachusetts where twenty poor victims were killed. They are well aware that the public generally does not know that the popes had been waging a campaign against "witches" for centuries that according to *Encyclopedia Britannica* resulted in hundreds of thousands being burned at the stake! Catholic authorities reduce the number somewhat. Vacandard, a very important Catholic historian, states that they burned thirty thousand witches in one hundred and fifty years (*The Inquisition,* Vacandard, 207). They were still burning them all over Europe at the same time they were being put to death in Massachusetts. We can only conclude from this that they were just as ignorant as other people.

Popes Were Astrologers

The pope's knowledge depends on learning and not infallibility. Due to inferior, or rather lack, of education, popes sought help from astrologers rather than their infallibility.

"In the Renaissance, religion also, was subordinate to the dictation of Astrology" (*Catholic Encyclopedia,* 11, 22).

"Emperors and popes became votaries of astrology—the Emperor Charles IV and popes Sixtus IV, Julius II, Leo X, and Paul III. When these rulers lived astrology was, so to say, the regulator of official life; it is a fact characteristic of the age, that at the papal and imperial courts ambassadors were not received in audiences until the court astrologer had been consulted. . . Another well-known man was Lucas Gauricus, the court astrologer of Popes Leo X and Clement VII, who published a large number of astrological treatises. . . Even the victorious progress of the Copernican system

289

could not at once destroy the confidence in astrology" (*Catholic Encyclopedia*, II, 22-23, XII, 768).

Catholic Psalters were ornamented with the signs of the Zodiac (*Catholic Encyclopedia*, I (facing) 766).

Belief and faith are interchangeable and translated from the same word in the Greek New Testament. Catholics tell us that the Pope is infallible in faith and morals. There are hundreds of examples where the popes believed what was false. This is incontestable evidence that he is not infallible in faith. Doctrine is teaching. The pope has nearly always been in error in doctrine also!

Popes and Hierarchy Were Alchemists!

Alchemy was the ignorant belief of the Dark Ages, that by a magical formula, base metals like iron and lead could be changed into gold. The popes and hierarchy were leaders in this stupid belief. During these Dark Ages, which Catholics prefer to designate as the *Golden Age,* the popes and the hierarchy regulated every important thing by Astrology, and were burning countless thousands of unfortunate women as witches. The Inquisition, the benighted Catholic Court, charged these women with putting spells on people, of causing cyclones, famines, pestilences, riding broomsticks through the air, etc.

"Many clerics were alchemists. To Albertus Magnus, a prominent Dominican and bishop of Ratisbon, is attributed the work *'De Alchimia,'* though this is doubtful authenticity. Several treatises on alchemy are attributed to St. Thomas Aquinas. He investigated theologically the question of whether gold produced by alchemy could be sold as gold, and decided that it could, if it really possessed the properties of gold. A treatise on the subject is attributed to Pope John XXII, who is author of the Bull *'Spondent quas monehibent'* (1317) against dishonest alchemists" (*Catholic Encyclopedia,* 1, 273).

For centuries the Catholic Church has been filling its coffers with money from world-wide gambling, the world's most extensive liquor manufacture and sale, confiscating the riches of those many millions burned at the stake as heretics and witches, the universal robbing of widows and orphans by the ugliest of swindles, pretending to get people out of purgatory by selling masses, prayers and candles, renting graves in the "Consecrated cemeteries" and many other Dark Ages frauds. In view of this, I think Thomas should not have been worried about the gold made by alchemists being put into their treasury.

Catholic authorities do not champion alchemy and astrology any more. It is not divine guidance but general enlightenment that brought about this change!

If I were going to make an effort to prove papal infallibility, I would not choose any of these cases!

Perhaps the most embarrassing case involving the claim of infallibility is that of Galileo. For centuries popes had followed the teaching of Aristotle, considered the greatest of the Greek philosophers, who lived more than three hundred years before Christ. Aristotle taught that the sun moves around the earth. Copernicus, a Catholic priest, began to teach just the opposite, that the earth moves around the sun. Later Galileo began to teach this new doctrine and was brought before the court of the Inquisition with Pope Paul V as the chairman. He condemned Galileo as a heretic for, as he said, "teaching contrary to the sacred and divine scripture." *Catholic Encyclopedia* says:

"In thus acting, it is undeniable that the ecclesiastical authorities committed a grave and deplorable error, and sanctioned an altogether false principle as to the proper use of the Scripture" (VI, 344).

Think how this negates the popular claim made for the pope in the following:

Pope To Decide All Doubtful Points!

"It is that of having a fundamental authority in all ages, for a means of deciding all doubtful points, not a book alone, or a book with authorized interpreters, *but simply authorized interpreters of the faith* such as the Apostles were, with a book perhaps to help them, but still not absolutely needing that book for the discharge of their office any more than the Apostles themselves" (*Plain Facts for Fair Minds,* Searles, 33).

Galileo Right—Pope Wrong!

"To take a particular example, if Galileo, who happened to be right, while the ecclesiastical tribunal which condemned him was wrong, had really possessed convincing scientific evidence in favor of the heliocentric theory, he would have been justified in refusing his internal assent to the opposite theory, providing that in doing so he observed with thorough loyalty all the conditions involved in the duty of external obedience" (*Catholic Encyclopedia,* VII, 792).

This can only mean that Catholics *must* say that the pope is right when they know from facts that he is wrong! This is Catholic "loyalty"! All of which brings us back to:

Catholic "Prophecies" Better Than Bible!

"Miracles and prophecies have in truth never ceased, though with the close of the Apostolic age prophets have not the same public office as before, and therefore are not usually called by that name; still more is often known about the saints who have prophesied than about the Old Testament prophets, so that they offer a valuable study even for strictly Biblical purposes, and to neglect their experiences is not scientific" (*Back to the Bible,* Cuthbert Lattey, 72).

Mary Worship Promoted by Revelations

"The honor of this institution (Immaculate Conception) is generally conceded to England, for having celebrated it toward the close of the seventh century, in consequence of a revelation made to an abbot of that country named Elsin or Heribert" (*Life of the Blessed Virgin,* Monsignore De Gentilucci, 104-105).

Illusions in Catholic "Revelations"

"As for giving an infallible decision about the authenticity of a vision, that is not within the province of ecclesiastical authority, which, can merely declare that pending further investigation the faithful may accept it. For instance, the Church may have approved some unauthentic place of pilgrimage (as actually happened in Palestine) because it had no means of deciding the archaeological truth about it; but the veneration of the faithful (if they are properly instructed) is not directed to the place itself, but to the mystery that is conceived to be connected with the place. It is the same with visions. Whether the mystical phenomenon is individual or collective, there is always room for illusion. Prudent examination may decide that there is probably no fraud or illusion on the part of the visionary, if also the content of the vision is edifying, if its spiritual results are undeniable and the cures affected seem to surpass the powers of nature, the Church then authorizes a public cult. It may happen that the seer is canonized; if so, it is not for his vision alone, but for the heroic virtues of his life; it is for his charity, not for his having 'prophesied' or 'spoken in tongues.' Suppose the worst: imagine facts come to light which throw serious doubt on the genuineness of the vision, or suppose a better acquaintance with natural forces throws doubt on the reality of what has been supposed to be miracles. That would take nothing at all from the truths this particular vision represented. These would not depend on any new vision: the Church already possessed them in her deposit of faith. Nor would it detract from the graces received where the vision occurred" (*The Virgin Mary,* Guitton, 100). Catholics must follow these visionaries even though they falsified!

Prophecies of St. Malachy—Forgeries

"These prophecies were first published in 1559, by Arnold Wion, a Benedictine monk, four hundred and fifty years after the death of their supposed author. This circumstance favors the belief that they were forged to further party interests in the conclave of 1590, which elected Gregory XV (evidently XIV), for the prophecies relating to that Pontiff's predecessors are remarkably clear and precise" (*General History of the Church,* Chevalier, Artaud de Montor III, 238).

Revelations—Errors

"Whatever opinion we may form as to Mary of Agreda's revelations, taken as a whole, we are obliged to admit that they contain some errors. Thus. . . she says that the earth's radius is 1251 miles" (*The Life of Mary as Seen by Mystics,* Brown, 15).

The fact is that the radius of the earth is 3950 miles, more than three times this! Still Catholics base many things on the false statements of this woman!

Pope Approves Erroneous Revelations

"The reserve which is ordinarily maintained on the subject of revelations really no longer has any reason to exist in relation to the Mystical City, since His Holiness Leo III has been so good as gladly to encourage the project of spreading among the faithful the science of the saints which is contained in that heavenly life of the Mother of God" (*The Life of Mary as Seen by Mystics,* Brown, 13, 14).

Catholic Fables

Paul tells us in 2 Timothy 4:3-4 that men would turn away their ears from the truth and be turned to fables. A fable or myth is an untrue story, an impossible story.

"But refuse profane and old wives' fables, and exercise thyself rather unto godliness" (1 Tim. 4:7). Would we not understand from this that if we accepted profane and old wives' fables we would be exercising ourselves rather unto ungodliness?

And now listen to Peter, who Catholics claim was the first Pope: "For we have not followed cunningly devised fables, when we made known unto you the power and coming of our Lord Jesus Christ, but were eyewitnesses of his majesty" (2 Peter 1:16).

I am sure that you will agree that the Catholic fables that I have cited, and hundreds more that could be cited, were cunningly devised.

"St. Gregory speaks of the deacon 'accepting the tower in which the mystery of the Lord's body (bread—O.C.L.) was contained' and which he was taking into the Church 'that he might place it upon the altar.' The Lord's Body (bread—O.C.L.), however, escaped from his hands and placed itself upon the altar—a miracle which was believed by those present to have indicated the unworthiness of the deacon in question" (*The Development of Christian Worship,* Steuart, 172).

"But how great was her consternation and grief when Our Lord in company with St. Catherine, her patroness, led her one day, in spirit, to Purgatory. There she beheld her father in an abyss of torments, imploring her assistance. At the sight of the pitiful state the soul of her father was in, she melted to tears; she cast herself at the feet of her Heavenly Spouse, and begged Him, through His precious blood, to free her father from his excruciating sufferings. She also begged St. Catherine for him, and then turning to Our Lord, she said: 'Charge me, O Lord, with my Father's indebtedness to Thy justice. In expiation of it, I am ready to take upon myself all the afflictions Thou art pleased to bestow upon me.' Our Lord graciously accepted this act of heroic charity, and released at once her father's soul from Purgatory" (*Purgatory,* Sadlier, 109).

Do we believe God? If not why not?

"Behold, all souls are mine; as the soul of the father, so also the soul of the son is mine: the soul that sinneth, *it* shall die." Ezekiel 18:4).

"So every one of us shall give account of *himself* to God" (Romans 14-12).

"I will recompense them according to their deeds, and according to the works of *their own hands*" (Jer. 25:14).

"Who will render to every man *according to his deeds*" (Rom. 2:6).

"We receive the due reward of *our deeds*" (Luke 23:41).

"Every man shall receive his own reward *according to his own labor*"

"The Lord shall reward the doer of evil according to *his wickedness*" (2 Sam. 3:39).

"For the Son of man shall come in the glory of His Father with his angels; then He shall reward every man *according to his works*" (Matt. 16:28).

"And, behold, I come quickly; and my reward is with me, to give every man *according as his work shall be*" (Rev. 22:12).

You will note that this last quotation comes from the last chapter in the Bible. It is included in the last warning of the Bible, and along with all the other quotations were given us by divine revelation. They are for our admonition and learning, and are not to be taken lightly. We are told in these passages what we may expect and depend upon after our earthly life comes to an end. If we have failed to keep the commandments, or heed the warnings, it will then be too late for our destiny to be changed. Our relatives, our friends, the priests, or anyone else will be unable to do anything for us. It would be well for the reader to take time out at this point, and read carefully the story of the Rich Man and Lazarus as found in Luke, chapter sixteen.

CHAPTER XVI

The Sacraments

Catholicism has invented seven rites, which she admits are not only unscriptural, but were unknown in history for nearly a thousand years after the Catholic Church was first mentioned, which was in the fourth century. She has endowed these fictions with magical powers with which to awe the laity and make gods of the priests. These are the chains that are used to shackle the minds of the laity and provide the hierarchy with a shameful source of enrichment. They make up a powerful sort of spiritual blackmail. The priests learn all the questionable conduct of Catholics, and claim the right either to forgive or not to forgive: to open or to close the gates of heaven. This system makes the priests indispensable. There is only one being that could invent such a perfect means of enabling a bad man to debauch Catholic wives and daughters and furnish a means of contact with the worst type of people. The truth of this can be gained from a study of her own writers and their frank admission that this is so.

We are told that these seven sacraments are Baptism, Confirmation, Eucharist, Penance, Holy Orders, Matrimony, and Extreme Unction. The Catholic Church admits that no one in the Church ever heard of this idea for centuries, but like nearly every other feature of Catholicism some visionary back in the Dark Ages would suggest it, then for centuries thereafter others would, from time to time, add to it and finally it would formally be made a part of Catholic theology. It is admitted that it was the Council of Trent, under pressure of the Protestant Reformation, that finally adopted this system of sacraments as binding on Catholics. This happened only four hundred years ago, which is much too late to be divine! None of the popes for twelve hundred years knew of it!

After this system was adopted and became a law in the Catholic Church an anathema was pronounced on all who refuse to follow it. Catholics have, in a thousand ways, changed God's will in the Bible but they do not allow any change in Catholic arrangements.

"In short, a legal document of such importance, and drawn up with such precision, must be interpreted according to what it says, not according to what it does not say" (*New Matrimonial Legislation,* Cronin, 148).

"The Council of Trent had already condemned as anathema anyone who held that it was lawful to ignore the rites approved by the church for use in the solemn administration of the sacraments or to substitute others for them" (*The Sacred Canons,* Abbo and Hannan, 415).

More than three hundred years later the pope allowed priests to leave off saliva, if they wished, in the administration of baptism! (*The Sacred Canons,* 415).

At this point it is appropriate to point out how incongruous, discordant, contradictory, inconsistent, and irreconcilable the whole Catholic system is. It is the stock explanation given for its unscripturalness that only a small part of the divine will was written and that most of it, though it was given at the same time, was doomed to be transmitted from one to another by word of mouth. They insist that there is nothing in "tradition" any newer than that written in the Bible. We are assured that the pope and the hierarchy are infallible custodians of tradition. How in the light of such claims can Catholics account for one hundred and seventy-five of their pretended line of infallible popes knowing nothing of all the sacraments?

Catholics readily admit that the *sacraments* are not Scriptural. They do this in addition to the Catholic Bible which says that the Scripture (written word) furnishes completely to every good work. This Bible statement can only mean that if a thing is not in the Scripture it is not a good work.

298

Bible Silent on Sacraments

"The Bible is silent or at least is not clear on a number of matters such as baptism of infants and the exact number of the sacraments, concerning which the Church follows tradition" (*National Catholic Almanac,* 1943, 128).

Catholics disregard all the Bible warnings against adding to the Scripture.

Sacraments Not in Scripture

"*We* are given to understand that the Apostles themselves or the plenary councils—whose authority in the Church is most wholesome—have commanded and have decreed that those sacraments are to be retained which are not recorded in Scripture" (*Sources of Christian Theology,* Palmer, 1, 88).

This is not only true of sacraments, but with reference to practically all Catholic teaching and practice.

Catholics Mistranslated Bible to
Make Men Accept "Sacraments"

For three hundred years after the *Douay Version* was issued, priests pointed proudly to Ephesians, 5:32: "This is a great sacrament," as Scriptural authority for this system.

An Admitted False Translation

"The same council (Trent, 1545-1563 A.D.—O.C.L.) speaks of Scripture as insinuating (innuit) this truth, and more can scarcely be said. One text indeed, so translated in our *Douay Bible,* would certainly seem to settle the question—viz. Ephesians 5:31-32, 'For this cause shall a man leave his father and his mother, and shall adhere to his wife; and they shall be two in one flesh. This is a great sacrament, but I speak jn Christ and in the Church.' But we venture to think that this is not the true sense of the Vulgate. . . Indeed, though the word 'sacramentum' occurs in fifteen other places of the Vulgate, it cannot possibly mean a sacrament in any one of them. We translate, accordingly, 'This mystery is great, but I speak with reference to Christ and the Church.' . . . We have the authority of Estius for this interpretation, which is that adopted by modern scholars, and he denies that the ancients appealed to this text to prove marriage a sacrament" (*Catholic Dictionary,* Addis and Arnold, 545, 546).

It was in 1884, that this learned work stated that Catholic scholars had abandoned the Catholic English Bible as being a false translation of the words of Paul. But it was not until nearly sixty years later (1941 A.D.) that the Catholic English Bible was corrected on this point. The present English Catholic translation says "mystery" just as Protestant versions have always read! This is only one of the many like instances.

We have in earlier pages of this book presented admissions to having mistranslated the Bible many times in order to support Catholicism and in their pretended explanation of Scriptural passages to have forced into the Bible meanings not intended by the divine writers.

Let us hear them again:

". . . There was no systematic sacramental theology before the scholastic period" (*Catholic Encyclopedia,* V, 719).

The scholastic period here referred to is really the Dark Ages.

Two Sacraments

"In tracing the history of the numeration within the Church, we may distinguish four different stages. Till about the end of the fourth century we find usually two, and sometimes three rites placed together as sacraments" (*Catholic Dictionary,* Addis and Arnold, 735).

". . . the enumeration of *seven sacraments* was unknown for nearly twelve centuries of Church history" (*Catholic Dictionary,* Addis and Arnold, 734).

"In the thirteenth century, the term sacrament, which until them had been applied to various religious rites, was reserved to designate only the seven sacraments properly so-called" (*History of the Catholic Church,* Brother Gustavus, 106).

"When about the twelfth century the true nature of the sacraments had become better understood and more clearly defined; theologians, principally after Alexander of Hales, reserved the name of sacrament to the sensible signs of divine institution and that of sacramental to those of ecclesiastical origin" (*Legislation on the Sacraments,* 398).

"Prior to the twelfth century the name 'sacrament' was applied to sacred rites and to sacramentals as well as to the seven sacraments" (*The Sacred Canons,* Abbo and Hannan, 414).

Peter Lombard First Spoke of Seven Sacraments!

"Most probably this honor belongs to Peter Lombard (d. 1164) who in his fourth book of *Sentences* defines a sacrament. . . and then enumerates the seven Sacraments" (*Catholic Encyclopedia,* XIII, 299-300).

Reformation Produced Sacraments

"The new errors of the Reformation gave occasion to the explicit teaching of the Church concerning Justification, the Sacraments, Indulgences, Veneration of Saints, the existence of Purgatory" (*The Question Box,* Conway, 139).

Such admissions as the above never cease to amaze me.

Council of Trent Decreed Seven Sacraments

"If any one saith that the Sacraments of the New Law were not all instituted by Jesus Christ our Lord, or that they are more or less than seven . . . let him be anathema" (*Council of Trent,* Quoted by Pastor's *History of the Popes,* IV, 144).

"The Council of Trent defined that the seven sacraments of the

New Law were instituted by Christ. This settles the question of fact for all Catholics" (*Catholic Encyclopedia,* XIII, 298).

How is it possible to harmonize the above teaching with that of the inspired Apostle Paul, given twelve hundred years earlier to the Churches of Galatia?

"I wonder that you are so soon removed, from him that called you into the grace of Christ, unto another gospel: which is not another, only there are some that trouble you, and would pervert the gospel of Christ. But though *we,* or an *angel* from heaven, preach a gospel to you besides that which *we have preached* to you, let him be anathema. As we said before, so now I say again: If *any one* preach to you a gospel, besides that *which you have received,* let him be anathema" (Galatians, 1:6-9, *Douay Version*).

Catholics Must Accept Falsehood for Fact!

The Council of Trent more than fifteen hundred years after the Lord's church was established, told this falsehood, and now Catholics must accept it as the truth!

Seven Sacraments—Twelve Centuries Late

"Again, though it is quite true that the enumeration of seven sacraments was unknown for nearly twelve centuries of Church history" (*Catholic Dictionary,* Addis and Arnold, 734).

Seven Channels of the Blood

"They are the seven precious channels of the blood and merits of the atonement, flowing from the cross upon the hearts of sinful men to wash away their sins" (*Question Box,* Conway, 1913 Edition, 346).

How did Catholics get the blood for the hundreds of years when nobody knew anything about the channels?

No Sacraments for 1200 Years

"Actually, it was not until the twelfth century that the word "sacrament" was defined with sufficient precision to disengage the seven rites, and only seven, from the numerous ceremonies that had been celebrated in the Church for centuries, and to apply to just seven sacraments of the New Law. . . This will explain, perhaps, why there is no mention of the sacraments in the early creeds of christendom" (*The sources of Christian Theology,* 1, Palmer, 72).

Sacraments Greatest Avenue to Heaven!

"At this instant, by far the greatest amount of earth's intercourse with heaven is carried on directly or indirectly through the sacraments" (*Teachings of the Catholic Church,* Smith, 10).

Is it not strange, that for twelve hundred years, the Catholic Church, which claims to have always had the truth and all the truth, knew nothing of this greatest avenue to heaven? It is not only strange but incredible.

CHAPTER XVII

Marriage

Marriage Not a Sacrament Before Thirteenth Century

"It is therefore historically certain that from the beginning of the thirteenth century the sacramental character of marriage was universally known and recognized as a dogma. . ." (*Catholic Encyclopedia*, IX, 707).

Another Catholic Contradiction

"The Catholic Church has always taught that marriage is a sacrament" (*Marriage*, Morrison, S.J., 40).

"The reason why marriage was not expressly and formally included among the sacraments earlier (thirteenth century) . . . is to be found in the historical development of the doctrine regarding the sacraments" (*Catholic Encyclopedia*, IX, 707).

In spite of this admission by Catholics, we see that the laity is told the falsehood, and led to believe that if they are not married "before the priest" they are not really married! The "sacraments" are the chains by which the consciences of Catholics are bound to the priesthood. They make the priests, regardless of how wicked they may be, indispensable!

Protestants Not Married!
Must Be Before Priest To Be Marriage!

"Can any one administer the sacraments in your Church?

"No; the Catholic Church believes, with St. Paul, in a ministry ordained by Christ for that purpose, and therefore limits the administration of the sacraments to those in Holy Orders, with the exception of baptism in cases of necessity, it being necessary for salvation—'So let a man think of us as the ministers of Christ and the dispensers of the mysteries of God' (1 Cor. 4:1)—and that of matrimony, in which the parties themselves are the ministers of the sacrament, while none the less obligated to be married in the presence of their pastor" (*Question Box,* 349, 350).

None But Catholics Participate in Sacraments

"Again, no outsider has a right to participate in the sacraments of the Catholic Church" (*Question Box,* 363).

"Thus she claims exclusive control over the sacraments" (*Question Box,* 504).

"Of course baptized persons alone receive the sacrament" (*Catholic Encyclopedia,* IX, 700).

Marriage Inseparable from the Sacrament!

"The opinion of several canonists, who, wishing to justify this view, taught that the contract of marriage might possibly be separated from the sacrament, was condemned in the Syllabus of Pius IX in 1864 (number 65 and 66)" (*Catholic Encyclopedia,* IX, 700).

"Under the Christian law, therefore, the marriage contract and the sacrament are inseparable and indivisible" (*Catholic Encyclopedia,* IX, 700).

"The Church does not consider merely civil marriage as marriage in any sense" (*Penal Legislation in the New Code of Canon Law,* 1918, p. 298).

"Those who attempt to contract matrimony otherwise than in the presence of the parish priest or of another priest with the leave of the parish priest or of the ordinary, and before two or three witnesses, the Holy Synod (Council of Trent) renders altogether incapable of such a contract, and declares such contracts null and void" (Council of Trent, as reported by *Catholic Encyclopedia,* IV, 1).

Protestant Mothers Concubines!!!!

"But impious laws taking no account of the sacredness of this great sacrament, placed it on the same level as all merely civil contracts; and the deplorable result has been that citizens, desecrating the holy dignity of marriage, have lived in legal concubinage instead of Christian matrimony" (Leo XIII, in *Life of Leo XIII,* 332).

Decry Shameful Divorces—Would "Annul" Every Protestant Marriage!!!

A certain portion of marriages end up in the divorce court, which is a cause of shame to every God-fearing man or woman, but Catholics would separate every couple not married by the priest. I abhor such things just as much when they are called "annulments." As we have already abundantly proven by their own testimony that they do not consider one who has not been married by the priest as being really married, it will not be a surprise to read the following:

"If two unbaptized persons have contracted marriage, this marriage, even if consummated, may be dissolved, supposing one of the parties embraces the Christian religion and the other refuses to live peaceably and without insult to the Christian religion in the married state" (*Catholic Dictionary,* 268).

CHAPTER XVIII

Extreme Unction

Extreme Unction Twelfth Century

"Only about the twelfth or thirteenth century did the people commence in the Western Church (Roman Catholic, O.C.L.) to look upon Extreme Unction as the sacrament of the dying" (*Legislation on the Sacraments in the New Code,* 300).

No Sacraments for 1200 Years

"Actually, it was not until the twelfth century that the word 'sacrament' was defined with sufficient precision to disengage the seven rites, and only seven, from the numerous ceremonies that had been celebrated in the Church for centuries, and to apply to just seven sacraments of the New Law. . . This will explain, perhaps, why there is no mention of the sacraments in the early creeds of christendom" (*The sources of Christian Theology,* I, Palmer, 72).

Catholics Must Accept Falsehood for Fact!

The Council of Trent more than fifteen hundred years after the Lord's church was established, told this falsehood, and now Catholics must accept it as the truth!

Seven Sacraments—Twelve Centuries Late!

"Again, though it is quite true that the enumeration of seven sacraments was unknown for nearly twelve centuries of Church history" (*Catholic Dictionary,* Addis and Arnold, 734).

Extreme Unction (Anointing)

"Crowds in heaven shall owe their endless bliss to that one communion" (*Teachings of the Catholic Church,* Smith, 7, 11).

I trust that the reader understands the meaning of "Extreme Unction" and the part it plays, as a sacrament, in the system of Catholicism. The following shows us that this unscriptural, nauseating doctrine and practice claims to enable the priest to do something to save one even after the sinner is unconscious, or dead!

"Baptism can justify the child whose reason has not downed. Extreme Unction can deal with the relics of sin in a sinner who lies insensible" (*Teaching of the Catholic Church,* Smith, 9, 10).

"God frequently works miracles through the ordinary administration of the sacrament of Extreme Unction" (*Question Box,* 1913 Edition, 389).

Die in the Act of Sinning—Forgiven!

"The intention to be anointed is *implicitly* contained, e.g., in the will to live and die a Catholic. Thus one may anoint him who has lived a Christian life; and, one, too, who has not lived much like a Christian or even whom death overtakes in the act of sinning" (*Moral Theology,* Jone and Adelman, 446).

Obliterates Sin!

"Extreme Unction, which obliterates the traces of sin and invigorates the power of the soul" (*Teaching of the Catholic Church,* Smith, 9, 10).

What Constitutes Extreme Unction?
Anointment of Parts That Sinned!

"As administered in the Western Church (Roman Catholic— O.C.L.) today according to the rite of the Roman Ritual, the sacrament consists (apart from certain non-essential prayers) in the unction of oil, specially blessed by the bishop of the organs of the five external senses (eyes, ears, nostrils, lips, hands), of the feet, and, for men (where the custom exists and the condition of the patient permits of being moved), of the loins or reins; and in the following form repeated at each unction with mention of the corresponding sense of faculty: 'Through this holy unction and His most tender mercy may the Lord pardon thee whatever sins or faults thou hast committed by sight (hearing, smell, taste, touch, walking, carnal delectation).' The unction of the loins is generally, if not universally, omitted in English-speaking countries, and is of course everywhere forbidden in the case of women" (*Catholic Encyclopedia,* V, 716).

Why are Catholic people frightened by the prospect of dying without the priest being present to recite those "non-essential prayers"? If the anointing of the loins is important for men why is it forbidden for women? Why is the anointing of the loins practiced in other countries but is being discontinued in English-speaking countries? The implication is clear that the anointing of different parts of the body is to get rid of the sins committed by the use of those parts. If this is beneficial for men, why deny this benefit to women?

The Bible gave no authority for all this and Catholic authorities knew nothing of all this for twelve hundred years, and Catholic doctrine had not developed to this point, yet all the time there was in existence a religion that was not only "complete" but "perfect." This complete and perfect system did not include Extreme Unction nor any of the thousands of the distinctive Catholic doctrines and practices. God's religion never grows into something else.

One of the corner-stones of Catholicism is the anti-scriptural idea that the priest can do something for us after we are unconscious, or dead, that will prevent our being charged in the judgment with OUR misdeeds.

This pernicious idea enables the priesthood not only to pose as pre-eminent, but also enrich the Catholic Church by their terrifying, pagan mumbo-jumbo! The following scriptures show how false this is:

"For the Son of man shall come in the glory of his Father with his angels; and then shall he reward every man according to his works" (Matt. 16:27),

"And no marvel; for Satan himself is transformed into an angel of light. Therefore it is no great thing if his ministers also be transformed as the ministers of righteousness; whose end shall be according to their works" (2 Cor. 11:14-15).

"And I saw the dead, small and great, (that means all who die—O.C.L.) stand before God; and the books were opened: and another book was opened, which is the book of life: (the record of our life—O.C.L.) and the dead were judged out of those things which are written in the books according to their works" (Rev. 20:12).

"Work out your own salvation with fear and trembling" (Phil. 2,;12).

"So then every one of us shall give account of himself to God" (Rom. 14:12).

"For we must all appear before the judgment seat of Christ; that every one may receive the things done in his body, according to that he hath done, whether it is good or bad" (2 Cor. 5:10).

It is a terrifying thought that *no one* after we are unconscious, or dead, *can do anything* to change our destiny.

"Behold, now is the accepted time; behold, now is the day of salvation" (2.Cor. 6:2).

After the rich man died nothing could be done for him (Luke 16: 23-26). The wise virgins could not help the foolish who had not made proper preparation themselves (Matt. 25:1-12). The wicked servant could do nothing to save himself after his master returned (Matt. 24:44- 51). So the Lord's admonition was "Therefore be ye also ready" (Matt. 24:44).

"He that is unjust, let him be unjust still: and he which is filthy, let him be filthy still: and he that is righteous, let him be righteous still: and he that is holy, let him be holy still. And, behold, *I come quickly; and my reward is with me, to give every man according as his work shall be"* (Rev. 22:11-12).

This certainly does not encourage men to believe that the priest, by giving Extreme Unction can benefit one who "dies in the act of sinning"!

No Possible Danger of Deception

Compare the following statements.

"The people are in no possible danger of deception" (*Catholic Dictionary,* Addis and Arnold, 738).

"Be not *deceived;* God is not mocked; for whatsoever a man soweth, that shall he also reap" (Gal. 6:7).

It is easy for one to walk in darkness or to be deceived, but oh so dangerous to do so.

CHAPTER XIX

Baptism

The Catholic Bible is very clear as to what baptism is, but it is nowhere called a "sacrament."

"Then went out to him Jerusalem and all Judea, and all the country about Jordan: and were baptized by him *in* the Jordan, confessing their sins" (Matt. 3:5-6, *Douay*).

"And Jesus being baptized, forthwith came *out of* the water" (Matt. *3:16, Douay*).

"And John also was baptizing in Aennon near Salim; because there was much water there"(John 3:23, *Douay)*.

"Know you not that all we, who are baptized in Christ Jesus, are baptized into his death? For *we are buried* together with him by baptism into death; that as Christ is risen from the dead by the glory of the Father so we also may walk in newness of life. For if we have been *planted* together in the likeness of his death, we shall be also in the likeness of his resurrection" (Rom. 6:3-5, *Douay*).

"Buried with him in baptism, in whom also you are risen again by faith of the operation of God, who hath raised him up from the dead" (Col. 2:12, *Douay*).

"Then Philip, opening his mouth, and beginning at this scripture, preached unto him Jesus. And as they went on their way, they came to a certain water; and the Eunuch said: See, here is water: what doth hinder me from being baptized? And Philip said: If thou believest with all thy heart, thou mayest. And he answering, said: I believe that Jesus Christ is the Son of God. And he commanded the chariot to stand still; and they *went down into* the water *both* Philip and the Eunuch: and he baptized him. And when *they* were come *up out of* the water, the Spirit of the Lord took away Philip;

and the Eunuch saw him no more. And he went on his way rejoicing" (Acts 8:35, *Douay*).

Immersion

"Catholics admit that immersion brings out more fully the meaning of the sacrament, and that for twelve centuries it was the common practice" (*Question Box,* 240).

"Baptism took place by immersion in ancient times" (*New Interpretation of the Mass,* Borgmann, 120).

Catholics Change from Bible Practice!

"The Scripture makes it clear enough that water is to be used, but it is not so plain at first sight that sprinkling or pouring of water will suffice. *In Apostolic Times the body of the baptized person was immersed,* for, St. Paul looks on the immersion as typifying the burial with Christ, and speaks of baptism as a bath. Immersion still prevails among the Copts and Nestorians, and for many ages baptisms was so given among the Latins also for even St. Thomas, in the thirteenth century, speaks of baptism by immersion as the common practice of his time" (*Catholic Dictionary,* Addis and Arnold, 60).

Lord's Way Inconvenient

"The present mode of pouring arose from the inconvenience connected with immersion, frequent mention of which is made in writings of the early Church fathers" (*Question Box,* 366).

Students of the Bible know that God has never consulted man in making his plans or considered man's convenience in carrying out his commands. An example of this is found in the twelfth chapter of First Kings and the second chapter of Acts. It was God's command that the children of Israel go to Jerusalem to worship him. For some this was not convenient, so they set up altars at Dan and Bethel and began to worship there. As a result of this evil, God brought evil upon them along with Jeroboam the one who had led the people to do this terrible thing. "It is a fearful thing to fall into the hands of the living God"! (Hebrews 10:31, *Douay*).

"And he shall give Israel up because of the sins of Jeroboam, who did sin, and who made Israel to sin" (1 Kings 14:16).

Immersion Practically Obsolete!

"Immersion (Lat., immergere), the act of dipping or plunging the subject into the water used in the administration of Baptism: called the triple or trine immersion when the candidate is dipped three times, in the name of each person of the Holy Trinity. Immersion was the method generally employed in the early Church. The Greeks still retain it; but though valid, for obvious reasons immersion has become practically obsolete in the Latin Church (Roman Catholic)" (*Catholic Dictionary,* Vatican Edition, 471).

The Element of Baptism

In an emergency baptize with tea, coffee, or carbonated drinks" (Leaflet, *Sacraments in Pictures*).

Try to imagine how much Coca Cola or beer would have been needed to baptize the thousands that were baptized in Bible times. After that, contemplate the countless emergencies that could have occurred during the almost two thousand years since that time. Those who believe and rely on the Bible are not disturbed, for the Bible says *water!*

Infant Baptism
Catholics Rarely Obey Bible!

"Baptism, nowadays, is given almost exclusively to children" (*Our Priesthood,* Bruneau, 154).

". . . baptism of adults . . . a thing of rare occurrence" (*General History of the Church,* Darras, 11, 135).

Cannot Prove Infant Baptism by the Bible

"It is difficult to give strict proof from the scripture in favor of it" (*Catholic Dictionary,* Addis and Arnold, 61).

"There is no express mention of the baptism of infants in the New Testament" (*Question Box,* 1929 Edition, 243).

"The baptism of infants is not positively directed in the Gospels" (*Teaching of the Catholic Church,* Smith, *Sacraments and Sacramentals,* 23).

Infant Baptism Not in Bible
Who Then Should Be Baptized?

"Going therefore, teach ye all nations: baptizing them" (Matt. 28:19, *Douay*).

"He that believeth and is baptized shall be saved" (Mark 16:16, *Douay*).

"Repent and be baptized every one of you" (Acts 2:38, *Confraternity*).

Catholic Teaching Not in the Bible

"Catholic controversialists soon proved to the Protestants that to be logical and consistent they must admit unwritten tradition. Otherwise by what right did they rest on Sunday and not on Saturday? How could they regard infant baptism as valid, or baptism by infusion?" (*Catholic Encyclopedia,* XV, 7, Also *Question Box,* 368, 369).

Immersed Only in Early Church!

"Ecclesiastical custom with regard to the administration of Baptism has undergone a change in the course of history. Whereas the early Church baptized adults only, the baptism of children soon became the usual practice. But for a long time it was the rule to

315

baptize only children who had been born. At a later period, however, it was found desirable, in cases of difficult birth, to administer Baptism before birth was completed" (*Pastoral Medicine,* Ruland-Ratter, 32-33).

"A miscarried fetus or embryo, no matter how small, must always be baptized" (*Spiritual First Aid Procedures,* Gerald H. Fitz Gibbons, S.J. 3).

Catholic Reason for Infant Baptism

"When all fear of persecution had passed away, and the empire had become almost entirely Christian, the necessity for a prolonged period of trial and instruction no longer existed, about the same time the fuller teaching on the subject of original sin, occasioned by the Pelagian heresy, gradually led to the administration of baptism to infants. In such cases instruction was, of course impossible, though traces of it are still to be seen in the rite of infant baptism, where the godparents are put through a sort of catechesis in the name of the child" (*Catholic Encyclopedia, N,* 78).

"Where in the fourth and fifth centuries the doctrine of original sin became better known, the practice of infant baptism progressed rapidly" (*Legislation on the Sacraments in the New Code of Canon Law,* Ayrinhac, 72).

"Anciently, when baptism was constantly given to adults and the rite of immersion prevailed, it was inconvenient to baptize in the Church itself, and hence after the conversion of Constantine separate buildings for the administration of baptism were erected and attached to the Cathedral Church" (*Catholic Dictionary,* Addis and Arnold, 64).

Catholics Have Laws for Babies!

The Bible has no command to or for babies. They have no need for one. When speaking of little children Jesus said: "Of such is the kingdom of God" (Luke 18:15). When speaking to his disciples

Jesus said: "Unless you be converted and become as little children, you shall not enter into the kingdom of heaven" (Matt. 18:3). And again he said: "See that you despise not one of these little ones: for I say to you, that their Angel in heaven always see the face of my Father who is in heaven" (Matt. 18:10, *Douay*).

Think how absurd is the following Catholic law!

"The present law of the Church (Cannon 1262, 2) prescribes that women who assist at sacred functions should cover their heads and be dressed modestly, especially when they approach the Lord's table. So women and girls should wear a hat or a scarf or a veil or a babushka. Girl babies should wear a bonnet. It is, of course, not a mortal sin to disregard this ruling in itself. Since feminine headgear is sometimes extraordinary, grotesque, and rather startling, of a kind that could hardly be called a covering of the head at all, it would probably be discreet not to notice whether the women in our churches have their heads covered or not" (*Our Sunday Visitor*, August 25, 1963).

Origin of Sponsors

"At the end of the second or beginning of the third century Tertullian refers to the responsibilities assumed by sponsors in baptism and represents their office as an already ancient institution. (*De Baptismo C.* XVIII.) Some have tried to find for it a biblical foundation or seen in it an imitation of some Jewish rite. Necessity suffices to account for its introduction from the beginning" (*Legislation on the Sacraments*, Ayrinhac, 45).

Catholics Baptize Unbelievers

"Valid reception does not require faith. . . Therefore, an unbeliever who so desires may be validly baptized even tho he have no faith" (*Moral Theology*, Jone-Adelman, 320).

Compare the above quotation with the following:

"But without faith it is impossible to please God. For he that cometh to God, must believe that he is, and is a rewarder of them that seek him" (Hebrews 11:6, *Douay*).

How far from truth can a man get, or maybe I should ask; How far from truth can a man be led?

"Sanctify them in truth. Thy word is truth" (John 17:17, *Douay*).

Catholics "Baptize" the Unconscious

"They would admit the same rule for pagan as for Christian countries and baptize any person found unconscious and in a dying condition" (*Legislation on the Sacraments,* Ayrinhac, 32).

Baptize the Unwilling! Babies Enemies of God!

"*We* begin with the solemn rite of Baptism. Many priests find this ("baptizing" babes—O.C.L.) the least spiritualizing of all their works in the Church. The fact that the recipient of the sacrament is unconscious of what is being done, and often in consequence be-haves in a manner not befitting the occasion, undoubtedly detracts from the solemnity of the rite. Yet there is much to suggest itself of special interest, for the sacrament involves the whole history of mankind. The child arrives not a member of the Church, even in positive enmity—though unconsciously—to Almighty God, and in the power of the enemy of mankind. As a result of the priest's min-istration, the devil is expelled, and the child acquires the state of one of the faithful" (*The Priestly Vocation,* Ward, 89).

Bible Faith and Catholic Faith Different

The Catholic Bible (*Douay* Version) tells us that faith comes by hearing the word of Christ. But even common reason shows clearly that an infant is incapable of believing.

"Faith then cometh by hearing; and hearing by the word of Christ" (Romans 10:17).

The following are but a few of the hundreds of instances where

318

Catholics reverse the divine order:

"Many receive their faith in their infancy" (*Catholic Encyclopedia*, V, 757).

Having authority for the fact that most Catholics are now "baptized" in infancy we are prepared for Catholic assertion that infants receive faith "through baptism" (*Explanation of Catholic Morals,* Stapleton, 77).

"It is baptism that makes faith possible, for faith is a gift of God" (*Explanation of Catholic Morals,* 90).

So, according to the Catholic Bible faith comes by hearing the words of Christ, but according to Catholic theology a few drops of water on the head of an unconscious infant will give him faith!

Catholic Encyclopedia (V, 753-757) and *Explanation of Catholic Morals* (94) speak of the "habit of faith."

Must Baptize All Babies in Hospital Against Parents' Wishes!

"*Dying Infants and Babies*—must always be baptized, i.e., *any* child below the age of reason. If you are not absolutely sure the baby was baptized at all, or correctly and validly baptized, and a priest cannot be had in time, baptize without delay. . . The child is dying! Its rights to heaven have complete priority over all other rights and considerations—even those of parents who, though perhaps here and now unwilling because not informed or misinformed, assuredly wish everything done to guarantee for their baby the vision of God in all eternity. The baptism is easily taken care of: If visitors cannot be asked to leave the room, the doctor or nurse facing away from them uses a towel with clean water to bathe the child's forehead, then squeezes it; when water is seen to flow, the words are said audibly but in a whisper" (*Spiritual First Aid Procedures,* Fritz Gibbon, S.J., 3).

All the "baptisms" must be recorded (*Ibid,* 4). This is one of the ways which enable the Catholic Church to claim such frightening numbers!

Forever Branded Indelibly

"Three Sacraments, Baptism, Confirmation and Orders, besides grace, produce in the soul a character, i.e., and indelible spiritual mark by which some are consecrated as servants of God, some as soldiers, some as ministers" (*Catholic Encyclopedia,* XII, 301).

Confirmation

"A sacrament of the new law by which grace is conferred on baptized persons which strengthens them for the profession of the Christian faith. It is conferred by the bishop, who lays his hands on the recipients, making the sign of the cross with chrism on their foreheads, while he pronounces the words 'I sign thee with the sign of the cross and confirm thee with the chrism of salvation, in the Name of the Father, and of the Son, and of the Holy Ghost.' Besides conferring a special grace to profess the faith, it also sets a seal or character on the soul, so that this sacrament cannot be reiterated without sacrilege" (*Catholic Dictionary,* Addis and Arnold, 208).

Can't Really Leave the Catholic Church!

"But though those who have been baptized can outwardly throw off their allegiance to the Church, abandon her communion, and so lose all rights to those spiritual benefits and advantages which the Church bestows so bountifully upon her faithful children, nevertheless they can never free themselves from the bond of subjection and obedience to the authority and jurisdiction of the Church—a bond that came into being in and through the Sacrament of Baptism, and continues in existence by virtue of the baptismal character which is sealed permanently and indelibly upon the soul. No subject is considered to be released from his obligation of allegiance and submission to lawful authority by the fact that he has committed an act of rebellion, though thereby he has forfeited his rights and privileges. Still less can a creature effectually repudiate and cast off the ties with which the law of God has bound him. Consequently the Church always has and retains her power over all who have been baptized, even though they have attempted to throw off her sweet yoke and have gone out from her. They are therefore subject to her laws, in so far as she wishes and intends them to be subject; and this is shown too by the constant practice of the Church and by the explicit declarations of the Roman Pontiff" (*New Matrimonial Legislation,* Cronen 244-245).

This quotation should be read and reread many times. It should be carefully studied, analyzed and digested. Let us consider a few of the things that this quotation tells us about the Roman Pontiff and *his* Church. This tells us that all those "baptized," whether conscious or unconscious, willingly or unwillingly, can *never* free themselves from the bond of subjection and obedience to the authority and jurisdiction of the Catholic Church.

With God's church it is different. First, it was given to Christ, His Son, and not to the pope. "And hath put all things under his feet, and *gave* him to be the head over all things to the church, which is his body, the fullness of him that filleth all in all" (Ephesians 1:22-23). Man is not a mere machine. He can make a choice (Josh. 25:15; 1 Kings 18:21; Prov. 27:1). The first choice is to accept Christ's way of life (Matt. 16:24; 7:13-14). Should our choice be sin and yielding to Satan we choose the things of the flesh in every walk of life (Rom. 8:13; Gal. 5:24; 1 Cor. 9:27). In choosing Christ we make a choice and then meet the conditions (Matt. 11:28-29; Rev. 22:17). Believe the gospel (Mark 16:15-16; Heb. 11:6). Repent of your sins (Acts 17:30-31; Acts 2:38). Be baptized into Christ (Acts 2:38; Rom. 6:3; Gal. 3:27). ". . . be thou faithful unto death, and I will give thee a crown of life" (Rev. 2:10). But this does not mean that man ceases to be a free moral agent. He can still choose to do right or wrong, following after the spirit or after the flesh.

"For after they have escaped the pollutions of the world through the knowledge of the Lord and Saviour Jesus Christ, they are again entangled therein, and overcome, the latter end is worse with them than the beginning. For it had been better for them not to have known the way of righteousness, than, after they have known it, to turn from the holy commandment delivered unto them. But it is happened unto them according to the true proverb, The dog is turned to his own vomit again; and the sow that was washed to her wallowing in the mire" (2 Peter 2:20-22).

Once a Catholic Always a Catholic

I am sure that practically all Protestants are familiar with the following saying: "Once a Catholic always a Catholic." But I doubt very seriously if they have the faintest idea of its origin or implications. Someone wondered about that as the following will show.

(Question) "When a person is baptized a Catholic isn't he a Catholic always even though he joins up with a Protestant Church?"

(Answer) "Yes. The catechism describes one of the effects of Baptism as imprinting an indelible mark or character on the soul. . . Baptism is not the initiation of a person into a club or an organization which a person can leave later if he wishes" (*The Question Box Column,* in the *Tablet,* Feb. 27, 1954). This same question and answer appeared in the Brooklyn *Tablet,* March 2, 1957.

The *Lone Star Visitor,* July 27, 1958, stated that one-third of the Catholics fall away. Yet, the Catholic authorities claim that those who have left the Catholic Church are still under her authority and jurisdiction, and are bound to obey her laws.

Pius IX a Kidnapper!
The Mortara Affair

Illustrating what Catholics mean by being "branded" by baptism, we are told that the infant of a Jewish couple named Mortara at Bologna, was "baptized" by a nurse, of course without the knowledge or consent of its parents. This child was taken away from its parents, carried to Rome, raised as a Catholic and finally made a priest. This is what "branding" means, and how it terminates when Catholics dominate (*The Life of Pius IX,* Shea, 243).

Must Baptize the Unborn!

"A miscarried fetus or embryo, no matter how small, must always be baptized—absolutely if certainly alive, conditionally if doubtfully alive. Maceration (putrefaction or advanced general decomposition) in this case is the only certain sign of real death. Break the membranes, or open the blood clot or mole, surrounding the embryo. Immerse it in a pan of water making sure the water contacts the fetus itself. Then, while moving it about in the water so that there will be a washing or flowing or 'baptizing' say the words, usually those for conditional baptism: 'If you are capable, I baptize you in the name of the Father, and of the Son, and of the Holy Ghost.' Finally, remove it from the water.

"Never fail to follow this procedure even though told in a hospital to take the clot, etc., intact to the medical lab. The water must contact and flow on the fetus or embryo itself. Baptism on the covering membrane is no baptism. Those in a medical lab are not in fact interested in the 'intactness' of the membranes. Hence break membranes, baptize, and if necessary explain afterwards" (*Spiritual First Aid Procedures,* Gerald H. Fitz Gibbons, 3).

"The obligation imposed extends to even the smallest fetus, even though it is aborted immediately after conception" (*The Sacred Canons,* Abbo and Hannan, I, 753).

Intra-Uterine Baptism

"If, during the actual process of birth, there is an obstruction, and the child is in danger of death before complete delivery, what is to be done?

"The general rule is, of course, that a child should not be baptized until fully born. But if there is danger that the child will die of suffocation or from some other cause before complete delivery, it should be baptized on the first available members. If the head emerges first, the child should be baptized conditionally on that member, and again conditionally on the head after delivery" (*Quizzes on Hospital Ethics,* Rumble, 56).

Morally Compulsory

"First, it is morally compulsory to follow the safer course when there is a question of means to be taken to save a soul. Thus, an infant which was baptized in the uterus may be born in a dying condition. It is only probable that the uterine baptism fulfilled the requirements for the valid reception of the sacrament. The infant *must,* therefore, be baptized again conditionally.

"Second, it is morally compulsory to follow the safer course when there is a question of the validity of the sacraments. A nurse, for example, comes across an unbaptized infant who is obviously dying. An emergency baptism is an immediate necessity" (*Medical Ethics,* McFadden, 23).

How Intra-Uterine Baptism Is Given

"A syringe should be filled with boiled water, which has first been cooled to body temperature. If plain water is dangerous, one part of bichloride of mercury to a thousand parts of water may be added to it.

"The membranes surrounding the fetus must be ruptured, discharging the amniotic fluid, since the water must come into contact with the fetus itself" (*Quizzes on Hospital Ethics,* Rumble, 56).

"If the fetus was baptized in the mother's womb, the child shall: when born, be baptized again conditionally" (Canon 746).

"Care should be taken that every fetus born prematurely, no matter at what stage of pregnancy, be baptized absolutely, if life is certain, but conditionally, if life is doubtful" (Canon, 747) (*The New Canon Law,* Woywood, 153).

Obligation of a Physician

"Theologians generally acknowledge the obligation of a physician to perform a Caesarean operation after the death of the mother for the purpose of procuring baptism for the child, though there is a doubt about this obligation if the mother's death occurs during the first four months of pregnancy, inasmuch as pregnancy is not certain during that period while it is morally certain that a fetus of that age cannot survive its mother. Similarly, there is doubt about this obligation if the time of delivery is close at hand when the mother dies, since the child cannot be baptized in the womb. In the later case, however, the physician is obligated to perform the operation to save the child's life. The common opinion holds that the mother is not obligated to undergo a Caesarean operation to procure baptism for the child, since the latter can be baptized in the womb" (*The Sacred Canons,* Abbo and Hannan, 752).

Obligation for Midwives

"Hence the obligation for midwives, surgeons, or physicians to take great care of the fetus in cases of premature birth or miscarriage and to examine closely the blood that has issued from the mother's womb, as the fetus is sometimes very small and may have the appearances of death although really living. Physicians themselves find it difficult to discern signs of fife, and some give as the only sure evidence of death, advanced putrefaction or decomposition.

"For the baptism of a fetus expelled prematurely from the

womb and still enveloped in the secundine membranes they suggest to open these and expose the fetus to view in tepid water whilst pronouncing the words of the form" (*Legislation on the Sacraments,* Ayrinhac, 25).

Let Mother Die!

"Question: If it is morally certain that a pregnant mother and her unborn child will both die if the pregnancy is allowed to take its course, but if, at the same time, the attending physician is morally certain that he can save the mother's life by removing the inviable fetus, is it lawful for him to do so?

"Answer: No it is not" (*Moral Problems in Hospital Practice,* Finney, 3).

"Direct abortion is intrinsically evil and therefore morally unlawful, and, consequently, a physician has no professional obligation to resort to it in order to save the mother, but he has a most positive obligation to refrain from it" (*Moral Principles in Hospital Practice,* Finney, 42).

One Fetus Worth More Than 10,000 Mothers!

"The first fact in the world is that justice, law, order, should be observed no matter what the cost, better that ten thousand mothers should die, than one fetus should be unjustly killed" (*Moral Problems in Hospital Practice,* Finney, 47).

Mothers Duty to Die!

"In this instance, it is the mother's duty to die rather than to consent to the killing of her child" (*Moral Problems in Hospital Practice,* Finney, 46).

In view of these Catholic laws, one is made to wonder why good Catholic women will take a chance and risk this tragedy by going to a Catholic hospital.

Why all this disgustingly, nauseating doctrine? It is because it

326

is a Catholic doctrine that even the unborn fetus is a horribly guilty person and cannot possibly go to heaven unless a little water is poured upon it!

"No Catholic parent who loves his child will defer its baptism. What will he not do to shield it from disease, the eternal loss of the beatific vision in case early death threatens it" (*Teaching of the Catholic Church,* Smith, 24).

Catholic theology and practice contradicts the Catholic Bible on every hand but there is none so heartbreaking as that concerning the little babies.

Jesus said of little children, "Of such is the Kingdom of heaven" (Matt. 19:15, *Confraternity*).

"Amen I say to you unless you turn and become like little children you will not enter into the Kingdom of heaven" (Matt. 18:3, *Confraternity*).

If we ask what sins infants and even the unborn have committed, we are told that they have not committed any *actual* sins, but are only guilty of their parents sins, clear back to Adam! The doctrine is that the little infant inherits sin! What a God-dishonoring doctrine! The belief could only be from one of two causes: gross ignorance of the Bible, or total disregard for its plain teaching.

". . . the son shall not bear the iniquity of the father, and the father shall not bear the iniquity of the son" (Ezek. 18:20, *Douay*).

Practically every time a person is sentenced to death, for some horrible crime, the priest goes in, and if the criminal is willing, he can go through his performance and the bad man or woman can go to heaven! The only person the priest cannot say masses for, and pray for, and bum candles for, is an innocent little baby. If it was not baptized it cannot be buried in the consecrated cemetery with the murderer, drunkards, whoremongers and the like, but must be put outside in the potter's field, as it were. The devil can take a vacation as long as that sort of performance goes on!

Limbo—The Little Baby Hell!

"Holy Mass cannot be offered for ("unbaptized" infants) because it cannot benefit the lost in hell, nor the souls in limbo, nor the blessed in heaven.

"We know that in limbo dwell children who died without baptism; for these we do not offer the Holy Sacrafice" (*Legislation on the Sacraments,* Ayrinhac, 105). See also *Radio Replies,* Rumble and Carty, 1, 167; *Manual of Christian Doctrine,* 145, 147-148, 399; *Manual of Moral Theology,* 11, 48; *Pastoral Medicine,* Sanford, 90).

Limbo

There was no mention of Limbo before the Dark Ages.

"The latin word Limbo was used in the Middle Ages for that place in which the just who died before Christ were detained till our Lord's resurrection from the dead" (*Catholic Pocket Dictionary,* 128).

"The existence of the Limbo of Infants has never been defined by the Church" (A *Catholic Dictionary,* Addis and Arnold, 519).

Catholic Treatment of Babies

"As baptism is the door of the Church, the unbaptized are entirely without its pale. As a consequence: (1) Such persons, by ordinary law of the Church, may not be buried in consecrated ground. This includes the infants of even Catholic parents" (*Catholic Encyclopedia,* 11, 267).

All kinds of evil people are gladly accepted in Catholic cemeteries, but not innocent babies!

"All persons who certainly die without baptism are excluded from ecclesiastical burial (Canon 1204) even children born of Catholic parents" (*Administrative Legislation,* Ayrinhac, 87).

328

Unbaptized Babies

"A fetus which has been baptized either absolutely or conditionally should be buried in consecrated ground. A fetus which has died without baptism should be buried in unblessed ground" (*Medical Ethics,* McFaddin, 245).

"Question: "Are there any special rules concerning the disposal of a dead fetus, or of a full-term still-born child?

"Answer: "Yes. If the mother dies also, the fetus or child should be buried with the mother. If the mother does not die, the fetus or child, if baptized, should be given Catholic burial in consecrated ground; if not baptized, it should be buried in unconsecrated ground; without any religious rites" (*Quizzes on Hospital Ethics,* 57-58).

Innocent Jewish Babies Cannot Be Saved Without Baptism—Sinful Jewish Adults Can!

"Would a good and practicing Jew go to heaven, despite his not being a baptized Christian?

"Yes, provided through no fault of his own he did not at any time advert to the truth of Christianity, and to the necessity of actual baptism; and provided he sincerely believed Judaism to be still the true religion, and died truly penitent of all serious violations of conscience during life" (*Radio Replies,* Rumble and Carty, III, 43).

Answer of a Good Conscience

"By which also he went and preached unto the spirits in prison; which sometimes were disobedient, when once the long-suffering of God waited in the days of Noah, while the ark was a preparing, wherein few, that is, eight souls were saved by water. The like figure whereunto even baptism doth also now save us (not the putting away of the filth of the flesh, but the answer of a good conscience toward God,) by the resurrection of Jesus Christ" (1 Peter 3:19-21).

329

How can a fetus, a stillborn child, or an unconscious person have a "good conscience"? The Bible has much to say of baptism. It tells who should be baptized and why. It gives examples and conditions surrounding them. But in all the cases of baptism mentioned in the word of God, there is not a hint of an infant. These things should furnish the reader with much food for thought and be reminded to:

"Carefully study to present thyself approved unto God, a workman that needeth not to be ashamed, rightly handling the word of truth" (2 Tim. 2:15, *Douay*).

CHAPTER XX

The Eucharist

Catholicism has its own punctuation, its own pronunciation and its own vocabulary. This is one of the results of a separate school system. Hundreds of words found in Catholic literature rarely appear anywhere else. Because of this a few of my readers have contacted me regarding what they thought, were errors along this line. In each case I felt it necessary to explain to them, that to be authentic a quotation must be given exact in every way. Even mistakes, if such there be. I would like for the reader of this book to keep that in mind. This does not mean that the book is without grammatical error. I am human along with the printer and proof-reader. But I can assure you that the quotations given have been checked and double checked and will stand up under any criticism that may be found with them.

Eucharist is really a Greek word meaning thanks. The Lord's Supper is nowhere in the Bible called "thanks." I am glad that the multiform adulteration, Eucharist and Mass, is not called the Lord's supper, even by Catholics.

"The Mass is the complex of prayers and ceremonies that make up the service of the Eucharist in Latin rites" (*Catholic Encyclopedia,* IX, 790).

The Real Presence

Catholic writers insist that when Jesus said, ". . . this is my body" and ". . . this is my blood" (Matt. 26:26-28), that the only interpretation possible to put on this language is that he meant that the bread and fruit of the vine, after the ceremony of the priest, is transformed into the actual flesh and blood of Christ. When Jesus said this he had not yet been crucified and all his "actual" blood was still in his body. So, this fruit of the vine and the bread was not actually the flesh and blood. They admit that if it were chemically analyzed it would possess the analysis of bread and wine. They also readily admit that it would look and taste like bread and wine. In fact Jesus, after he had blessed it, called it the "the fruit of the vine" and not blood! It was still wine after he blessed it.

The *New Standard Dictionary* defines a Metaphor,

"The form of trope that is founded on a resemblance of relations; a figure of speech in which one object is likened to another by asserting it to be that other or speaking of it as if it were that other: distinguished from *simile,* in which a word of likeness is always expressed. Thus the sentence 'Roderick Dhu fought *like* a lion' contains a *simile.* 'He *was* a lion in the fight' contains a metaphor."

Pointing to a picture and saying, "This my mother" is a metaphor. To insist that this could only mean, "My mother *is* this picture" would be nonsense.

All sorts of fables are told to the laity about the bread, which they are told is now the body of Christ. Such as seeing it bleeding, or hearing it talking, etc. At the Feast of Corpus Christi (body of Christ) the bread is carried in a procession and worshipped. The laity is told that the same sort of worship should be accorded it as is given to God.

"The seven beautiful kine, and the seven full ears, *are* seven years of plenty" (Gen. 41:26, *Douay*).

The two wives of Abraham, Sarah and Hager are said to be the Old and the New Covenants. "For these *are* the two testaments" (Gal. 4:24, *Douay*).

"The rock *was* Christ" (1 Cor. 10:4).

"I *am* the door of the sheep" (John 10:7).

"I *am* the true vine" (John 15:1).

"The seven stars *are* the angels of the seven churches" (The

332

Apocalypse of Revelation, 1:20, *Douay*).

These are a few of the many of the metaphors in the Bible. All this effort to put the laity in awe of the bread and the priest.

"There is sometimes in such passages a hidden depth of meaning which the letter hardly expresses and which the laws of interpretation hardly warrant. Moreover the literal sense itself frequently admits other senses, adopted to illustrate dogma, or to confirm morality. Wherefore it must be recognized that the sacred writings are wrapped in a certain religious obscurity, and that no one can enter into their interior without a guide" (*Great Encyclical Letters,* Leo XIII, 285).

Catholics read into the Bible the meanings they wish, without regard to the laws of language!

No one ever heard of a Mass, or anything else characteristically Catholic, for hundreds of years after the Lord's church was established and the New Testament written.

"The first certain use of it (Mass) is by St. Ambrose" (*Catholic Encyclopedia,* IX, 791).

Ambrose died A.D. 397 and is revered by the Church as one of her greatest doctors.

This was at least three hundred and fifty years after the Lord's Church was established. But even then, and for a long time thereafter, it meant "dismissal," and not what it is now made to mean by Catholic writers.

Let us compare some of the features of the Eucharist and Mass with the Lord's Supper.

Lord's Supper	Eucharist and Mass
First day of the week	Every day
Everyone had wine	Priest drinks all the wine
Ordinary clothes	Ecclesiastical Robes
Ordinary tables	Altars

Ordinary plates	Paten
Ordinary drinking vessels	Chalice
Fruit of the vine	Wine spiked to 18% Alcohol
Break bread	Pellets
Vernacular	Latin
Face the people	Turned backs
Thanks	Prayers for the dead

Catholic authorities tell us, as we have already noted, that only about 2,000 copies of the Catholic Douay Bible are sold each year. This being true, we should not be surprised when they tell us that Bible language is strange to Catholics. The book referred to, in the following quotation, is one gotten out by a Catholic priest in the early days of this country.

"This book is remarkable for its apologetic notes, and still more so for some of the headings, the strangest being that which reads 'The celebration of the Lord's Supper, together with Holy Communion, commonly called the Mass'" (*New History of the Catholic Church,* Shea, 383).

This priest had either been reading his Bible, or associating with Bible-reading people, for as all Bible-reading people know the Lord's Supper is prominently featured in the New Testament.

The reason for all this is that the complete system of Catholicism has been arranged hundreds of years this side of the New Testament, and Catholic writers admit that no one ever heard of Mass until the seventh century.

No Mass in Early Church

"The word Mass (missa) first established itself as the general designation for the Eucharist Sacrifice in the West (Roman Catholicism—O.C.L.) after the time of Gregory the Great (who died in 604, O.C.L.) the early church having used 'breaking of bread'"

334

(*Catholic Encyclopedia,* X, 6).

Mass, Best Thing in Religion, Left Out of Bible!

". . . the best thing religion has" (*Catholic Facts,* Noll, 66).

"It is the holiest thing that can be done on earth" (*Prayer Book for Children*).

In New Testament All Had Fruit of the Vine, Now Priest Drinks All the Wine

"In like manner also the chalice, after he had supped, saying: This chalice is the New Testament in my blood: this do ye, as often as ye shall drink, for the commemoration of me. For as often as ye shall eat this bread *AND* drink the chalice, you shall show the death of the Lord, until he come. Therefore whosoever shall eat this bread, or drink the chalice of the Lord unworthily, shall be guilty of the body and of the blood of the Lord. But let a man prove himself: and so let him eat of the bread *AND* drink of the chalice" (1 Cor. 11:25-28, *Douay*).

"Communion under both kinds was the prevailing usage in Apostolic times" (*Catholic Encyclopedia,* IV, 176).

Catholics Formally Abolish Lord's Way!

Communion "under both kinds" was ". . . entirely and formally abolished in 1416 by the Council of Constance" (*Lives and Times of the Roman Pontiffs,* Chevalier Artaud de Montor, I, 111).

Lord's Way Now Strictly Forbidden

"The ". . . chalice is strictly forbidden to any but the celebrating priest" (*Catholic Encyclopedia,* IV, 175-176).

Those Who Want Lord's Way Called Heretics

"In the thirteenth session (1414 June 15) the lawfulness and expediency of giving communion to the laity under one species

335

were affirmed, and those who obstinately maintained the contrary were to be treated as heretics" (*Catholic Dictionary,* Addis and Arnold, 219).

John Huss was burnt at the sake at that council, so, to be treated as a heretic was to be burnt at the stake, for doing what the Lord taught!

Popes Contradict Each Other! Then and Now!

"True, Leo and Gelasius emphatically condemned persons who abstained from the Chalice" (*Catholic Dictionary,* Addis and Arnold, 202).

Bible Way Abrogated—Bible Way Heresy!

"John Huss held such fanatical views about the necessity of communion under both kinds that the whole land was disturbed by his teaching. According to him, the Church could not dispense with the obligation of receiving both species, for Communion under one kind was no Communion at all, and that all who received in that way were damned. Huss was supported in these views by his disciples, Jerome of Prague, Jacobellus of Misnia, and Peter of Dresden. To confound these heretics, and for other very wise reasons, the Council of Constance, assembled in A.D. 1414, declared that Communion under one species was as true a participation in the Body and Blood of the Lord, in virtue of what theologians called *concomitance,* as if both species were received; and that all who held differently were to be anathematized as heretics. A decree was then issued by said council *abrogating the species of wine;* and from this date our present discipline in this respect" (*History of the Mass,* O'Brien, 373-374).

"It is heretical to say that communion must be given under both kinds" (*Radio Replies,* Rumble and Corty, II, 191).

Catholic Changes

About one thousand years after the New Testament period two changes took place in Catholic "discipline." Up until this time the priests had been married men. Now their wives were taken from them causing thousands of homes to be broken up. The Bible statement, "What God hath joined together let not man put asunder," was totally disregarded and thereafter their wives were considered as concubines. This arbitrary measure was attended by bloodshed everywhere. About this same time the wine was taken from the laity and given to the priests. At which time the priests were authorized to spike the wine to 18 percent or 36 proof, which is nearly half the strength of whiskey (*Catholic Encyclopedia,* III, 562).

Why No Mass After Noon!

"In the course of the past ages Mass has been celebrated at any hour of the day or night, forenoon or afternoon, midday or midnight. Since the Council of Trent Mass may not be said after the noon hour. Originally Mass was said at the hour in which Our Lord celebrated the First Mass at the Last Supper. They said it as they had seen Him say it in the evening" (*New Interpretation of the Mass,* Borgmann, 206).

I am quite sure that the reader will have no difficulty in seeing the reason for this change soon after the one giving the priest the privilege and authority of spiking the wine. Most everyone knows what the effect of several goblets of spiked wine would have upon a person, and a priest is no exception. After serving at several morning Masses he is probably incapacitated for a long time. How then do Catholics spend Sunday afternoon and Sunday night? It is the usual custom of the Church to arrange for Bingo and other gambling in the afternoon and dancing for Sunday night. It is true that not all Catholics attend these afternoon and evening functions but a great number of them do. It does not worry them or bother their conscience, since they have been taught since childhood that no element of immorality is involved in so doing.

Mortal Sin to Do What Lord Ordained!

"The reason which actuated the Church in prescribing communion under one species of bread alone were very grave; and it would be a mortal sin to violate this law" (*Eucharist, Law and Practice*, Durieux, Translated by Dolphin, 207).

Bible Example Now A Mortal Sin!

In the early church residences were frequently used for Church services.

"And the Church which is in their house" (Romans 16:5, *Douay*).

"Aquila and Priscilla salute you much in the Lord, with the Church which is in their house" (1 Cor. 16:19, *Douay*).

"Salute the brethren who are at Laodicea, and Nymphas, and the Church that is in his house" (Col.4:15, *Douay*).

It is now declared to be a mortal sin to do as these early Christians did:

Dishonor Eucharist to Take Lord's Supper in Homes!

"St. Basil expressed the view, often echoed by his fellow bishops, that it would ordinarily dishonor the Eucharist to have it celebrated in a private home" (*The Mass of the Future*, Ellard, 70).

"Thus, about 350, a council at Gangra forbade bishops and priests to celebrate any Masses in private homes" (*The Mass of the Future*, Ellard, 69).

Now "a mortal sin" (*Eucharist, Law and Practice*, Durieux, 214).

Admit Changes

"There are, however, certain differences on this point between the ancient and modern discipline. In the early ages, especially in times of persecution, the Christians often received permission to

338

keep the Holy Eucharist in their homes; they even took *It* with them on their journeys. To do this in these days one must have a very special permission from the Holy See. According to the *Codex,* no one has the right to keep the Blessed Eucharist in his home or to carry *It* with him when traveling. It would be a mortal sin to disregard this prohibition" (*The Eucharist, Law and Practice,* Durieux, 214).

Notice that this author capitalizes "It" when referring to the bread. The reader, new to Catholic doctrine, may imagine that this is a mistake of mine. Nothing of the kind. Catholics are taught that the bread used in the Eucharist *is* Christ! Believing that this bread is actually God they capitalize the word referring to Him.

I may tire the reader by tediously giving Catholic statements, to the effect, that in the *New Testament* Church an ordinary table, with an ordinary plate and cup were used for the Lord's Supper and that those who carried on the worship wore ordinary clothes. Catholic writers admit also that it was hundreds of years before the Catholic arrangement began of having an altar of special material, a chalice of precious metal and the elaborate priestly garb. It is now declared to be a mortal sin to do as the *New Testament* Christians did.

"Theologians pronounce it a grave sin to give communion without the stole and surplice, and a light one to omit either" (*Legislation on the Sacraments,* Ayrinhac, 157-158).

Early Church Commemorated Resurrection on the First Day of the Week, Catholics Once a Year—Easter

"Further, there seems much to suggest that the Church in the Apostolic Age designed to commemorate the resurrection of Christ, not by an annual, but by a weekly celebration" (*Catholic Encyclopedia,* IX, 152).

"The first Christians apparently partook of the Holy Eucharist whenever they assisted at its consecration, which took place once a week" (*Legislation on the Sacraments in the New Code,* Ayrinhac, 180).

Catholics Change

"In the beginning Mass was celebrated once a week, then three or four times, and finally in the fifth and sixth century, every day" (*Legislation on the Sacraments,* Ayrinhac, 87).

Early Church Broke Bread

The following Bible references all speak of "breaking bread": Acts 2:42, 46; 20:7 and 1 Cor. 10:16. In the Catholic Church this *New Testament practice* is prevented because the bread, which the priest dispenses, is made up in little pellets.

"Up to the eleventh century the custom was almost general of communicating the people from particles of the large Host which the priest used; hence this must have been of far greater proportions than is now (Kozma, 239). When the custom of thus communicating the people ceased, small Hosts were introduced which still bore the name of particles, and the priest's Host became smaller in size" (*History of the Mass,* O'Brien, 158).

"For the first six centuries of the Christian Church it was on paten that the Hosts used to be consecrated and broken, and from it distributed to the people at Holy Communion" (*History of the Mass,* O'Brien, 274).

In the early Catholic Church the laity brought money, now the bread is shaped like money.

". . . the altar bread now began to be made like coins, cut like coins, stamped like coins to bring out the direct relationship between the coin offered by the worshipper, and the sacrificial gift prepared for transubstantiation" (*The Mass of the Future,* Ellard, 88).

340

Catholic Practice Dangerous to Health!

For centuries now the members of the laity have not been allowed to touch the bread, or "break" bread as the Bible teaches. The priest takes the pellet in his hands and places it on the tongue of the laity, a very unsanitary practice, transplanting all the disease germs everyone might have. So of many Catholic practices, which were formulated in the Dark Ages, as kissing the Pope's ring and his foot, the clerical garb, kissing the altar, kissing relics, kissing sores of the afflicted, the unsanitary "Holy Water" basin, that everyone's fingers have contaminated, baptismal ritual of blowing in the face, using saliva, the babies sucking wine from the priest's fingers! See *Radio Replies,* Rumble and Carty, I ,279; *Pastoral Medicine,* Ruland and Rattler, 168-171; and *Catholic Encyclopedia,* IV, 170 for Catholic verification.

"Manner of Receiving—With very little exception, it was customary during the first five or six centuries to place the sacred Host in the hands of the communicant and let him communicate himself" (*History of the Mass,* O'Brien, 375). Now priests must place bread on the tongues (*Externals,* 107).

Not Necessary to Understand Prayers

Question: "Why does the Catholic Church insist that even the nuns must pray in Latin, a language they cannot understand?"

Answer: "Even if the nuns did not understand, it would not matter. The Church knows full well the meaning of the prayers she asks her nuns to say for her, and God certainly understands the worship being offered to Him in the name of all the faithful. . . But the chief thing to remember is that, in these official prayers, it is the Church praying through the instrumentality of her religious orders" (*Radio Replies,* Rumble and Carty, III, 322).

"I will pray also with the understanding" (1 Cor. 14:15, *Douay*).

One more instance where Catholic practice contradicts the

Catholic Bible!

Hurried Mass

"I have attended Mass when it would all be over in 12 or 14 minutes. I believe that is entirely too fast to say Mass. I believe that if a priest is in such a hurry he should not even start Mass. You and I know that it is the greatest act of praise and adoration we can give to God. I can't begin to keep up with the priest. If I thought that the Masses I attend are not pleasing to God because I miss some of the prayers I would feel like a hypocrite. What should I do? Please answer.

"I receive many complaints like that from good people like you. All I can say is that that is too fast, approximately about 30 minutes for a low Mass, not including sermon, Communion, etc., being the ideal" (*Operation Understanding,* August 9, 1964).

From this we learn that priests often leave out about two-thirds of the Latin prayers, and because these prayers are in Latin the people do not know that this is being done!

We had occasion, elsewhere in the book, to comment on the convenience of the Latin language. Canon Law is not allowed to be translated into English. By so doing much that is ugly in Catholicism remains hidden. Latin serves another purpose: it prevents the laity from checking on the hypocrisy of the priest in pretending to carry out the Catholic ritual as if it were a sacred and necessary thing.

"I do not know that it has ever been demonstrated that the magicians incantations of "hocus-pocus' is really a corruption of *'hoc est corpus* meum,' but this would be a period and a milieu to greet such an imitation with mocking favor" (*The Mass of the Future,* Ellard, 93).

Sold to American!

"Comedian Joe E. Brown loves to tell the story of a little boy attending his first High Mass. The lad looks and listens with wonder at all these new sights and sounds.

"Then the priest begins to sing an oration. At the end of the prayer, and before the choir can stamp its affirmative 'Amen', the little urchin shouts, 'Sold, American!'

"The story is always told in good taste and unfailingly tickles his audience. But, like all good humor, there is a subtle and disturbing element of truth here.

"It is unfortunately true that most of the chant drifting down from the altar bears a striking resemblance to the drone of a tobacco auctioneer. Whether this is due to the foreignness of the Latin or vocal idiosyncrasies of the singer is a question most moot.

"Anyway it is a little odd that we have been carrying on this way for so many centuries. And it is not a little surprising that people have come so faithfully to Mass when it takes the expertise of a tobacco buyer—to return to our metaphor—to understand what's going on" (*Michigan Catholic,* Detroit, Reprinted in *Green Bay Register,* Green Bay, Wis. Nov. 20,1964).

Absurdities of Latin Mass

"This is, specifically, not a modern fault, but it is one of three signalized as deplorable by Pius XII. Under pressure of hurry bows become bobs, genuflexes resemble bounces, and signs of the saving cross, wavy jerks of the hand. At the 1946 American Liturgical Week, Reverend Joseph Newman of the Louisville Diocese, while on other grounds favoring some use of the vernacular, deprecated its introduction into the liturgy on the ground that it would shock and scandalize people to find out how priests mangle the text that they read. As a matter of fact, a layman himself often so shocked, had been quoted in *America* as saying:. . . The plain fact is that they (the prayers) are not enunciated, as an altar boy soon discovers. It is not only the race of responses that begins at the foot of the altar, when the servers sometimes have to be chisel swift to get

343

their answers in at all. In the body of Mass prayers I have heard elisions and omissions of Latin. . . that are possible only in Latin— in English its incongruity would be bare. . . Priests are blamed precisely for mumbling and hurrying: one layman is quoted as saying: 'One often sees nothing, hears nothing, says nothing, does nothing . . . but is very bored'. . . 'The blessed mutter of the Mass' is rubrically correct for only a few words during the whole Mass rite. The so-called secret tone, the directions say, should (normally) be audible to the priest himself, inaudible to all others" (*The Mass of the Future,* Ellard, 190-191).

Absurd Burden of Catholicism Fasting Before Communion

Until a few months ago the following was Catholic law:

"(A) Time is reckoned physically not morally; the obligation of abstaining from food begins *exactly at midnight, at the first* stroke of the clock *according to some, at the last according to others, not one second later.*

"The law permits here following the local time, mean or true, or the legal time, regional or extraordinary (Can. 33), and to depend on any clock which is probably correct. In case of doubt, whether or not he has taken anything after mid-night, a priest is not obligated to abstain from saying Mass.

"(b) *Any kind of food* or drink, even if taken in the *smallest quantity,* breaks the natural or Eucharistic fast, but it must surely have the nature of digestive food or drink and be taken as such, entering the mouth *ab extrinseco* and penetrating into the stomach, per *modum cibi et potus,* not by way of saliva or breathing.

"A person does not break his fast if he swallows blood from the gums or particles of food which had remained between the teeth from the previous evening meal; nor if, when washing his mouth, a drop of water becomes mixed with the saliva and passes into the stomach" (*Legislation on the Sacraments in the New Code,* Ayrinhac, 98-99).

Few Drops of Water Sinful After Midnight

"It (fast before communion) consists in this, that the communicant has not taken, since midnight, any food or drink or medicine, even the least possible quantity. It would be a mortal sin to receive Communion after having intentionally taken a few drops of water after midnight; even an error of good faith (v.g., the taking of a drink of water at two o'clock in the morning because the clock had stopped at a quarter before twelve) does not dispense from the law" (*Eucharist Law and Practice,* Durieux, 179).

"But if a man had no wife, but a concubine instead of a wife, let him not be refused communion" (*Catholic Encyclopedia,* IV, 207).

So it follows that if a Catholic takes one drop of good sweet milk he cannot have communion, but if he spent Saturday night with a concubine, he can!

Straining Out a Gnat—Swallowing a Camel!

"It is not breaking the fast, then to swallow even voluntarily, blood which flows from the gums, or from the nose through the back of the mouth or from a wound in the mouth itself,. . . the fast would be broken if the blood came from the outside, v.g., from the lips, the nose; or if abundant tears flowed into the mouth. . . the same holds true if one eats, without adverting it, a mouthful of food, or swallows a mouthful of water during one's sleep.

"On the other hand it is permitted, without breaking the fast, to wash out one's mouth, to put in place false teeth which are wet with water,. . . nor is any account of an insect, a drop of rain, a snowflake etc.

"It is also permitted to smoke, to take snuff, to chew tobacco, even though some fragment may mix with the saliva and enter the stomach" (*The Eucharist Law and Practice,* Durieux, 180-181).

According to this it would be a terrible sin if the clock happened to be a few minutes slow or fast or should stop, and the person should drink a swallow of good, cold sweet milk!

Catholic authorities strain out a gnat in demanding complete obedience to the commandments of men, but swallow camels when discarding the Bible!

A few months ago it was decreed that Catholics could eat up to three horns before Communion. Since then Pope Paul VI has changed to even a shorter time.

"In a surprise move, Pope Paul VI has changed the Eucharistic fast regulations, reducing the time of fasting from solid foods before Communion from three hours to one hour.

"Archbishop Pericle Felici, secretary general of the Council, made the announcement at the Council's closing session. He said the new relaxation applies to priests as well as to the faithful, and was made 'at the request of Bishops of many countries'" (Green *Bay Register,* November 11, 1964).

All this is based upon the Catholic teaching that when the priest pronounces his "Hocus Pocus" over the bread that it actually becomes Christ.

"Recall what you learned about the Real Presence of Christ in the Eucharist. Our Lord is present, Body and Blood, Soul and Divinity. . . therefore in order to become united with our Divine Savior in the Eucharist, it is necessary that we take Him into ourselves by swallowing the Host as soon as we receive" (*Brooklyn Tablet,* July 1, 1961).

Never Handle or Chew Christ!

"It is well to remark here that the teeth must never be applied to the sacred Host when it enters the mouth. It must be swallowed by the sole aid of the tongue; and if a difficulty should be experienced in this respect, on no account must the finger be introduced to overcome it" (*History of the Mass,* O'Brien, 367).

346

Must Not Spit All Day!

"Out of respect for the Holy Eucharist, the communicants are cautioned against expectorating during the entire day" (*History of the Mass,* O'Brien, 384-385).

Breaks Fast to Lick Postage Stamp!

"The following are digestible (and forbidden O.C.L.): pieces of bone, beeswax, earth, chalk, green wood, linen threads, gum paper, etc." (*Eucharist Law and Practice,* Durieux, 182).

I am sure that all will agree that a postage stamp is made of gum paper.

Must Lick up Wine!

"In cases when through negligence a little of the Precious Blood falls on the ground, or on the altar stone, the Corporal, the altar clothes, or the clothing of the priest, it must be taken up at once by the lips" (*Eucharist Law and Practice,* Durieux, 149).

Eucharist Remits All Sin

"The Lord being propitiated by the celebration of the Eucharistic Sacrifice, imparts the grace and gift of penance, remits sins and crimes, be they ever so great" (*The Holy Sacrifice of the Mass,* Gihr, 161).

Vernacular in Mass Mixed Blessing

"Boise, Idaho—The use of the vernacular at Mass will not be an unmixed blessing, but it can be a blessing, Bishop Sylvester Treinon, Bishop of Boise, wrote last week in the *"Idaho Register":*

"There will be grave dangers to overcome, both on the part of the people and priest; according to the Bishop.

"Hurrying the prayers will be very scandalous. Stumbling over words and mispronouncing words will be a public confession of something; he noted.

347

"'Why the vernacular in the liturgy?' he asked. 'The whole purpose must be for better understanding, for greater devotion, for more worthy worship of God. If these results are not forthcoming, we may as well go back to the Latin.'

"'Nor are these fruitful results going to be automatic.'

"'If anyone thinks that merely having the liturgy in the mother tongue is going to press a button that will guarantee a well said prayer, he is thinking wishfully.'

"'Having distractions during the Rosary? Finished with the litany before you knew it? There is just no substitute for effort, effort, effort, during prayers, is there?' Bishop Treinen wrote" (*Green Bay Register*, June 5, 1964).

Yes, there is a grave danger on the part of the people should the Mass be said in the vernacular. They would know that the priest was hurrying the prayers and skipping part of them. Their true ability would be revealed in their stumbling over words and the inability to pronounce them correctly. Much of the respect and reverence shown these priests by the laity would evidently be lost. There would be the possibility of the people discovering that their "Fathers" had "feet of clay."

Mass Wards Off Calamities

"The Mass, moreover, wards off calamities, scourges, evils of all sorts, as well as the spiritual miseries which God would have justly inflicted on us, if the Eucharistic sacrifice had not appeased His anger" (*Eucharistic Law and Practice*, Durieux, 25).

Mass For Successful Lawsuit

"If, for example, the Mass is requested for a successful operation, a happy death, successful lawsuit, or examination, etc" (*Moral Theology*, Jone and Adelman, 377).

This seems to encourage Catholics to believe that if they pay the priest for Masses it would miraculously enable them to win in

348

a lawsuit!

Mass Remits Sins—Costs Money!

". . . The possibility of meriting and of satisfying in a strict sense ceases with death; hence the holy souls in purgatory can only suffer enough, that is, endure their punishment until the requirements of Divine Justice are satisfied and the last farthing has been paid. The living, on the contrary, when in the state of grace, can by prayer, fasting, ALMS and other penitential works satisfy the Divine justice, that is, merit the remission of those punishments which otherwise they would be obliged to undergo in purgatory. To this distinction Holy Church appears to allude, when she says that the Sacrifice of the Mass is offered 'for punishments and satisfactions' (*pro poenis et satisfactionibus*): the propitiatory virtue of the Mass supplies for the punishment otherwise to be undergone by the departed (*poena satispassio*); but for the living the propitiatory power of the Sacrifice supplies principally for the satisfaction to be rendered (*satisfacts*). For both it removes the last impediment to their entrance into heavenly glory.

"If those for whom the Mass is celebrated are susceptible thereof, they always and infallibly receive the satisfactory fruit of the remission of punishment, and this applies not only to the living, but also to the dead. For the rest, it is not known in what degree and measure this punishment is each time cancelled; but it is certain that the punishment due is not always entirely and completely removed by one Mass: for this complete remission not infrequently the repeated offering of the Mass is required" (*Holy Sacrifice of the Mass*, Gihr, 1964).

Mass Stipends—Eighth Century

"Shortly after the low Mass had established itself, Mass stipends (preforming Mass for pay, O.C.L.) came into being, the eighth century provided the first instance, and therewith a social institution of such far-reaching consequences" (*The Mass of the*

Future, Ellard, 71).

Different Kinds of Mass

Just in case the reader is not familiar with the names and the many excuses for preforming the different kinds of Masses, a brief description follows. For a fuller and more complete description read: *History of the Mass,* O'Brien, 3-17.

Solemn High Mass.—It is called HIGH from the fact that the greater part of it is chanted in a high tone of voice. It is called Solemn when celebrated with deacon and subdeacon and a full corps of inferior ministers.

Low Mass.—Low Mass is so called from it being said in a low tone of voice.

Conventual Mass.—Conventual Mass, strictly speaking, is that which the rectors and canons attached to a cathedral are required to celebrate daily at about nine o'clock.

Bridal or Nuptial Mass.—A Mass offered in behalf of a newly-married couple in order that Almighty God may bless their union and favor them with happy offspring.

Golden Mass.—A Solemn High Mass celebrated on the Wednesdays of the quarter tenses of the Advent in honor of the "Mother of God."

Private Mass.—Strictly speaking, a Private Mass is one in which only the priest himself communicates.

Solitary Mass.—When Mass is said by a priest alone, without even a server.

Votive Mass.—A Mass celebrated to satisfy either the pious wishes of the priest himself or of some member of his congregation.

Dry Mass.—A Mass celebrated, using neither bread or wine.

Evening Mass.—A Mass celebrated on Thursday evening in memory of the institution of the Blessed Sacraments on that day.

Midnight Mass.—Best known as a Christmas Mass.

Mass of the Presanctified.—A Mass celebrated once a year on Good Friday.

Mass of Requiem.—A Mass celebrated in behalf of the dead.

Mass of Judgment—A Mass used in determining the innocence or guilt of a person.

Some of these Masses are not very much in vogue in the Catholic Church today, but at various times in their long history they were practiced very religiously.

We will point out a few of the Masses giving authoritative quotations concerning them.

Mass of Requiem—Burial Fees—Double Talk!

"As a price for burial, the parish priest can demand nothing without incurring the suspicion of simony. Burial is a spiritual right belonging to the faithful; and the parish priest, in virtue of his office, is bound to perform this duty for his parishioners. Nevertheless, if there is a legitimate custom which allows offerings to be made, or if the bishop should have established a *fixed scale of offerings,* the parish priest may *demand* such fees provided he in no way incurs suspicion of extortion. . . The bishop is authorized to prescribe, in regard to funerals, what portion should belong to the parish priest and to others assisting at the altar; how much should be given to those who accompany the body to the grave; to those who toll the bells; likewise the number and weight of the candles used during the burial service, the remuneration for the use of funeral ornaments, etc. . . With regard to the fees for burial in our own time, there is no customary uniform fee, and the enactments of provincial synods contain nothing very definite on the matter. Generally speaking if a Church has a cemetery attached, a scale of fees is drawn up and approved by the bishop of the Church, and charges varying to the degree of solemnity with which the funeral is carried out" (*Catholic Encyclopedia,* VI, 321).

Six Dollar Stipend Established for Masses

"Marquette, Mich.—Bishop Thomas Noe has established a six dollar stipend for High Masses and Community Masses in the Marquette diocese.

"The High Mass is the usual sung Mass which has been offered as a regular part of the worship of the Church through the years.

"The Community Mass is a Low Mass in which the congregation participates in the recitation of the common parts of the ceremony with the priest and at least three English hymns are sung.

"Bishop Noe has declared that after September, 30 priests of the Marquette Diocese are free to offer either High Mass or a Community Mass for six dollar stipends" (*Green Bay Register,* November, 27, 1964). "The Bishop can forbid the acceptance of a smaller stipend" (*A Moral Theology,* Jone and Adelman, 375).

Big Sums for Masses!

"I do give and bequeath unto the Roman Catholic Bishop of the Diocese of Green Bay, Michigan, the sum of $4150, the said sum to be used and applied as follows: For Masses for the repose of my soul, $2,000, for Masses for the repose of my deceased wife, etc, etc." (*Catholic Encyclopedia,* X, 33).

Sue at Law for Funeral Fee!

"Originally, as burial was a Spiritual function, it was laid down that no fee could be exacted for this without simony (*Decretum Gratiani*). But the custom of making gifts to the Church, partly as an acknowledgment of the trouble taken by the clergy, partly for the benefit of the soul of the departed, gradually became general, and such offerings were recognized in times as *jura stoloe* which went to the personal support of the parish priest or his curates. It was, however, distinctly insisted upon that the carrying out of the rites of the Church should not be made conditional upon the payment of the fee being made beforehand, though the parish priest could recover such fee afterwards by process of law, in case it were withheld" (*Catholic Encyclopedia,* III, 71).

"Children who die unbaptized are excluded from the benefits of the Mass" (*Catholic Encyclopedia,* X, 23).

"But there were also false prophets among the people, even as there shall be among you lying teachers, who shall bring in sects of perdition, and deny the Lord who bought them: bringing upon themselves swift destruction. And many shall follow their luxuries, through whom the way of truth shall be evil spoken of. And through covetousness shall they with feigned words make merchandise of you" (2 Peter 2:1-3, *Douay*).

Devour Widows Houses!

"Woe to you Scribes and Pharisees, hypocrites: because ye devour the houses of widows, praying long prayers" (Matt. 23:14, *Douay*).

"For they bind heavy and insupportable burdens, and lay them on men's shoulders; but with a finger of their own they will not move them" (Matt. 23:4, *Douay*).

Contrast this cold, unfeeling, commercial conduct of Catholic funerals with the respectful, gentle burial of Christians who perform this last tender service out of respect for the departed and for the comfort and consolation of the bereaved. It must be truly shocking to Christians to learn that there are those who speak at such a service, or walk behind the casket, and demand money for this service and claim the right to recover these fees in a court of law!

"The love of money is the root of all evil" (1 Tim. 6:10).

CHAPTER XXI

Penance

Under this head we encounter a number of terms characteristic of Catholicism, such as Auricular Confession, Easter duties, Father Confessor, the Confessional, Seal of Confession, Indulgences, Treasury of Merit, Venial and Mortal sins, Absolution, Purgatory, solicitation in the confessional, forgiving an accomplice, etc. Suppose we notice briefly some of these terms before we go into a more searching examination in which we allow Catholic writers to outline the sordid details of this central arrangement of all this satanic system.

Auricular Confession

This means whispering in the ear of the Catholic priest every sinful thought or act, in every lurid detail, prompted by a devastating, unprintable system of questions.

Easter Duties

Catholics are told that if they confess to the priest daily they are exemplary Catholics. If they confess only once a year, at Easter, they are still good Catholics. They must make confession at Easter and go to Communion. This, no doubt, has given rise to the almost universal church-going at Easter. Since they go only at this time new clothes are necessary. This has become quite lucrative to the dry goods merchants. This along with many other Catholic inventions has been adopted by most Protestants also.

Father Confessor

The priest, we learned formerly in this book, is "God." The

Catholic is supposed to go to him regularly and accuse himself with the expectation that this man can forgive every sin. According to John Laux's *Church History* Catholics first used the expression "Father Confessor" in 589 A.D. (page 206).

The Confessional

This is a booth, one side for the "Father Confessor," and the other for the penitent, in which the regular confession is supposed to be made. Charles Borromeo in the seventeenth century introduced it (*Legislation on the Sacraments,* Ayrinhac, 269).

Seal of the Confession

This means that the priest to whom confession is made is not supposed to ever reveal the sins confessed. This arrangement is clearly for the purpose of encouraging a confession of everything. But this admittedly is not of *New Testament* origin.

"The first express mention of the Seal of Confession, so far as we know, occurs in Canon 20 of the Armenian Synod at Dovin, in 527" (*Catholic Dictionary,* Addis and Arnold, 756).

"In case of doubt the priest must always do the safer thing (i.e., favor the seal), since he must absolutely see to it that no one be deterred from the confession" (*Moral Theology,* Jone and Adelman, 435).

Indulgences—Treasury of Merit

"Whereas an indulgence places at the penitent's disposal the merits of Christ and of the saints, which form the 'Treasury' of the Church" (*Catholic Encyclopedia,* VII, 783).

Venial and Mortal Sins

No such distinction is even hinted at in the Bible. The "Father Confessor" is reputed to forgive both.

Absolution

A priest, even the vilest, is supposed by his mere word to forgive "the guilt and penalty" for sins, even of his accomplice!

Purgatory

This is the place between Heaven and Hell into which all Catholics are "presumed" to go at death. Superstitious Catholics are made to believe that the ministrations of the priests, Masses, prayers, candles, etc., can help those who are there to get out earlier.

"So we *presume* all Catholics who die to be in purgatory; although it may often seem more probable for a particular soul that it is in heaven or hell" (*Plain Facts for Fair Minds,* Searles, 125).

Solicitation in the Confessional

A great deal of Catholic literature, including a large section of Canon Law, deals with the priests who induce women to commit adultery with them. This "solicitation" is often done in the "Confessional," that booth in which there are only two people; the priest and the woman. We will deal with this most diabolical and demoralizing part of Catholicism a little later.

Forgiving an Accomplice

The suggestion that any mere man can forgive sins is blasphemy. The idea that a priest may commit adultery with a Catholic woman, some man's wife or daughter, and immediately thereafter forgive her sins is the limit of this dreadful system!

Bible Doctrine of Confession

"Confess therefore your sins one to another: and pray one for another, that you may be saved. For the continual prayer of a just man availeth much" (James 5:16, *Douay*).

How different the Catholic Bible is from the Catholic Church! The Catholic Church, as we will presently see, teaches that we must confess to a priest, even the vilest, and the word of this vile man "availeth much"!

The Catholic doctrine is that people generally must not know of the sins of other people. The priest must perjure himself, if necessary to shield, not only an ordinary sinner, but even a criminal. The Catholic Bible demands that all must know of sins!

"Them that sin rebuke before all: that the rest also may fear" (1 Tim. 5:20, *Douay*).

Catholic writers admit that for hundreds of years Catholic writers advocated and practiced open confession.

"As St. Augustine (400 years after the birth of Christ) also declares, 'If his sin is not only grievous in itself, but involves scandle given to others, and if the bishop judges that it will be useful to the Church (to have the sin published), let not the sinner refuse to do penance in the sight of many or even the people at large, let him not resist, nor through shame add to his mortal wound a greater evil" (*Catholic Encyclopedia*, XI, 630).

"When St. Cuthbert (635-87) on his missionary tours preached to the people, 'they all confessed openly what they had done'" (*Catholic Encyclopedia*, XI, 633).

This humiliation before the public sometimes lasted for years (*Catholic Encyclopedia*, XI, 629-633).

Catholic Encyclopedia admits that even in the "Middle Ages" Catholics sometimes confessed to "laymen" (*Catholic Encyclopedia*, XI, 623-24).

"Auricular confession is nowhere expressly mentioned in the Bible" (*Question Box*, 1929 edition, 287).

"In the primitive Church there was no concept of the reconciliation of the Christian sinner by the authority of the Church, but the Church by very slow degrees only grew accustomed to this concept. Moreover even after penance came to be recognized as an institution of the Church, it was not called by the name of sacrament" (*Catholic Encyclopedia*, XI, 620).

"Still the doctrine was not fully established in the West (Roman Catholic Church—O.C.L.) till the time of Gregory the Great" (*Catholic Dictionary,* Addis and Arnold, 706).

Leo 1 ("The Great") Forbad What Bible Teaches!

"In 459 he forbad public confession as never having been commanded by the Church. . . presumption against the Apostolic rule, secret confession being sufficient" (*Lives and Times of the Roman Pontiffs,* 1, 103-4).

Bible Doctrine "Unreasonable"!

"'I determined to have by all means suppressed (public confession, O.C.L.), so that the confession of the kind of sins committed by individuals should not be published in a little book, since it suffices that the guilt of their consciences be made known to the priests only, in secret confession . . . let so unreasonable a custom be done away: lest many should be repelled from the remedies of penitence, either because they are ashamed, or because they fear that their deeds may be disclosed to their enemies" (Appendix Note 104—*History of the Confessional,* Hopkins, 293, page 143 for above statement).

"By the middle of the next century (ninth, O.C.L.), when secret had generally replaced public confession" (*Legislation on the Sacraments,* Ayrinhac, 264; See also *Canon Law (Corpus Juris),* 260).

"With the spread of secret Confession the administration of penance became more a matter of the strictly internal forum, not so closely connected with the external government of the diocese or parish" (*Legislation on the Sacraments,* Ayrinhac, 259).

"2. When and why did Holy Mother Church dispense with public penance?

"A. The mitigation of public penance is first indicated in a letter of Pope St. Innocent in the year 405. A similar trend of leniency is found in the East (Greek Catholic, O.C.L.) at the turn of the fifth

358

century. One reason is due to the scandals which were sometimes consequent to public penance. For about a thousand years, there were modifications of the ancient usage. By the middle of the sixteenth century (Council of Trent, O.C.L.), public penance had practically disappeared. The Church found the patient more willing to accept exercises of prayer, piety and alms-giving which, in her clemency, she commuted from the enjoined penances once so severe" (*Brooklyn Tablet,* Jan. 20, 1962).

So, by this time a Catholic was willing to pay the priest money to keep his sins a secret. This is a very effective way of enriching the Catholic Church!

A Sample of Catholic Wresting of Scripture

"But if thy brother shall offend against thee, go, and rebuke him between thee and him alone. If he shall hear thee, thou shalt gain thy brother. And if he will not hear thee, take with thee one or two more: that in the mouth of two or three witnesses every word may stand. And if he will not hear them: tell it to the Church. And if he will not hear the Church, let him be to thee heathen and publican" (Matt. 18:15-17, Douay).

This is a clear command to deal with impenitent sinners so that every member of the Church not only knows of the sin, but has a part in the discipline. The way Catholic writers attempt to evade the force of this plain statement is to make the absurd claim that "Church" here only means the priesthood!

"He reminds them (the laity) that they (the priests) and other orders of the clergy make up the mystical body of the Catholic Church" (*Externals of the Catholic Church,* Sullivan, 81).

Indulgences

We will now make reference to two very closely related Catholic ideas: "Indulgences" and "The Treasury of Merit."

"All the faithful should hold in great reverence the indulgences

359

which the ecclesiastical authority grants from the treasury of the Church. Indulgences given to the living are granted in the form of absolution from temporal punishment due for sins already pardoned as to their guilt, and if granted to be gained for the faithful departed they are applied in the form of suffrage, because the Church has no longer jurisdiction over the faithful once they have passed this life (Canon 91)" (*The New Canon Law,* Woywood, 183).

Indulgences in Advance!

The priest pronounces "absolution," which, they claim remits both the guilt and penalty of sin but in addition gives "indulgences" which, they claim remits all or part of the time a sinner must boil, fry, bake, stew and bum in purgatory. The living sinner who obtains this "indulgence" may keep it for himself or send it on for the benefit of those already in "Purgatory."

"Plenary Indulgence"

"By a plenary indulgence is meant the remission of the entire temporal punishment due to sin so that no farther expiation is required in Purgatory" (*Catholic Encyclopedia,* VII, 783).

Indulgence for the Dead!

". . . over the dead she (The Catholic Church) has no jurisdiction and therefore makes the indulgence available by way of suffrage, *i.e.,* she petitions God to accept these works of satisfaction and in consideration thereof to mitigate or shorten the suffering of the souls in Purgatory" (*Catholic Encyclopedia,* VII, 784).

Plenary Indulgence for Killing!

"We therefore, by the mercy of the omnipotent God, trusting in the authority of the Blessed Apostles Peter and Paul in virtue of that power of binding and loosing which God has conferred on us. Though unworthily, grant to all who aid in this work (Crusades) personally and at their own expense, a full remission of their sins" (Fourth Lateran Council as given in *Disciplinary Decrees of the General Councils,* Schroeder, 295).

Pope Urban II ". . . granted a plenary (full) indulgence to all Crusaders" (*Lives and Times of the Roman Pontiffs,* Chevalier Artaud de Montor, I, 319).

"The pope granted indulgence to all who carried on this pious work" (*The Inquisition,* Vacandard, 43).

"The period of the Crusader marks a turning point in the history of indulgences, for they were given more and more freely from that time onward . . . For example at the Council of Siena, in 1425, a plenary indulgence was offered to those who took up arms against the Hussites; while wars against the Waldenses, Albigenses, Moors and Turks were stimulated by the same means" (*Catholic Dictionary,* Addis and Arnold, 442).

So we see the popes and councils gave a full remission of all sins to those millions who went to war against the enemies of Catholicism. Many of them died on the battlefield or by disease, but they were thus encouraged to believe that their sins and even their stay in "Purgatory" were all taken care of in advance! Their sins were remitted before they left home! Catholic writers now assume the air of injured innocence and cry that Protestants slander them by making this charge! But we see that this is true, nevertheless!

The Treasury of Merit

All this fable is based on the theory that the more than nine thousand "Catholic saints" each had all the merit of goodness he needed, and a great deal to spare. This is so clearly an assumption contrary to reason and the plain teaching of the scriptures.

No One 100% Good!

"There is none that doth good" (Psa. 52:2, *Douay;* Psa. 53:1-3, *King James*).

"For there is no man that sinneth not" (3 Kings 8:46, *Douay*, or 1 Kings 8:45, *King James'*).

"For there is no just man upon earth, that doeth good and sinneth not" (Eccl. 7:20, *Douay*).

"If we say that we have no sin, we deceive ourselves, and the truth is not in us . . . If we say that we have not sinned, we make him a liar, and his word is not in us" (1 John 1:8, 10).

"There is not any man just. . . there is none that doth good, there is not so much as one. . . For all have sinned, and do need the glory of God" (Rom. 3:10, 12, 23, *Douay*).

"Doth he thank that servant for doing the things which he commanded him? I think not. So you also, when you shall have done all these things that are commanded you, say: We are unprofitable servants; we have done that which we ought to do" (Luke 17:9-10, *Douay*).

So Catholic authorities falsify when they say more than nine thousand had all the goodness they needed, and had a "superabundance" of goodness to give away!

What Kind of Catholic "Saints"?

Pope, "St." Hormisdas was the father of Pope "St." Silverius. (*Catholic Encyclopedia,* VII, 470).

"St." Pope Makes Bigamists Priests

"Pope St. Siricius authorized penitents and bigamists to exercise the functions of orders which they had received unlawfully" (*General Legislation in the New Code,* 179).

Thirty "St. Popes" used forgeries to further their claims (*Catholic Encyclopedia,* V, 778; IX, 224; *General Legislation in the New Code,* 34).

Pope "St." Leo I ("the Great") believed heretics should be put to death (*Catholic Encyclopedia,* VIII, 27).

"St. Thomas Aquinas" "advocated the death penalty for the relapsed heretics in the name of Christian charity" (*The Inquisition,* Vacandard, 126).

Killers Made "Saints!"

"History shows us how far the inquisitors answered to this ideal. Far from being inhuman, they were, as a rule, men of spotless character and sometimes of truly admirable sanctity and *not a few of them* have been canonized by the Church" (*Catholic Encyclopedia,* VIII, 31).

"We know the names of many of the inquisitors, monks and bishops. There are some whose memory is beyond reproach; in fact, the Church honors them as saints, because they died for the faith" (*The Inquisition,* Vacandard, 133).

Many of the "saints" were killers, liars and used forgeries.

About the Prayers of Souls in Purgatory

"I have read many of your articles and enjoyed them but your last one on the Poor Souls got me twisted up. Should I ask some of those worldly unsavory characters that are in purgatory to intercede for me, such as gangster murderers? I have found that roughly 60% of the tough gangster murderers of the past 30 years belonged to the Catholic faith, and most of them lie in consecrated soil, the rites of the Church having been granted. Your article seems to make it clear that these unsavory characters got their ill-gotten gains here below at the expense of a longer stay in purgatory; and yet in your article you class them as fit to pray to for help. I think St. Catherine of Bologna refers to such in that statement of hers that you made.

"It is an article of faith that there is a purgatory and that the souls detained therein can be aided by the prayers of the living faithful and of the Church. And it is common Catholic teaching

363

that the souls in purgatory can pray for us." (*Operation Under-standing*, 4/4/65).

So we ask where is that "superabundance of Merit" which Catholics are told will be theirs if they pay the priests to dispense to their credit?

To show further how shadowy are the claims of priestly power to get people out of Purgatory we note the following:

"The Church does not pretend to know how much of Purgatory God remits by a partial indulgence of so many days, years, etc." (*Question Box*, 1913 edition, 413).

"The efficacy of such prayers will not be known until the day of judgment" (*Question Box*, 1913 edition, 474).

"The Catholic Church does not pretend to know anything about the duration of the suffering of Purgatory" (*Question Box*, 1913 edition, 567).

"The Catholic Church does not claim to directly apply the infinite merits of Jesus Christ and the superabundant merits of His saints to the souls in Purgatory over whom she has no jurisdiction. She can only offer these merits to God by way of suffrage, and leave the application entirely to His good pleasure. Thus a Catholic may gain a plenary indulgence and offer it up for a particular soul, but God is not pledged to apply it" (*Question Box*, 1913 edition, 414).

Catholics May Work for Nothing!

"I would say that the Catholic Church claims no jurisdiction over souls in the other world, and professes absolute ignorance regarding God's particular application of the infinite merits of the passion and death of His Son to the souls in purgatory. All Masses and prayers for the dead are applied 'by way of suffrage'—that is are dependent on God's secret mercy and will, who in His infinite justice may apply to another soul altogether the Masses said for a certain individual" (*Question Box*, 1913 edition, 460-461).

No Bible For It!

"We would appeal to those general principles of Scripture, rather than to particular texts often alleged in proof of Purgatory. We doubt if they contain an explicit and direct reference to it" (*Catholic Dictionary*, Addis and Arnold, 704).

"The Council of Trent expressly declares that penance was at all times necessary for the remission of grievous sin. Theologians have questioned whether this necessity obtains in virtue of the positive command of God or independently of such positive precept. The weight of authority is in favor of the latter opinion" (*Catholic Encyclopedia*, XI, 618).

"Auricular confession is nowhere expressly mentioned in the Bible" (*Question Box*, 1929 edition, 287).

Purgatory not only is unknown to the New Testament writers, and Catholics now try to prove it by Origen (called by Catholic writers a heretic) and by acknowledged forgeries such as *Apostolic Constitutions* (*Catholic Encyclopedia*, XII, 577).

Purgatory Borrowed from Pagans

Catholic doctrine on Purgatory is very similar to teaching of Plato and Virgil (*Purgatory*, Sadler, 318).

"A Catholic, therefore, would no more question the doctrine of auricular confession. . . than a mathematician would the fact that two sides of a triangle are greater than the third" (*Question Box*, 1913 ed., 116).

Claim Priest Is God!

The system of Catholicism, an accumulation of fifteen hundred years, is so interwoven that it is impossible to deal with it without considerable repetition. I will now refresh the readers mind on the fantastic claims for the priesthood: that the priest is above angels, to be obeyed rather than Christ, that the penitent cannot possibly do wrong when obeying the priest. Catholics are cautioned to obey

365

him blindly, and even force themselves to obey him in spite of the fact they feel they should go to hell for doing so. The priest is said to "command Christ" who "humbly obeys" the priest! The power of the priest is said to be unlimited!

Bad Priest Forgives Sin!

All these points are asserted by Catholic authorities. The reader should go back to Chapter XI and read again the blasphemous claims for Catholic priests, to see how slavishly Catholics are taught to submit to them.

We have cited a number of Catholic statements as to how difficult it is for a young priest's chastity to survive the confessional.

Absolution

I have had Catholics, in an effort to sidestep the blasphemous claim of priests to being able to forgive sin, to say he only asks God to forgive. To clarify this, so there can be no possibility of a quibble, I now present several quotations.

Really Forgive Sins!

"In the institution of the sacrament our Lord did not say to His Apostles, 'Whose sins you shall ask to be absolved, shall be absolved,' but he instituted as the form of the sacrament, 'Whose sins *ye shall* forgive, they are forgiven them.' These words show that the minister of the Sacrament of Penance does not pray for the absolution of the penitent, but pronounces the absolution as a judicial sentence, as one having judicial authority" (*Catholic Dictionary,* Addis and Arnold, 5).

"The Church which has received from Christ the power to forgive sins, both as to the guilt and penalty, and who has the distribution of the spiritual treasures accumulated by Our Lord and the members of His mystical body, can satisfy the claims of divine justice by taking from the superabundant satisfactions of Christ and His saints and applying them to sinners" (*Legislation on the Sacraments,* 273).

"The priest must be mindful that at the very moment he speaks these precious words, the forgiveness of heaven is granted, the Blood of the Lamb is applied to the penitent, and the life of grace is restored to his soul."

"First, the confessor must tell the sinner what a great favor he has just received in having his sins forgiven and in being snatched from the jaws of hell. The priest should remind the sinner that a moment ago he was a child of the devil, and now he is a son of God, and that the deliverance which has just come to him surpasses even the deliverance of an afflicted man freed from the most grievous suffering" (*The Priest, His Dignity and Obligations,* Eudes, 165).

One of the advertisements put out by the Knights of Columbus is entitled, "Yes . . . A Priest Can Forgive Your Sins!"

"Its minister purifies souls from sin by an act of absolution, and as the Council of Trent defined, this absolution is not a mere declaration of what has taken place as effect of other causes, but a real efficacious judicial sentence actually freeing the sinner from guilt" (*Legislation on the Sacraments,* Ayrinhac, 190).

"The use of such absolutions in Rome in the ninth century is attested by Amalarius" (*New Catholic Dictionary,* Vatican edition, 6). Why was an earlier instance not cited? There was none!

Claim Bad Priest Forgives Sins!

"It teaches also that even priests who are in mortal sin, exercise through the virtue of the Holy Ghost which was bestowed in ordination, the office of forgiving sins as the minister of Christ; and that the sentiments of those is erroneous who contend that this power exists not in bad priests" (*Teachings of the Catholic Church,* Smith, 79).

"Is the state of grace requisite for the validity of the sacrament?

367

"No; a minister may confer a sacrament validly even if he be in the state of mortal sin" (*Manual of Christian Doctrine,* by a Seminary Professor, 392-393).

"If anyone says that a minister who is in mortal sin, though he observes all the essentials that pertain to the effecting or conferring of a sacrament, neither effects nor confers a sacrament, let him be anathema" (Canon 12 of Council of Trent, *Canons and Decrees of the Council of Trent,* Schroeder, 52-53).

"This power is transmitted by ordination and is inamissible. Unworthiness, heresy or schism do not affect it; suspension, excommunication, and degradation do not take it away" (*Legislation on the Sacraments,* Ayrinhac, 80).

If a priest commits all the sins in the catalog he can still forgive sins, they say!

One can readily understand why the hierarchy arranged this. They want the laity to feel certain that their sins are gone. This puts a vile man between a Catholic and God, and puts the laity completely at the mercy of the priest, and willing to pay for his services!

"The people are in no possible danger of deception" (*Catholic Dictionary,* Addis and Arnold, 738).

But really, according to the Catholic arrangement, no Catholic could be certain he was married, that he was "baptized" or that his sins were actually forgiven, for it all depends on the intention of the priest, and no Catholic could be certain on this point.

"*Intention* (for the sacraments). The minister of a sacrament must determine the purpose of his action by an act of his will, called intention. Therefore for a valid sacrament, the minister must have the intention of making and administering a sacrament, at least doing what the Church does" (*New Catholic Dictionary,* Vatican edition, 486).

Priest Can Forgive an Accomplice!

Not only are Catholics assured that the priest they know to be a drunkard or an adulterer, is the only one who can admit them to God's mercy, but they are also taught that a priest can forgive one who is helping him to rob a bank or that the priest he got drunk with Friday night can forgive his sins on Saturday!

"Absolution of an accomplice in danger of death is valid" (*Legislation on the Sacraments,* Ayrinhac, 208).

Priest Can Still Forgive in Hell!

"The fires of hell cannot in all eternity burn out the sacerdotal character imprinted on our (priests) souls in ordination; but the splendors of heaven will make that sacred character shine out with so much greater lustre" (*The Holy Sacrifice of the Mass,* Gihr, 207).

Priest Commits Adultery—Forgives Woman

"But a priest might happen to share in a sin committed by his subjects, e.g. by knowledge of a woman who is his subject . . . If however, he were to absolve her it would be valid" ("St." Thomas Aquinas, *Summa Theologica,* Part III, Fourth Number, 274, 276).

This was seven hundred years ago but it is still Catholic doctrine.

A priest is said not to break his "vow of chastity" "by sinning against the sixth commandment (adultery)" (*Explanation of Catholic Morals,* Stapleton, 149).

We are also informed that "there is no element of immorality" in having a "permanent" concubine!

"Permanent concubinage, though it lacked the ordinary legal forms and was not recognized by the civil law as a legal marriage, had in it no element of immorality" (*Catholic Encyclopedia,* IV, 207).

"If a man had no wife, but a concubine instead of a wife, let him not be refused communion, only let him be content to be united with one woman, whether wife or concubine" (*Catholic Encyclopedia,* IV, 207).

According to this it ought not to be wrong for a priest to have a concubine!

Priest Should "Persuade" to Commit Fornication

"If I (a priest) know that someone has made up his mind to commit sin and there is no other way of preventing him, I may lawfully induce him to be satisfied with some less offence of God than he was bent on committing. And so, if a man was determined to commit adultery, I do nothing morally wrong, but rather the contrary, by persuading him to commit fornication instead" (*Manual of Moral Theology,* 1, Slater 201-202).

With all this immoral teaching it ought to be comparatively easy for a priest to seduce wives and daughters, and the most likely place is in the confessional. So we should not be surprised that a big section of Canon law is given over to a discussion of...

Solicitation in the Confessional

According to Canons 2367, 884, 2252, and 2254, we have the following: "There must have been complicity in *peccats turpi,* which supposes a sin against the sixth commandment, grave and external, whatever be the specific nature otherwise, committed by the free, mutual and externally manifested consent of two parties *whether of* different or the same sex.

"The confessor must not only hear the confession of his accomplice but also absolve or pretend to absolve him" (*Penal Legislation in the New Code,* Ayrinhac, 317).

This applies not only to the priest who commits adultery with a Catholic woman, but also when he commits sodomy with a Catholic man!

370

One of the Knights of Columbus Advertisements is entitled "Confession? *Ask The Man Who Goes There!*" The probabilities are that he will not give you much information though!

Questions in Confessional Dangerous to Children

"The harm done both to religion and morals by this early confession (seven years old) is obvious to anyone who is not blinded by the dogmatic and hieratic conceptions of Ultramontanism . . . If he is of a delicate and timid nature, confession becomes a torment, a source of doubt and trouble; if made of coarser stuff, the mechanism of confession tends to destroy what little delicacy of conscience he possesses. Again it impairs the confidential relation with parents, above all with the mother. A child loses the habit of taking refuge with her when he has committed a fault or is troubled by doubt. A strange element—the priest in the darkness of the confessional—steps between mother and child, and all the 'divinity' which attaches to it is incapable of replacing the childish naturalness and simplicity which formerly sent the little culprit full of shame and penitence to his mother to seek peace for his troubled spirit. . . Natural sexuality is distorted into something unnatural and sinful; innocent naturalness scarcely exists. Everywhere the Ultramontane Catholic suspects vice. In this way he either helps to cultivate it, or produces such unhealthy and tormenting ideas about the human body and its functions that all, especially young persons, in whose head and heart such unnatural, or rather perverted, views have taken root are greatly to be pitied . . ."

"At night we had to wear a closed night-dress made like a sleeping sack. This prevented us from even seeing or touching our naked bodies. And if one of us took a bath by himself in the bathroom, he had to put on a bathing costume reaching to his feet" (*Fourteen Years a Jesuit,* Baron Van Heensbroech, 34-39).

Solicitation in the Confessional

Since it is admitted that many priests are bad, it is easy to see

371

what advantage a bachelor priest would have over women in the privacy of the Confessional. Couple this with the vile system which the Catholic Church provides him. It will be well now to examine the questions which the priest must put to the wives and daughters of other men. Talking of the searching questions we have this:

". . . glossing over nothing omitting, minimizing or withholding nothing, but making a full and clear accusation of every mortal sin of which he believes himself guilty" (*The Priest, His Dignity and Obligations,* Eudes, 150).

This is conversation unbecoming a bachelor and one of the opposite sex.

Translations of Priests Questions Unlawful!

"Tell us not, that the corrupting influence of the Confessional have been conclusively established by publishing extracts from our own accredited theologians, Dens, Liguori, and others. Such 'no-popery' champions as Sparry, the driveling apostate Smith, and many more of the same stamp, have indeed flooded our land with such publications, teeming with obscenity, said to be translated from our own authors; and Sparry, for acting as traveling peddler of such books, was arrested by the civil authorities in Pennsylvania. . . Do they not know that those works are strictly professional, and as such not at all blame-worthy? And why will they not have the candor and honesty, to make the same allowance in regard to Catholic theological works—written in Latin, withdrawn by this circumstance and by their very nature from the popular gaze, and strictly professional in their character and tendency? Or is it proper to enter into those details *in English,* a language accessible to all, —for the purpose of unfolding *human* laws, treating the ills of the body and not proper to do the same in Latin,—a language hidden from the multitude,—and for a much higher and nobler purpose of developing the *divine* law, and unfolding the necessary remedies for the maladies of the soul?" (*Miscellanae,* Archbishop Spalding,

372

450-451).

There could hardly be a more incriminating statement. This does not attempt to deny that those excerpts and translations of the questions this bachelor priest asks the wives and daughters. The fact that the Archbishop thought it was criminal to print those things in English is a sufficient acknowledgement of their baseness. He admits they are "teeming with obscenity"!

Sordid and Salacious Details

"The confessor must not ask useless questions, but examine the penitent on necessary points. He must insist on important details, such as the number of times each mortal sin has been committed, and the length of time that has elapsed since his last confession" (*The Priest, His Dignity and Obligation,* "St." John Eudes, 168).

Frighten Them To Tell All!

"It is related that a young girl of great virtue consented to a sin against chastity; she concealed the sin three times in confession, and went to communion; after the third communion she suddenly fell dead. Because she was considered to be a saint, her body was laid in a particular part of the Church of the Jesuits; but after the obsequies were finished, and the Church closed, the confessor was conducted by two angels to the place of interment. She came forth, fell on her knees and threw from her mouth into a chalice prepared for them, the three consecrated hosts which had been sacrilegiously received and miraculously preserved in her breast. The angels stripped her of the scapular; the miserable girl instantly presented a horrible aspect, and was carried out of sight by two devils" (*The True Spouse of Christ,* "St." Ligouri, 337).

"For example, if you notice that a person seems to be ashamed to confess his sins, encourage him by reminding him that priests are not angels but men who, being human themselves, understand the faults and frailties of others" (*The Priest, His Dignity and Obligations,* "St." John Eudes, 151).

373

Confessions of Bad Women Bad for Priests!

"No doubt General Confession is in many cases necessary. This necessity will occur in the case of women more frequently than of men, because invalid confession, for lack of contrition or of sincerity, are more frequently made by the former than the latter. When, therefore, there is need of General Confession in the case of a female, the confessor is, of course, obliged to hear the same. But great precaution is required in this matter, as it not infrequently happens that females misuse General Confession and are prompted by discernable motives. Such motives are, for instance: 1. curiosity regarding the ways of a new confessor; 2. infatuation, which caused the penitent to seek opportunity for long conversations with the confessor; 3. jealousy, the person endeavoring to stay longer in the confessional than other penitents of her sex; 4. now and then malicious intentions, either of confusing young and inexperienced confessors, or even to lead them into temptations, by inventing sins *contra sextus, etc."* (*The Casuist,* 111, 211).

Priest a "Destroyer"!

"Yet, the priest, who is in truth the physician of souls, can become their destroyer if he is not fitted for the work of the confessional."

"He would cause innumerable sins, making false consciences, obliging people to make restitution when they are not bound, refusing absolution when it should be given, granting it when it should be withheld. Truly, the Scripture says; 'If the blind lead the blind both fall into the pit'" (*The Priest, His Dignity and Obligations,* Eudes, 147).

Priest Ravening Wolves!

"The most evident mark of God's anger and the most terrible castigation He can inflict upon the world are manifested when He permits His people to fall into the hands of clergy who are priests

374

more in name than in deed, priests who practice the cruelty of ravening wolves rather than the charity and affection of devoted shepherds. Instead of nourishing those committed to their care, they rend and devour them brutally. Instead of leading people to God, they drag Christian souls into hell in their train. Instead of being the salt of the earth, and the light of the world, they are its innocuous poison and its murky darkness" (*The Priest, His Dignity and Obligations,* Eudes, 9).

"The experiences I have had with them (prelates, priests and religious) have unhappily—and I mean unhappily—sorely tested my faith in the Church . . . I must cling, of course to the fact that the production of one saint could triumphantly vindicate them. But why have I yet to see one?" (A Catholic's question in *Operation Understanding,* 5/26/63).

"The unworthy confessor. . . instead of being another Christ, he is a very devil. 'No tongue can tell the evil the bad confessor commits'" (*The Priest, His Dignity and Obligations,* Eudes, 129-130).

"Obey (The confessor) blindly, that is, without asking reasons. Be careful, then, never to examine the directions of your confessor . . . In a word, keep before your eyes this great rule, that in obeying your confessor you obey God. Force yourself then, to obey him in spite of all fears. And be persuaded that if you are not obedient to him it will be impossible for you to go on well; but if you obey him you are secure. But you say, if I am damned in consequence of obeying my confessor, who will rescue me from hell? What you say is impossible" (*True Spouse of Christ,* "St." Liguori, 352).

The reader will remember the many statements concerning the "saints," how just the sight of a woman put such evil thoughts in their minds that they had to roll in briers, snow or ice water to quell their evil passions. You can see that this unnatural system including the celibacy of priests, and the privilege of engaging in detailed recital of sins is a perfect arrangement for the seduction of women. It is easy to see why the Lord left all this out of the New Testament.

The Confessional is the perfect propaganda arrangement and also for raising money.

"Prelates are commanded to use their influence in their sermons and in the confessional to induce the faithful to leave in their testaments something for the assistance of the Holy Land" (*Disciplinary Decrees of the General Councils,* Schroeder, 310).

Confession—Wholesale Blackmail

"The secret source of obedience and reverence which has been discovered by Catholicism is confession.

"Every man, whoever he may be, prince in power and knowledge, if he would have any part in the mystery of Christ, must kneel to confess his sins, to ask for pardon and to receive penance: an exercise of obedience and reverence which reveals him to himself, purifies him, humanized him, and bends him without breaking him" (*Political and Social Philosophy,* Lacordaire, 173-174).

"The proud spirit consents to be dominated; the wild heart, ever ready to revolt, accepts unity, order, and power under the only form possible, the form of authority. Confession linked to the public action of the hierarchy, has created in the world an enormous store of obedience and reverence . . ."

"The Catholic spirit has produced in the world, even in the sphere of human authority, something altogether new, altogether unknown to antiquity, the middle term between the Eastern system and the Western system; it has produced the Christian monarchy" (*Political and Social Philosophy,* Lacordaire, 175).

"This mysterious aroma was confided to the Church; she alone possesses the secret of penalties which reinstate the offender, and this is not the least among the evidence of her Divine institution.

"The most important of the Divine penalties with which the Church is armed is confession, voluntary confession. . . And yet this justice is merciful; for it is not to the world, that you are directed to confess your faults, but to a single man, under the most absolute secrecy. . . When Protestantism has abolished confession, when it has sent away the priest, and sent men to confess to God, what has it done but left the soul alone with its guilt, and driven away mercy by the fear of justice. . . allow men to come to the feet of the priest, and you will do more than all your chains, your executioners, and your dreams can ever do" (*Political and Social Philosophy*, Lacordaire, 209-211).

"Nevertheless, cannot the civil authority, which holds the power of the sword, make vigorous use of it, not to obtain faith, which is a fruit of grace and persuasion, but to defend the Church against the attack of her enemies, and to prevent all external demonstrations against the faith. This, Gentlemen, is a new point of view from which we must consider the question.

"For all ancient communities religion was considered to be a fundamental law of the State, and whoever insulted religion was punished as a violator of the most sacred laws of the country. Now, had the civil community the right to make religion a fundamental law of the State? There is no reason to doubt it, for civil society is free to set up any laws that are not unjust, and it does not appear to be unjust to prevent the commission of any external act against the religion unanimously practiced in a country" (*Political and Social Philosophy*, Lacordaire, 219).

This means that if the confessional were universally bound on people, the civil government would be administered by Catholics under the priesthood. This has always been the ideal and the goal of the hierarchy. All freedom would disappear. The very core of this world domination is the confessional.

The Seal of Confession

There are many instances of priests revealing things learned in the confessional, such as the Gunpowder Plot to blow the Parliament houses in London in 1604 (*Autobiography of a Hunted*

Priest, Gerard, 302).

"Catholic Priest to Bare True Story of Lamar Bank Robbery" (*Port Arthur News,* July 16, 1930).

"The next account is Relation 1., made for S. Peter of Alcantara, and was probably seen by many; for that Saint had to defend her, and maintain that the state of her soul was the work of God, against those who thought that she was deluded by Satan. Her own confessor was occasionally alarmed, *and had to consult others, and thus by degrees, her state became known to many;* and there were some who were so persuaded of her delusions, that they wished her to be exorcised as one possessed of an evil spirit, and at a later time her friends were afraid that she might be denounced to the Inquisitors" (St. Teresa's *Autobiography,* XXXI).

"At the time the discipline of the seal of confession was in certain details less strict than it has since become. It was then considered lawful for a confessor to bear witness in general terms to the exceptional virtue of a penitent" (*Autobiography of a Hunted Priest,* Gerard, 187).

"In the West (Roman Catholic, O.C.L.), there was no mention of penalties for breaking the seal til very late" (*Catholic Dictionary,* Addis and Arnold, 756).

The present arrangement demands that a Catholic Priest perjure himself, if necessary to protect guilty criminals.

"From this obligation (not to reveal what is learned in the confessional) he cannot be excused either to save his own life or good name, to save the life of another, to further the ends of human justice, or to avert any public calamity" (*Catholic Encyclopedia,* XI, 29).

"The priest would violate his Christian obligations did he betray his penitent under any circumstances whatever from knowledge secured in the confessional . . . If Catholics are subject to the obligation of confessing their sins in order to secure God's forgiveness, they must know that they can do so with absolute confidence and security. Any betrayal of a penitent who has come to Confession in order to fulfill a conscientious obligation imposed by God would be outrageous. And the Catholic law that the seal of Confession obliges everywhere, and always, and permits of no exception whatever, is the only just law.

"What if the priest's own innocent father or brother or mother were condemned? Could he expose the real murderer then?

"If a man confessed to me that he had sinned in resolving to shoot me, I would simply have to commend myself to God's protection. Did I know where the man kept his revolver, I could not even go and remove it; for I would be making external use of knowledge secured in the Sacrament of Confession . . . If people thought that under certain circumstances, the priest could reveal what he hears in the confessional, they would either stay away, or be gravely tempted to conceal their sins, which would turn a Sacrament meant for their good into grave spiritual injury. . . Any priest who presumes to reveal a sin manifested to him in Confession must not only be deposed from his priestly office, but must be sent to an enclosed monastery, there to do penance for the rest of his life" (*Radio Replies*, Rumble and Carty, 182).

"So sacredly is confession regarded that if my father had been recently murdered, and you confessed to me that you were the murderer, I would not be allowed to report you; more than that, I would not be permitted to allude to it, nor act differently toward you, if you called at my house immediately after the confession" (*Father Smith Instructs Jackson*, Noll, 171).

"Gerson would not permit an exception to the rule, even to save an empire or to preserve the whole Church from heretical infection; even if the penitent declared his intention of killing the king or the Pope, said Cajeton, in spite of the teaching of not a few doctors to the contrary" (*Legislation on the Sacraments*, Ayrinhac, 219).

Revealing the Truth far Worse Than Lying!

"He who dares to reveal a sin confided to him in the tribunal of penance, we decree that he be not only deposed from the sacerdotal office but also relegated to a monastery of strict observance to do penance for the remainder of his life" (Fourth Lateran Council, Canon XXI, as recorded in *Disciplinary Decrees of the General Councils,* Schroeder, 259).

When we poor mortals, who are not Gods, as priests claim to be, withhold material evidence or shield known criminals, we are punishable as accessories. Why should the Catholic Church be allowed citizenship in our land while they shield criminals, and give perjured evidence to protect them? The Confessional is the most reprehensible and lawless of this detestable system!

Priests Perjure To Protect Criminals

"If, however, he can see no other effectual way of evading the question or of averting suspicion from the penitent, he (the priest) can and must declare even upon oath, that the penitent has not confessed to him what is in question, that he knows nothing at all about it. Such a statement is not a lie nor is it in consequence, a perjury if made upon oath, for it is a case of lawful use of the implicit reservation that the confessor, as a private individual, the only capacity in which he can be expected to answer, has no knowledge of a subject revealed to him as a representative of God" (*Theory and Practice of the Confessional,* Schieler-Henser, 468-469).

So a priest who perjures himself to protect a guilty criminal is looked upon as God, but if one told the truth and helped to punish the guilty he is put in jail for life.

This is not only un-American but satanic also.

EPILOGUE

We have now come to the end of this long journey through the labyrinth of the Catholic system. The reader should have no difficulty seeing with noon-day clearness, the difference between this most elaborate manmade religion and the simple *New Testament* Church. Let me say again that this has been a labor of love. Nothing short of that heavenly principle could have encouraged me to go on through all the weary years.

It is my hope that the general public can know how false the accepted image of the Catholic Church is: how inimical this institution is to our political philosophy. This is the institution that has finally, through the help of an uninformed public, been given tax money for its schools, so that it may further entrench itself in our land.

I cannot say too often, nor emphasize too much, the fact that this opposition is not toward the laity of the Catholic Church, but toward this system and toward those who have framed it, and those who, knowing its nature, conspire to perpetuate it.

With a prayer for our land and for all good people we come to the end.

BIBLIOGRAPHY

Administrative Legislation, Ayrinhac, Longmans, Green & Co., 1930

American Culture and Catholic Schools, McLoughlin, Lyle Stouart, N.Y., 1960

Apocryphal and Legendary Life of Christ, Donohoo, Macmillan Co., N.Y., 1903

Autobiography of a Hunted Priest, Gerard, Doubleday, Garden City, N.Y., 1952

Back to the Bible, Lattey, Burns, Oates & Washboume, London, 1944

Brooklyn Tablet (Diocesan Newspaper)

Carmel, Official Story of Discalced (barefooted) Carmelites, P.J. Kenedy, N.Y., 1927

Catholic Breviary (Volumes I to IV), Benziger Brothers, Inc., 1951

A Catholic Commentary on the Holy Scriptures, Thomas Nelson & Son, N.Y., 1953

Catholic Dictionary, Addis and Arnold, Catholic Publication Society, N.Y., 1887

Catholic Dictionary, Vatican Edition, Universal Knowledge Foundation, N.Y., 1929

The Catholic Doctor, Bonner, P.J. Kenedy & Sons, N.Y., 1937

Catholic Encyclopedia, The Encyclopedia Press, N.Y., 1913

The Catholic History of Great Britain, Wilmot-Buxton, Burns, Oates & Washboume Ltd., Glasgow, 1921

Catholic Facts, Noll, Our Sunday Visitor, Huntington, Indiana, 1927

The Church in Modern Society, Bishop John Ireland, Pioneer Press

Mfg. Depts., St. Paul, Minn., 1905

Canonical and Civil Status of Catholic Parishes, Augustine, B. Herder Book Co., St. Louis, 1926

Catholic Versions of Scripture:

Confraternity, St. Anthony Guild Press, Patterson, N.J., 1941

Douay, C. Wildermann Co., Inc., N.Y., 1938

Kleist and Lilly, The Bruce Pub. Company, Milwaukee, 1954

Knox's Sheed and Ward, N.Y., 1945

Spencer's, Macmillan Company, N.Y., 1951

Westminster, Longmans, Green and Co., N.Y., 1931

Catholic Apologetics, Deviviers-Messmer, Benziger Bros., N.Y., 1903

Commentary on Canon Law, Augustine, (Volumes I-VIII), B. Herder Book Co., St. Louis, 1931

Constitutions of the Catholic Church, Ayrinhac, Longmans, Green and Co., N.Y., 1930

Canons and Decrees of the Council of Trent, Schroeder, B. Herder Book Co., St. Louis, 1941

Campbell and Purcell Debate, McQuiddy Ptg. Co., 1914

The Casuist (Volumes I-III), Jos. F. Wagner, N.Y., 1906

Church History, John Laux, Benziger Bros., N.Y., 1930

Development of Christian Worship, Steuart, Longmans, Green and Company, N.Y., 1953

Devotion of the Holy Rosary, Muller, Benziger Bros., N.Y., 1876

Disciplinary Decrees of the General Councils, Schroeder, B. Herder Book Company, St. Louis, 1937

Encyclical, *Light of Truth,* Pius XI

Eucharist, Law and Practice, Durieux, Oliver Dolphin, Faribalt,

Minn., 1926

Eusebius's History, Geo. Bell and Sons, London, 1889

Explanation of Catholic Morals, Stapleton, Benziger Bros., N.Y., 1904

Externals of the Catholic Church, Sullivan, P.J. Kenedy and Sons, N.Y., 1919

The Faith of Millions, O'Brien, Our Sunday Visitor, Huntington, Indiana, 1938

Faith of Our Fathers, Gibbons, John Murphy Co., Baltimore, 1917

Father McShane of Maryknoll, Catholic Foreign Mission Society, N.Y., 1932

Father Smith Instructs Jackson, Noll and Fallon, Our Sunday Visitor, Huntington, Indiana, 1947

General History of the Church, Darras, (Volumes I-IV), P. O'Shea, N.Y., 1865

General Legislation, Ayrinhac, Longmans, Green and Co., N.Y., 1930

Glories of Mary, Liguori, P.J. Kenedy and Sons, N.Y., 1902

Green Bay Register (Diocesan Newspaper, Green Bay, Wis.).

Great Encyclical Letters, Pope Leo XIII. (Title page missing).

History of the Catholic Church, de Courcy and Shea, P.J. Kenedy and Sons, N.Y., 1879

History of the Mass, O'Brien, Catholic Publication Society Co., N.Y., 1879

History of the Catholic Church, "Brother Gustavus," Chaminade College, Clayton, Co., 1915

History of the Catholic Church, Brennan, Benziger Bros., N.Y., 1881

History of the Church, Noethen, John Murphy and Co., Baltimore, 1870

History of the Church of God, Spalding, Schwartz, Kirwin &

Fauss, N.Y., 1883

History of Christian Philosophy, Gilson, Random House, N.Y., 1954

History of the Church, Birkhaeuser, Fr. Pustet and Co., N.Y., 1903

History of the Protestant Reformation, Spalding (title page missing)

History of the Confessional, Hopkins, Harper and Bros., N.Y., 1850

The Holy Sacrifice of the Mass, Gihr, B. Herder Book Co., St. Louis, 1946

Hughes-Breckenridge Debate, Isaac Bird, Phila., 1833

The Inquisition, Vacandard, Longmans, Green and Co., N.Y., 1908

Legislation on the Sacraments, Ayrinhac, Longmans, Green and Co., N.Y., 1928

Life of Pope Pius IX, O'Reilly, Peter F. Collier, N.Y., 1878

Life of the Blessed Virgin, Gentillucci, Thomas Kelley, N.Y., 1856

Life of Mary as Seen by the Mystics, Brown, Bruce Publishing Company, Milwaukee, 1951

Life of St. Francis Assisi, Magliano, P. O'Shea, N.Y., 1867

Lives and Times of the Roman Pontiffs, Chevalier Artaud de Montor, D. & J. Sadlier, N.Y., 1869

Lone Star Visitor (Texas edition of Our Sunday Visitor').

Lone Star Catholic (Texas edition of Our Sunday Visitor').

Manual of Christian Doctrine, "A Seminary Professor," John Joseph McVey, Philadelphia, 1909

Manual of Moral Theology, Slater, Benziger Brothers, N.Y., 1918

Marriage, Morrison, Bruce Pub. Company, Milwaukee, 1934

The Mass of the Future, Ellard, Bruce Pub. Co., Milwaukee, 1948

Medical Ethics, McFadden, F.A. Davis Co., Philadelphia, 1949

Miscellanae, Spalding, Gill and Levering, Louisville, 1855

Moods and Truths, Sheen

Moral Problems in Hospital Practice, Finney, B. Herder Book Company, St. Louis, 1922

Moral Theology, Jone and Adelman, The Newman Press, Westminster, Maryland, 1956

National Cath. Almanac, (1937, 1943, 1955, 1961), St. Anthony Guild Press, Patterson, N.J.

New Interpretation of the Mass, Borgmann, John Murphy Company, Baltimore, 1933

The New Canon Law, Woywood, Joseph F. Wagner, Inc., N.Y., 1918

New Knowledge and Old Truths, O'Brien, The Paulist Press, N.Y., 1935

New Matrimonial Legislation, Cronin, Benziger Bros., N.Y., 1919

Operation Understanding (Our Sunday Visitor')

Our Faith and the Facts, Donovan, Patrick L. Baine, Chicago, 1925

Our Priesthood, Bruneau, John Murphy, Baltimore, 1929

Our Sunday Visitor, (Catholic paper, Huntington, Indiana)

Pope Innocent III and His Times, Clayton, Bruce Publishing Company, Milwaukee, 1941

Political and Social Philosophy, Lacordaire, Kegan Paul, Trench Trubner and Company, B. Herder, St. Louis, 1924

Pastoral Medicine, Sanford, Jos. F. Wagner, N.Y., 1904

Pastoral Medicine, Ruland & Rattler, B. Herder, St. Louis, 1936

Pageant of the Popes, Farrow, Sheed & Ward, N.Y., 1946

The People's Padre, McLaughlin, Beacon Press, Boston, 1954

Pastor's History of the Popes, (19 volumes), B. Herder, St. Louis, 1933

Plain Facts for Fair Minds, Searle, Paulist Press, N.Y., 1915

The Priest, His Dignity and Obligations, Eudes, P.J., Kenedy and Sons, N.Y., 1947

The Priestly Vocation, Ward, Longmans, Green and Company, N.Y.

A Popular History of the Catholic Church, Hughes, Image Book-Doubleday, Garden City, N.Y. 1947

Pulpit Commentary on Cath. Teaching—The Creed, Gerrard, Joseph F. Wagner, N.Y., 1908

Purgatory, Sadlier, D. & J. Sadlier, N.Y., 1886

The Question Box, Conway, Columbus Press, N.Y., 1913

The Question Box, Conway, Paulist Press, N.Y., 1929

Question Box Column (in Catholic Diocesan newspapers)

Quizzes on Hospital Ethics, Rumble, Radio Replies, St. Paul, 1946

Radio Replies, Rumble and Carty, (Volumes I, II, III) Radio Replies Press, St. Paul, Minn.

The Sacred Canons, Abbo and Hannon, B. Herder, St. Louis, 1952

Short History of the Catholic Church, Wedewer and McSorley, B. Herder, St. Louis, 1916

Sources of Christian Theology, Palmer, Newman Press, Westminster, Maryland, 1955

Spiritual First Aid Procedures, Queen's Work, St. Louis, Fitz Gibbons

St. *Francis of Assisi,* Magliano, B. O'Shea, N.Y., 1867

The Story of American Catholicism, Maynard, Macmillan Company, N.Y., 1942

The State and the Church, Ryan and Millar, Macmillan Company, N.Y., 1922

St. Teresa's Autobiography, Columbus Press, N.Y., 1911

Strange but True Column (in Brooklyn Tablet)

Summa Theologica, Thomas Aquinas, Thomas Baker, London, 1911

Teachings of the Catholic Church, Smith, The Teachings of the Catholic Church and Its Divine Founder, Office of Catholic Publications, N.Y., 1886

Teachings of the Catholic Church, De Ligney, The Teachings of the Catholic Church and Its Divine Founder, Office of Catholic Publications, N.Y., 1886

Theory and Practice of the Confessional, Schieler-Henser

Trials of a Translator, Knox, Sheed and Ward, N.Y., 1949

True Devotions of the Blessed Virgin, De Montfort, P.J. Kenedy and Sons, N.Y., 1909

True Spouse of Christ, Liguori, Benziger Brothers, N.Y.

Twentieth Century Encyclopedia of Catholicism, (150 volumes), Hawthorne Books Publishers, N.Y., 1959

The Virgin Mary, Guitton, P.J. Kenedy, N.Y., 1952

www.ingramcontent.com/pod-product-compliance
Lightning Source LLC
Chambersburg PA
CBHW070901120626
46546CB00001B/94